Morgan County
Public Library

Martinsville, Indiana

Presented in memory of

Doris Corns

By

Susan H. and Allan Smith

The Essential Career Guide to Becoming a Middle and High School Teacher

The Essential Career Guide to Becoming a Middle and High School Teacher

Robert W. Maloy
and
Irving Seidman

BERGIN & GARVEY
Westport, Connecticut • London

Library of Congress Cataloging-in-Publication Data

Maloy, Robert W.
   The essential career guide to becoming a middle and high school
teacher / Robert W. Maloy, Irving Seidman.
     p.   cm.
   Includes bibliographical references (p.   ) and index.
   ISBN 0–89789–559–2 (alk. paper)
    1. Middle school teaching—Vocational guidance—United States.
   2. High school teaching—Vocational guidance—United States.
   3. Middle school teachers—Training of—United States.   4. High
school teachers—Training of—United States.   I. Seidman, Irving,
1937– . II. Title.
LB1776.5.M35   1999
373.11'0023—dc21   98–44207

British Library Cataloguing in Publication Data is available.

Library of Congress Catalog Card Number: 98–44207
ISBN: 0–89789–559–2

First published in 1999

Bergin & Garvey, 88 Post Road West, Westport, CT 06881
An imprint of Greenwood Publishing Group, Inc.
www.greenwood.com

Printed in the United States of America

The paper used in this book complies with the
Permanent Paper Standard issued by the National
Information Standards Organization (Z39.48–1984).

10 9 8 7 6 5 4 3 2 1

Contents

PART II. PROFILES AND RESOURCES

Illustrations

Preface

Welcome to *The Essential Career Guide to Becoming a Middle and High School Teacher*. The goal of the book is to give readers step-by-step guidance about how to enter the field of secondary school teaching. Part One focuses on what prospective teachers need to know to begin a teaching career, including making the decision to become a teacher, analyzing secondary schools and the adolescent students who attend them, understanding the ins and outs of certification and licensing, choosing an excellent teacher education program, succeeding as a student of teaching, and finding a first job in the field. Part Two offers state-by-state information important to prospective teachers.

The book is intended for college students making choices about courses and programs of study, recent college graduates pursuing professional positions, experienced workers thinking about changing careers, and high school students planning for college. All will find essential information about becoming a teacher and thought-provoking perspectives about adolescents, teacher education, and middle and high schools within the pages of this book.

The turn of the new century may be the best of times and the worst of times for those who want to teach. Most forecasts indicate that there will be a high demand for qualified teachers. Yet, favorable job prospects are not the only reason to become a teacher. Many people are searching for jobs that combine a life-long pursuit of knowledge, a long-held dream of joining a field they respect, a chance to work with young people, and an opportunity to make a difference in society. Teaching is a way of combining significant personal and professional goals in a career that matters.

While a teaching career encompasses all these goals and more, its context is becoming more and more complicated. Some politicians and social commentators—who seem to be uninterested or unable to deal with the inequities in our society that are the root cause of much that ails social institutions—have chosen to see schooling itself as the problem. They find it easier to propose reforms in education than to alter employment patterns or address extreme disparities in wealth and income that pervade United States society.[1]

The preparation of teachers—long a subject of criticism at best, ridicule at worst, and misunderstanding most of the time—struggles to find its way amidst cries to eliminate it and demands to professionalize it. Some argue that despite its centrality as a common good to a democratic society, education should be privatized, and teacher education should be taken out of the hands of those who have made their careers working and reflecting on its issues. The complexities of the work of teachers, even without the arguments of ideologues who are making the schools their battleground, makes it important for anyone thinking about a teaching career to do so based on realistic, honest information. A key purpose of this book is to provide you with an informative and thoughtful view of issues you will face as you prepare to teach.

We, the authors of this book, are faculty members in the Secondary Teacher Education Program (STEP) of the School of Education at the University of Massachusetts Amherst. Robert Maloy coordinates history and social studies education and is co-director of *180 Days in Springfield*, an immersion teacher education program run in cooperation with the Springfield, Massachusetts, Public Schools. Irving Seidman is Director of Teacher Education on the Amherst campus and coordinates the English Teacher Education Program. Between us we have fifty years experience in teaching and teacher education.

We spend significant time teaching, advising, and mentoring students who hope to become middle or high school teachers. Some of our students are undergraduates who wish to include certification as part of their four-year college program of study; others are recent graduates who want to pursue a teacher education program within a few years after receiving their first degree. Increasingly, we teach students who, after working in one field or another for a few years, decide to switch careers and become teachers. Many are seeking a deeper level of personal satisfaction that was absent in their previous jobs.

ORGANIZATION OF THE BOOK

This book is organized to provide the reader with realistic guidance and essential information about how to become a teacher. In Part I, we present the essential steps to preparation, certification and employment as a middle and high school teacher. Chapter 1 examines the motivations that bring people to the profession, the current job market for teachers, and the issues of pay, worklife, and job satisfaction facing those entering the field.

Chapter 2 focuses on different views of teaching, the choice between teaching in middle or high schools, and some inherent dilemmas that affect the work of teachers in secondary schools today.

Chapter 3 guides you through the maze of certification and licensure policies. It reviews the essential steps of certification, defines key terms such as subject areas, grade levels, and state reciprocity, and discusses the teacher testing requirements you face in earning your license.

Chapter 4 examines how college and university teacher education programs typically work, the value of ratings, the importance of accreditation, and new developments in preparing teachers. In order for you to thoroughly assess your options, the chapter also looks at alternative paths to certification, emergency certificates, and Teach for America.

Chapter 5 tells you what you need to know about getting accepted to the program of your choice. It offers an insider's perspective on how to construct a successful application and how to make the admission system work for you.

Chapter 6 orients you to becoming a student of teaching as you prepare to teach. This includes building your subject field of knowledge and using tutoring and community service to improve your skills as a teacher. Models of student teaching, the power-laden role of cooperating teachers, and what to seek or avoid when you work in schools are also discussed.

Chapter 7 guides you to successfully attaining your first job, including use of the Internet in your job search; developing a strong job application and a teaching portfolio; preparing for an interview; and negotiating the best possible contract for yourself.

In Part II, we bring together essential facts from a variety of sources in a format that prospective teachers can use in making decisions about how best to prepare for a career in teaching. At the center of this section of the book are State-by-State Profiles for each of the fifty states, the District of Columbia, Puerto Rico, Guam, the Virgin Islands, and the Department of Defense Dependent Schools.

Each state page includes the mailing and Web addresses and phone numbers for the state's teacher licensing agency. It also includes the colleges and universities in the state that are approved to prepare secondary teachers, including those accredited by NCATE (National Council for Accreditation of Teacher Education) and/or ranked among the top fifty graduate colleges of education by *U.S. News & World Report* for 1999. Beginning and average teacher salaries, per pupil expenditures, number of students, number of teachers, and the tests that prospective educators must pass before they can teach are also part of the state profiles. Part

II also has a Directory of Resources with the addresses of important organizations connected to teacher education that are mentioned in the book.

NOTE

1. David Tyack and Larry Cuban, *Tinkering Toward Utopia: A Century of Public School Reform* (Cambridge, MA: Harvard University Press, 1995), 4.

Acknowledgments

We wish to first acknowledge our students in the Secondary Teacher Education Program of the School of Education, University of Massachusetts Amherst. Their seriousness of purpose, their love of learning, and their commitment to becoming the best teachers possible have made it a privilege, on the whole, to work with them.

We also wish to acknowledge present and former colleagues in our Secondary Teacher Education Program with whom we have had the pleasure of working to make sense of our efforts in teacher education: Portia Elliott, Allan Feldman, Atron Gentry, Kenneth Parker, J. P. Berwald, Helen Schneider, Marge Magourik Colbert, Patrick Sullivan, Richard J. Clark, the late Byrd L. Jones and Seth Kreisberg.

We are indebted to many individuals for their contributions to this book. Dr. Sharon Edwards, outstanding teacher and writer, reviewed the manuscript and provided critical feedback. Mary Gerard Edwards responded to early chapter drafts. Portia Elliott, our department chair, offered specific insight into the issues facing mathematics teachers today. Dr. Mario Cirillo, principal of the Chestnut Accelerated Middle School in Springfield, Massachusetts, illuminated the processes of school change and teacher job interviewing. Karen O'Connor and Manuela Fonseca provided information about teacher education throughout the nation. We also thank Kathy Gagne, Andy Effrat, Rob Shumer, Laura Holland, Linda Griffin, Daniel P. Schwartz, Linda Seidman, Rachel Filene Seidman, and Ethan L. Seidman for their support of this effort.

Through their active engagement with teacher education, our Dean Bailey W. Jackson and Associate Dean John Carey supported the work of this book. Lori Mestre, education reference librarian at the W.E.B.

Du Bois Library continued to be an expert resource for us. Michael Schwartz and Joyce Putnam of our Teacher Education Office were valuable resources to us. Sam Dean shared his knowledge of computers. Diana Ajjan, writer, editor, and prospective teacher, offered key editorial assistance to the final manuscript. Edward Knappman, our agent, guided us throughout the writing.

In particular the following students have contributed directly to this book: Michelle Cote, Amy Wallender, and Anathea Chartrand did outstanding work as research assistants. Irene LaRoche, Tricia Lea, Nicole Dokton, Kate Hojnicki, Sasha Aaronson, Jeffrey Beaulieu, Beth Wohlleb, Julieanne Eagan, Robin Weiner, Brian Dickey, Barbara Remington, Andy Hamilton, and Maricruz Badia Cestero shared many personal insights from their own experiences in becoming teachers.

On a more personal note, Robert Maloy acknowledges the loving support of his mother, Peg Maloy, and the memory of his father, Bill Maloy. Irving Seidman wishes to honor the memory of his parents Fanny and Phillip Seidman and the ongoing influence of his brothers, Alex and Louis, and sister, Sally Rubinstein. Each of these family members, in his or her own way, was influential in our becoming teachers, for which we are thankful.

PART I

BECOMING A TEACHER

1

Entering a Career That Matters

"I want to be a teacher. How do I become one?" Over the last twenty-five years we have spoken to and worked with close to two thousand people who have made that statement and asked that question. In this book we share with you many of the ideas we have been privileged to research, develop, and discuss with our students as they prepared to become middle and high school teachers.

People who express an interest in teaching typically want to make a good living, but do not base their lives on the pursuit of money. Most of them enjoy kids and sense that it is deeply compelling to develop students' potential and touch their lives. They want to excite individuals and classes about subject matter the way they had once been inspired by a teacher. They are concerned about the social and economic conditions of our country, and they recognize the importance of knowledge, understanding, and critical thinking to an equitable society. Some want to make education today better than it was for them.

Regardless of their driving goal, individuals interested in teaching want their work to make a difference, personally and professionally. For them, for us, and we hope for you, teaching holds the possibility of being a productive, rewarding career that matters.

WHO IS GOING INTO TEACHING?

Prospective middle and high school teachers come from a range of backgrounds, have a complex set of motivations, and are at different decision points in their lives. We briefly describe them to you so that you may recognize your connection to, and place yourself among, those entering the field.

Undergraduates

We work with undergraduates, usually juniors and seniors, who either entered college knowing that they wanted to be teachers or made the decision along the way. While they are not the majority in our teacher education program, a significant number of prospective middle and high school teachers nationwide are undergraduates.

They are mostly of traditional college age, majoring in an arts and sciences discipline and often pursuing teacher certification through the equivalent of an academic minor in education. Generally, these undergraduates fit certification into their four year program, although increasingly they take an extra semester or enroll in a five year program.

Some undergraduates pursue teaching because school made an enormous impact on their lives. Growing up, others cared for younger siblings, lifeguarded at a pool, counseled at a camp, or baby-sat children in the neighborhood. Teaching adolescents, therefore, seems like a natural career choice. A few of these college students view becoming certified as a back-up career option. They are not sure what they want to do professionally, and the thought of having a teaching certificate provides a sense of job security.

As they pursue certification, many undergraduates, little older than the students they may teach, wonder whether they are ready to take on the authority of a teacher. Others demonstrate an intellectual readiness to teach that defies the often-heard criticism about those just out of college being too young to enter the profession. A small number respond to the complexities of teaching by deciding they are not yet ready for the work.

Recent College Graduates

A second major group of people who are increasingly choosing to become teachers are recent college graduates. They pursued liberal arts degrees while undergraduates, preferring to leave their career options open. Some of them taught for a year or so in an independent school after graduation and then decided that they wanted to get certified. Others traveled, or took available jobs, as they sorted out what they wanted to do in their lives.

In their mid-to-late twenties or early thirties, this group has now decided that they truly want to teach. At our school, like many across the country, they apply to a master's level teacher education program or to a postbaccalaureate continuing education program which leads to certification only. Some pursue graduate degrees in their subject fields, instead of in education, and take certification courses along the way. A few opt for a Master of Arts in Teaching, a degree originally conceptualized in the 1960s as a way for outstanding students to gain both advanced study in their subject field and the education courses needed for teacher certification.

Each year, one or two students from arts and sciences Ph.D. programs apply to our program. They recognize that the job market at the college and university level is uncertain in many of their fields. Becoming certified is a way of increasing their options once they earn their doctorate.

Mid-Career Candidates

A steadily growing group of prospective teachers with whom we work are mid-career candidates. They are older students, usually in their thirties, forties, or fifties. Most earned an undergraduate degree five to fifteen-plus years previously, but decided against teaching when they completed college.

Some are women who initially thought about teaching but identified it as a traditionally female occupation, and pursued job opportunities in other fields. Now they are following their original interest in teaching. Other women are reentering the workforce after years as parents. They find teaching attractive, in part, because it allows them a schedule that is consistent with their children's.

Many career changers who originally chose more prestigious or prosperous lines of work now no longer consider profit their first priority. Sitting in a corporate cubicle pushing paper, making telephone calls, and sending faxes to broker a deal just does not touch their soul. Others seeking new directions in their lives are tradespeople who want work that perhaps is less repetitive and more sustainable as they grow older.

There are many variations on the theme of "mid-career candidates." In the past three years at our campus, for example, a retired Air Force colonel, a registered surgical nurse, a social security agency administrator, an attorney, a clinical psychologist, a high tech industry technician, a master carpenter, and a postal worker have joined our teacher education program. Each has a unique story, but common to all is that teaching now makes sense in ways it had not earlier in their lives.

These early-to-mid-career people must make a major transition in their lives, one that is often very difficult. Many have become accustomed to earning a certain salary, and living again as a student, while intellectually and spiritually uplifting, can be economically discouraging. Most of these individuals, perhaps originally skeptical of attending classes with younger students, find they enjoy being back in school. They are challenged by the complexities of teaching and learning, but also reassured by the transferability of many of the skills they developed in their former careers. They are serious about their study, and many faculty and younger peers welcome them for what they have to offer. Once certified, these older new teachers find many middle and high schools actively seeking their applications.

WHAT MOTIVATES PEOPLE TO TEACH?

While prospective teachers come from a broad spectrum of life stages, their motivations for teaching seem to converge around a number of themes.

Family

Many students in our program come from families in which one or both parents, aunts and uncles, or other relatives were teachers. They grew up listening to stories about classrooms and schools, and perhaps observing an adult grading papers and preparing for classes. Some even admit to having been jealous of the attention a parent gave to his or her students. They may even have declared at some point in the past, "I will never do what my parents do!"

Some students report that they are seeking to become teachers despite the attempts of parents, relatives, or friends to persuade them otherwise. They are comfortable with the thought of teaching because they were immersed in it when they were young. They came to know firsthand the demands and the joys, and to believe that teaching was valuable work.

Role Models

Many students, when asked how they came to teaching, tell us that they had a teacher who had inspired them, one who made their subject come alive by sharing the excitement of learning. These special teachers had reached out and communicated with their students personally, encouraging them when they were down, or listening when they were going through difficult episodes in their lives.

Some students recall a teacher who had recognized and appreciated something distinctive in their work. Others had teachers who taught them to think critically, challenged them to new levels of achievement, and created positive connections between school and life. Clearly, those who have been fortunate enough to have experienced such an inspirational influence may want to emulate that person as they become a teacher in their own right.

Working with Kids

Most of our prospective teachers feel an affinity toward adolescents. Smiling at their stories and antics, empathizing with their struggles, they respect teenagers' potential for growth, development, and learning. Some students want to reach kids who are on the margins—the unpopular, those who seem always to be in trouble, or the ones who go through school so quietly their voices are never heard. They also enjoy the energetic, hardworking, successful students, and recognize that these kids too face issues and struggles that need caring adult responses.

Just as many are inspired by teachers who did their job well, still others are motivated by negative experiences with educators. They seem fueled by the desire to provide to other youngsters the quality instruction they themselves were denied. Remembering past events, they say, "I'll be the kind of teacher whose door is always open so kids can talk."

A few individuals every year come to realize through their field experiences that kids annoy them too often and too easily. They may become frustrated if they are unsuccessful at managing adolescent behavior, and realize that teaching, or teaching at the middle or high school level, is not for them. They learn before they get too far down the road that they just do not have the patience, presence, or predisposition to work with teenagers every day.

Love of Learning

Embedded in many of the stories our students tell us about how they come to teaching is their love of learning. They are excited about the ideas inherent in their subject. They are passionate about new thoughts and fresh ideas. Unfortunately, it may not be easy to admit to a love of learning and ideas, a reflection of what Richard Hofstadter termed anti-intellectualism in America.[1] Ours is a society that is ambivalent about intellectuals. It places great emphasis on common sense and experience as being better teachers than books. For many, the idea of a teacher as intellectual sounds elitist; it seems to imply a withdrawal from the world of action.

When we ask a class of prospective teachers, "Are you an intellectual?" an unusually large number say, "No." Some are reflecting the societal discomfort with the word while others are shy about claiming something for themselves that they see as the preserve of people who are much more scholarly and learned than they are. As the discussion of that question progresses in our classes, students begin to affirm that their love of learning is actually a serious commitment in their lives, and that learning and teaching are inextricably linked. They sense and hope that as teachers they will remain life-long learners.

Educational and Social Change

A number of our students enter teaching because they want to make the world, country, and schools more equitable and positive places. For some, their commitment to change and reform is a response to their own negative educational experiences. Others, because of the paths their lives have taken, are particularly sensitive to inequities in our society. They want to work toward eradicating racism, and they recognize classism as especially pernicious because it is so commonly overlooked.

Still others are committed to gender equity. They want schools to address sexism and patriarchy in their curriculum, teaching methods, and staffing. These students are not radical ranters and ravers. They may be idealists, but they are also quite pragmatic. They want to become teachers to work within the system of education in order to change it. And they hope to instill in their students a sensitivity to injustice in society as well as a commitment to making democratic ideals real for all.

Reflecting on Motivations to Teach

What difference, you may ask, does it make how or why people enter the teaching profession? Is it not more important what they do once they become educators? Are some reasons for teaching better than others? You may wonder, if your thoughts about becoming a teacher are not reflected in the motivations just discussed, "Am I simply misguided in my choice of career?"

Motivation is highly complex. You may have identified with one or more of the themes just discussed, or you may have your own personal reasons for pursuing a career in education. It is important to examine your reasons for becoming a teacher. Well intentioned motives may clash with the realities of what it is like to work day-to-day in schools.

For example, individuals who grew up in a family of teachers may find that the norms of work in schools have changed considerably over time. Or some may realize that they entered teaching because they were familiar and comfortable with it, but at the same time, they want to pursue a path different from their parents. Many find they need to leave the familiar and venture into new directions before achieving a sense of fulfillment in their lives.

Prospective teachers who want to emulate a role model may find it difficult to do for many students what a single person did for them. Caring about kids, they may connect their sense of accomplishment as a teacher to the immediate or short-term responses of adolescents. But some youngsters may not be ready to hear what you have to say. It can be very frustrating when students seem unwilling to change their negative or self-destructive behaviors.

As a teacher, you may affirm the importance of being an intellectual, and realize that, as Hofstadter says, you are probably the major representative of the life of the mind to your students. But the structure of many schools and the conditions of a teacher's day do not fully support the intellectual work of teaching. Generally, you teach five classes per day, attend many meetings, perform hall and lunchroom duties, counsel students, and grade papers after school. Colleagues are rushed and seldom have time to discuss ideas. Many students are excited about learning, but because of peer pressure they have a tough time admitting it.

Finally, new teachers realize that being a teacher and acting as a change agent are not easy goals to combine in one job. Schools are very conservative institutions, tending to reflect the culture rather than lead it. They exist, in part, to socialize students into the existing society, not to develop a new one. School administrators and other teachers are often ambivalent about new approaches, and are reluctant to support changes in established routines. In some districts, the desire to teach controversial social issues creates intense political debates about what should be covered in the mandated curriculum. Teachers who work toward equity must be prepared for colleagues or community groups claiming they are too political in their methods.

The bottom line is whatever your motivations to teach, they may conflict with some aspect of the work of teachers. There is no one right motivation to teach and contradictions abound in the school setting. You must approach teaching with your eyes wide open and your heart and mind alert and ready to manage the complexities you will face in classrooms and schools.

THE JOB MARKET FOR TEACHERS

The United States needs teachers. The National Center for Education Statistics puts the number of new teachers needed at two million in the next ten years. Between a half and two-thirds of these educators will be first-time teachers, and the others will be re-entrants into the profession.[2] Some future teachers will take the place of current staff who are retiring or otherwise leaving the profession. Others will fill brand new positions created by growing numbers of students and changing school staffing patterns.

Importantly, for readers of this book thinking about middle and high school teaching, about half of the projected teacher openings will be for secondary educators. Starting now, the predicted need for middle and high school teachers will exceed 120,000 a year at least through 2005, a faster rate of increase than for elementary teachers.[3]

So if you are an undergraduate thinking about teaching as a career, a recent college graduate returning to get certified, or a mid-career person who had earlier thought about working in schools but hesitated because of ambiguous job prospects, the news is good. The prospect of getting a job in teaching is decidedly better than it has been in the last twenty years. At the same time, there are some key considerations about the job market that you need to know.

Ready or Not, the Students Are Coming

Right now, more children than ever before in American history are attending elementary and secondary schools in this country—approximately 52.2 million students in the Fall of 1997. That is 1.5 million more students than the year before. Increases in student enrollments are projected to be as high as 54.3 million by 2007.[4] This increase has been called a "baby boomlet" or "baby boom echo," in reference to the fact that children born to adults from the baby boom generation of 1946 to 1964 are now moving through the nation's school systems. Growing numbers of school-age children are also a result of growing immigration to the United States by people from all parts of the world.

A snapshot look at public school enrollment across the country shows that virtually every state is now gaining students.[5] In thirty-three states, increases will continue over the next decade, led by California where one million new students will enter the public schools by 2005. Other states with large, double-digit increases include Texas, Washington, Georgia, Virginia, North Carolina, New Jersey, Florida, and Maryland.

While elementary school enrollments have been on the increase since the mid-1980s, the wave of new students is just now reaching the secondary level. Between 1995/96 and 2011/12, the number of students graduating from high school will increase in every region, led by the West (31 percent), the South (23 percent), the Northeast (17 percent), and the Northcentral (10 percent).[6] (See Table 1.1 for projected state-by-state changes in high school graduation rates.) More students graduating from high school means increasing class sizes and hence the need for new and renovated school facilities, and the need for more teachers in grades 5–12. Part II provides another way to examine enrollment trends by listing the number of students and teachers along with per-pupil spending patterns by state.

A "Graying" of the Teaching Force

Those of you who are thinking of becoming a teacher at the turn of the twenty-first century are choosing to do so at a time when the nation's corps of teachers is growing older. One out of every four teachers is fifty or more years old, and the median age of school faculty is forty-five, its highest point in four decades. Using sixty-two as the average age when teachers retire, the National Education Association (NEA) estimates that one-third of the nation's current 2.5 million teachers are nearing the ends of their careers. Based on these figures, the number of educators retiring will increase dramatically over the next ten years.

In communities all across the country, the aging of the teaching force is changing the way schools recruit new teachers. In Boston, Massachusetts, for example, half of the city's 4,600 teachers are expected to retire in the next ten years.[7] These retirements come on top of an enrollment growth rate of about nine hundred new students a year (a modest 1.4 percent increase), as well as existing shortages in areas like science and bilingual education. To respond, the city has begun an aggressive recruiting campaign including a database of prospective teacher candidates.

Many small school systems must also face the realities of an older teaching faculty, even in communities where the size of the student population remains relatively steady. In these systems, a few teachers are likely to retire every year, and while the overall numbers are not as dramatic as a big city system like Boston, small schools must recruit new professionals to fill openings. Overall, as the teaching force ages, retirements may create as many as a million jobs for teachers in the next ten to fifteen years.

Cities Facing Shortages

One of the complexities of the developing job market for teachers is that the most serious shortages are likely to be in big cities. In August, 1997, as the school year was about to begin, a *New York Times* headline announced "Help Wanted in New York: 3,000 Teachers (Or Maybe 9,000)."[8] New York City is not alone in their teacher shortage. According to a recent study of forty-seven large urban districts, 77 percent reported having to hire uncertified teachers to meet existing demands.[9] The situation is getting worse as enrollments rise and teachers retire; areas of high demand include special education, science, mathematics, bilingual education, elementary education, and English as a second language education. Even in English and social studies, currently well supplied fields, future shortages are forecast by many urban districts. From coast to coast, city school superintendents are searching for well-prepared, certified educators; some systems, including Dallas and Fort Worth, Texas, have even started offering small signing bonuses to attract teachers.

The importance of urban teacher shortages is heightened by the fact that so many students attend city schools. In the major industrial states, urban schools enroll between 10 to 25 percent of all public school students, for example:

Table 1.1
Public and Non-Public High School Graduates by State

State	1996	2008	1996-2008 (% change)
Alabama	41,921	45,709	9%
Alaska	6,175	7,409	20%
Arizona	33,232	52,281	57%
Arkansas	26,257	30,232	15%
California	286,069	395,761	38%
Colorado	34,686	46,819	35%
Connecticut	31,394	43,180	38%
Delaware	7,075	9,141	29%
D. of Columbia	3,677	3,500	-5%
Florida	102,448	154,314	51%
Georgia	66,071	99,729	51%
Hawaii	12,441	15,564	25%
Idaho	15,139	17,367	15%
Illinois	119,146	145,319	22%
Indiana	62,430	69,368	11%
Iowa	33,797	35,671	6%
Kansas	27,052	30,882	14%
Kentucky	39,638	43,142	9%
Louisiana	44,195	43,628	-1%
Maine	13,999	16,052	15%
Maryland	48,257	67,949	41%
Massachusetts	58,580	74,628	27%
Michigan	94,264	119,176	26%
Minnesota	53,487	65,137	22%
Mississippi	26,597	28,185	6%

Table 1.1 (continued)

Missouri	54,721	63,952	17%
Montana	10,594	11,559	9%
Nebraska	19,643	22,277	13%
Nevada	10,771	22,761	111%
New Hampshire	11,662	16,595	42%
New Jersey	78,762	102,623	30%
New Mexico	16,659	19,239	15%
New York	159,481	199,064	25%
North Carolina	60,042	83,740	39%
North Dakota	8,442	7,618	-10%
Ohio	120,432	133,018	10%
Oklahoma	34,482	37,447	9%
Oregon	28,583	37,037	30%
Pennsylvania	122,610	145,112	18%
Rhode Island	8,978	11,611	29%
South Carolina	34,933	42,368	21%
South Dakota	9,099	9,821	8%
Tennessee	49,858	64,371	29%
Texas	184,363	229,364	24%
Utah	28,897	31,725	10%
Vermont	6,356	7,798	23%
Virginia	64,524	84,381	31%
Washington	47,727	66,408	39%
West Virginia	21,166	18,462	-13%
Wisconsin	57,706	66,319	15%
Wyoming	5,938	5,693	-4%

- 12 percent of Michigan's children go to school in Detroit
- 15 percent of Maryland's students attend Baltimore's schools
- New York City, Buffalo, Rochester, and Syracuse enroll 44 percent of New York's youngsters
- Los Angeles, San Diego, San Jose, San Francisco, Long Beach, Fresno, Sacramento, Oakland, and Compton have 24 percent of California's student population
- Houston, Dallas, San Antonio, El Paso, Austin, and Fort Worth account for 28 percent of students in Texas

State by state, enrollment statistics document the high number of students in urban schools, and these do not include the size of the suburban community school systems that surround most major metropolitan areas. Fairfax County, Virginia, Dade County, Florida, and many other suburban systems enroll thousands and thousands of youngsters.

It stands to reason, then, that if you want to teach, consider going where the students and the jobs are concentrated. To a significant extent, that will be in the nation's urban centers and the communities around them. Many prospective teachers would do well to investigate teacher education programs and routes to certification that would give them experience in urban areas. Unfortunately many new teachers are influenced to some degree, perhaps unduly, by the media and are hesitant to teach in urban schools.

A Lack of Certified Teachers

As the number of students increases, many school systems do not have enough qualified educators to teach all the different subjects in middle and high schools. To compensate, they ask teachers to conduct classes outside of their certification field. Such out-of-field teaching happens, for example, when a typing teacher teaches a civics class, or an English instructor teaches mathematics.

The National Commission on Teaching & America's Future soundly criticizes out-of-field teaching practices, reporting that 56 percent of high school students taking physical science, 27 percent of those taking math, and 21 percent of those taking English have teachers not licensed in the subject. In schools with high minority enrollments, students have less than a 50 percent chance of getting a science or mathematics teacher who holds a license and a degree in the field he or she teaches.[10]

The extent of the demands for qualified teachers by subject field may surprise you. Nationwide, more than one in three students take classes from an instructor who does not have a license and a major in the subject area of the course; just 48 percent of eighth graders take math from a teacher who has had sixteen or more hours of professional development course work in the field.[11]

Of course, lacking a degree in a teaching field does not automatically make someone a poor teacher. Many individuals do wonderful work in the classroom because of their commitment to education and their ability to connect and communicate to kids. Still, there is mounting pressure on superintendents, principals, and school boards to hire faculty with strong academic records and degrees in their teaching field. That demand should translate into more teaching positions open to those who take the time, spend the money, and make the commitment to become certified in their subject field.

There are other subject field shortages you should know about. After virtually disappearing from the curriculum of public and private schools in the 1970s, Latin is enjoying a remarkable resurgence. Enrollments are up more than 15 percent in grades 9–12, 34 percent in grades 7–8, and 113 percent in grades K–6, according to the Modern Language Association.[12] Significant increases were also found in the nation's private schools. As a result, a critical shortage exists of qualified Latin and Classical Humanities educators.[13]

Educators who speak more than one language are also in great demand. While nearly 14 percent of school-aged youth speak a language other than English at home, only 3 percent of current teachers have proficiency in a second language.[14] Looking ahead, it is estimated that the number of students who speak a language other than English will increase from just over two million in 1986 to more than five million in 2020.[15] Even if you are not going into bilingual education as a teaching field, the ability to speak English and another language will give you a competitive edge in the job market, and a pedagogical strength in the classroom.

Dilemmas of Ethnicity

The politics of skin color and ethnicity are being played out in the teaching force just as they are being played out in every segment of our society. The language of these politics reflects the complexity, the confusions, and the contradictions of the terms themselves. Amidst these debates are some troubling facts and trends about who is going into teaching.

In 1996, 87.3 percent of the teaching force was White as compared to 6.7 percent Black, 4.1 percent Hispanic, 1.1 percent Asian, and 0.7 percent American Indian/Alaskan Native.[16] The number of African American, Asian, Latino, and Native American college students going into teaching was even smaller, just 8 percent of the total number of certification candidates. At a time when one child in three comes to public school with a non-European heritage, the absence of a diverse teaching force is a major concern for educators and parents.

Many education reformers believe that students should have teachers of their own cultural heritage who will serve as role models while being sensitive to and respectful of cultural backgrounds. The reality is that the numbers of college students going into teaching from other than European American cultural backgrounds is not increasing. Some college students assume that since they have made it to college, they are going into careers that are more financially rewarding and offer higher status than education. Others remember public education as an inhospitable experience, and they do not want to return to schools as teachers.

The combination of psychological, social, and economic reasons leading to the dwindling of teacher candidates from diverse cultural backgrounds is seldom deeply explored. Instead, institutions of teacher education are urged to mount recruitment programs that must counter very strong tendencies in society in order to create a teaching force that is more diverse. This approach is becoming more and more difficult and even more complicated as affirmative action programs are being questioned across the country.

What do these dynamics of ethnicity mean for prospective teachers? From a statistical perspective, many of you will work in a school with significant numbers of ethnically and linguistically diverse students. If you are from one of these populations, you will find many districts actively recruiting you in their hopes of building a teaching force which can better serve the children in their schools. Regardless of your heritage, you will find that awareness of, respect for, sensitivity to, and belief in the potential of all students are key to your success in the classroom.

Issues of Gender

Since the mid-nineteenth century, the field of teaching has been a female-dominated occupation. The woman as nurturer in a well-knit family unit emerged as the ideal role of a school teacher. Presently, approximately 74 percent of the teaching force is comprised of women. At the secondary level, the ratio between genders is slightly more balanced, but in many subject areas it remains distinctively out of balance. For example, there are more male teachers in math and science departments and more women who teach in the humanities and arts.

What does this mean for those entering the field? There are job opportunities for women and men in what have been considered traditionally female or male-dominated disciplines. Schools are intent on finding more women to teach math and sciences to meet the challenge of the sexism that seems to be embedded in the instructing of these subjects.[17] While the same sort of purposefulness in recruiting does not seem to happen in the humanities, males who go into English, for example, are fewer and further between and may be in a more competitive position when it comes time for seeking a job.

A further complication inherent in the field of teaching is that while most teachers are women, over 90 percent of administrators are men. To the extent that male administrators in schools are in positions of power over female teachers, schools replicate the gender inequities of the society. Sexism can complicate the entry of women into the field and alter the experience of women teachers throughout the years they teach.[18] When men leave job openings to women, that may be a sign that the field is less valued by the prevailing power structure. If the conditions of teaching become even more difficult, and if the economic rewards of teaching do not improve, fewer men will likely enter the field. In this case, ironically, women may gain more opportunities for leadership in schools even as the conditions for success become more complicated.

Where Are the Jobs?

Some observers do not believe there will be a teacher shortage. They point to large numbers of already licensed teachers who are not teaching, as well as great interest in the field among college students, and conclude that there will be more than enough certified educators to go around.[19] They criticize existing teacher education programs, and suggest bringing mid-career professionals into teaching through alternative routes to certification to help meet local demands.

Despite disagreements about the size of the teacher shortage, it is important to remember that any one of the job market factors mentioned in this chapter—rising student enrollments, increasing teacher retirements, and large numbers of educators teaching outside their field—may create job openings in certain places at certain times. As a result, communities throughout the United States are going to be looking for teachers.

For example, perhaps you are considering a community or geographic region where the student population is not increasing. Does this mean your chances for a teaching position are nil? Not really! Retirements and the need for qualified teachers in high-shortage fields may well generate openings in the schools. At the same time, communities where one or more of these factors are present become promising places for you to look for a teaching position. They are more likely to have a steady need for teachers. Finally, places where other people are less likely to go are good possibilities for your job search. Since many prospective educators prefer to live in suburban areas, large urban districts and small rural communities will be needing teachers in the years ahead.

To get a general overview of what is happening in your field in different sections of the country, check out the yearly assessment of the regional supply and demand for new teachers done by the American Association for Employment in Education (AAEE). They divide the country into eleven regions: Northwest, West, Rocky Mountains, Great Plains/Midwest, South Central, Southeast, Great Lakes, Middle Atlantic, Northeast, Alaska, and Hawaii. Based on surveys of college and university career service centers, AAEE calculates the relative supply and demand using a one-to-five scale from "considerable surplus" to "considerable shortage" in forty-eight elementary and secondary level teaching fields.

Using this data, it is possible to see what the specific demands are in different parts of the country. For example, the 1997 AAEE report shows national shortages of teachers in mathematics, chemistry, and physics, but also regional shortages in biology (the West), languages (Rocky Mountains), and English as a Second Language (Great Lakes and Middle Atlantic). More information about job market trends can be obtained from AAEE or from your college career and guidance center.

What is clear about the developing picture is that the next decade should be one of the best of times for a new teacher to find a teaching job. To some degree the picture will be affected by the economy of the country. If it takes a serious downturn, school districts will increase class size, eliminate some subject areas, and hire fewer new teachers. Nonetheless, we believe the basic trend is toward significantly increasing job opportunity for those of you considering middle or high school teaching.

POLITICS, PAY, AND THE NATURE OF THE JOB

Ironically, at a time when job prospects seem to be the most positive they have been in two decades, teaching and teacher education, are under attack. In the 1950s the former Soviet Union's launching of Sputnik created a crisis in confidence in United States schooling. In 1983 the report entitled *A Nation at Risk* declared a crisis in American schools. In fact, for the entire twentieth century, the field of education has been in the throes of one reform or another.

Conservative critics have cited the problems of underachieving students, ill-prepared teachers, and inadequate schools. Responding to these criticisms, state legislatures and public policymakers have passed stringent new laws, including broader testing of students and prospective teachers, lengthening the school day and school year, implementing voucher programs, introducing competition between schools for status and funding, and expanding the number of charter schools.

David Berliner and Bruce Biddle argue that the current education crisis has been "manufactured" by a range of groups for political and ideological purposes.[20] In fact, American schools are successfully educating more students than ever before. At the same time, teachers are being scapegoated for problems that neither politicians nor society as a whole want to face: the inequitable funding of city schools; the difficulties of trying to meet the social, emotional, and academic needs of diverse youngsters in large classrooms; and the growing numbers of low-income and disadvantaged children who would not have been attending secondary schools fifty years ago. On balance, and considering the challenges they face, educators are doing remarkably well.

So you are considering entering teaching at a time when it has become an ideological and political football. Politicians curry votes by blaming schools for not preparing students for the world of work and hold teachers responsible for a significant proportion of students' failure. Some seem to be saying that public education should be replaced by a privatized system. Others argue that public education is the cornerstone of our democracy. They contend that rather than siphoning funds and energy away from the schools, we should offer public education the support it deserves. A smaller group says that if we attend to the social inequities of the country, the schools will improve.

Criticisms of Teacher Education

The call for change extends to colleges and universities as well. If teachers and schools are failing, the argument goes, then schools and departments of education must be doing a poor job in recruiting and preparing professionals for the realities of their jobs. Some of you reading this book may agree with this critique and wonder about the value of any teacher education program. Semester after semester, we work with students who enter our program with the attitude, "If it weren't for certification, I'd be teaching already."

Many education critics contend that the academic caliber of students entering college and university teacher-education programs is not as high as it should be. Low-achieving college students, they argue, lack the general literacy skills and sophisticated subject matter knowledge needed to teach secondary level courses in a rigorous, intellectually demanding manner. Education courses, these critics go on to say, inadequately prepare teachers to teach. Professors who have been out of classrooms for years focus on theoretical ideas without attention to practical applications or new methods of teaching. At many of the most selective institutions of higher education, the critique continues, the best and the brightest students do not even consider teaching because of the relative ineffectiveness of preparation programs and the bureaucratic demands of certification.

According to other commentators, the labor market for teachers will be improved when qualified people can bypass higher education teacher preparation programs and move more quickly into the profession. They support alternative routes to teaching now popular in virtually every state. Through alternative systems, mid-career professionals and recent college graduates have a way to enter the classroom prior to completing a prescribed program of study in a college or university department of education. Certification is earned through on-the-job performance, and either district or campus-based coursework. Placing individuals right into teaching is not seen as a problem by proponents of alternative routes. After all, they say, the performance of many educators in independent and private schools who did not become certified through college teacher education programs suggests that non-certified individuals can be successful as teachers.[21]

Each of these criticisms has its own counterpoint. The idea that teaching attracts lower quality applicants is widespread, but inconsistent with our experience. Most of our students, who may not have gone to the most selective and elite undergraduate schools, exhibit a driving intellectual energy and commitment to learning, even though, in some cases, those qualities may have emerged later in their careers and may not be demonstrated on standardized tests. Becoming an outstanding teacher is a complicated process. Grades and high test scores alone are desirable but not sufficient. Teachers must be literate and well versed in their subjects. But they also must have a disposition that is committed to bringing out the best in all their students.

Second, education courses are an easy target for criticism because they address complex variables that are difficult to measure. In meeting the learning needs of children and adolescents, prospective teachers grapple with a spectrum of human development that stretches the mind: cultural backgrounds, family structures, multiple languages, and widely differing performance levels and experiences. We cannot guarantee that every education course you take will be sterling. But the task of preparing yourself for the complexities you will face in the classroom is real. Some of your education courses will be better than others, just as in every field.

Many capable teacher candidates find that college or university education courses give them opportunities to start thinking through the complexities they will face in schools. By contrast, some individuals pursuing alternative routes find themselves placed in teaching positions without the prior preparation needed to succeed in the classroom. The danger for both groups, those prepared in higher education institutions and those entering through alternative routes, is becoming overwhelmed, discouraged, and ready to give up on teaching. Generally speaking, to be successful as a teacher, a person needs the time and the opportunity to become familiar with school settings before teaching, and the tools and perspectives to reflect productively on their work once they enter the field full time.

Teacher Salaries

Sooner or later, most people who are planning to teach end up thinking about the issue of teacher salaries. Teachers earn 20 to 30 percent less than other workers with the same amount of education and experience.[22] Among recent college graduates, only service workers had a lower beginning salary. Not only do engineers, computer programmers, and health professionals make more money than new teachers, but many technicians, laborers, and clerical workers earn more as well.

How will you make sense of your financial prospects as a teacher? Many who go into teaching often rationalize the discrepancies in income by saying, "I am not in it for the money," or, "Money is not what motivates me in my choice of a career." Others who turn away from teaching say the opposite: "I cannot afford to work for such a low salary," or, "I am worth much more than schools are willing to pay." It is hard to avoid thinking about the job of teaching in terms of its pay, although we want to suggest that this is not the only way to look at the work of teachers.

The average teacher salary nationwide, adjusted for cost of living, is $37,643 (see Part II for state by state teacher salary figures). New York, Connecticut, Illinois, Indiana, Pennsylvania, Michigan, and Wisconsin average over $40,000. Low-end states below $32,000 include Utah, North and South Dakota, Montana, Mississippi, Maine, Hawaii, and Louisiana. Remember these salaries vary from district to district, and it takes a person some years on the job to reach the higher numbers. Minimum beginning salaries average $24,507, with Alaska, New Jersey, Pennsylvania, New York, and Connecticut paying above $28,000. North and South Dakota, Montana, Louisiana, and Idaho are all below $20,000.[23]

There is no reason to try to make these numbers look better than they are. Many teachers cannot make ends meet on their school salaries. They must work two jobs, or in the case of married couples, both partners must work to generate a sufficient family income. For others, summer is a time for a second job by temping, building and painting houses, writing free-lance articles, or working at a company or lab. At the same time, many other Americans are facing the same economic realities. Most families need two wage-earners to generate even a modest lifestyle. It is also true that education salaries are up substantially from as recently as 1980 when the average teacher earned just $15,913. Plus, virtually all school districts have a negotiated salary schedule that increases slowly but steadily as you accrue years of teaching service and add professional development credits to your personnel file.

From a pay perspective, teachers have traditionally been paid less, but usually have more job and income security. In sales, your pay may go up or down depending on the success of the marketplace or the firm. Downturns can lead to layoffs. Individuals who hold lower-level managerial jobs, receive commissions for their work, or bill by the hour also see their salaries vary from year to year, even month to month. Other workers must worry about the impact of technology; for instance, bank tellers are being replaced by ATMs.

In a positive sense, teacher salaries are predictable in a way that many other fields are not. In addition, most teachers receive a benefits package including health and medical insurance, a retirement plan, sick days, and significant vacation time. At a time when nearly 40 percent of workers are in temporary or non-staff positions that usually do not include health and retirement coverage, relative security is an important benefit to the job.

Deciding to Teach

Teaching, like many other jobs, is a mix of negatives and positives. Contrary to popular misconceptions, teachers have long, fatiguing work schedules. The demands of preparing for, teaching, and assessing perhaps 125 students every day takes teachers to the limit of their physical and emotional stamina. To teach classes, plan lessons, advise students, grade papers, and meet with parents, most educators spend between forty-five and sixty hours a week doing the job of teacher.[24] They face an average schedule of five to six classes a day, twenty-three students per class. Teachers in urban schools have larger classes than teachers in rural areas; public school educators must instruct more students than their colleagues in private schools.

Job demands negatively affect many first- and second-year teachers who often get the largest classes and some of the most difficult students. Between one-third and one-half of all new teachers leave the profession within their first five years.[25] At least eight states—Connecticut, Oklahoma, Kentucky, Ohio, North Carolina, Indiana, West Virginia, and Louisiana—have funded state-wide induction programs for new teachers to help ease the transition from professional preparation to classroom practice. Too often, however, new teachers cannot find ways to balance the competing pressures of teaching adolescents, developing curriculum, managing time, and handling personal and family responsibilities. The field of education has not yet found the best ways to keep good teachers in the profession.

From a positive perspective, teaching can be a great career choice for parents who value being on the same schedule as their children. Moreover, summer vacation and other days off provide periods of rest, renewal, and rejuvenation after the demands and stresses of the school year. Many teachers spend their vacations learning more about their field and developing curriculum for their students. You will face decisions about how to spend your time when you are not teaching. You will still be working, but it will be a very different pace that offers the chances to reflect and reconsider how best to teach your students.

Teaching also provides opportunities to "practice what you teach" as well as "teach what you practice." We know of teachers who are also authors, news reporters, consultants for companies, small business owners, accountants, television and radio talent, summer theater performers and directors, recreation facility staff, language translators, or otherwise engaged in fulfilling "dual" lives as educators and workers. You too may be interested, for example, in becoming a teacher of science who is also a practicing scientist, or a teacher of writing who is also a writer.

On balance, we think teaching is an honorable and important way to make a living. Working in middle and high school classrooms can bring together personal, intellectual, and professional goals in a career that matters. It is creative and stimulating intellectual work. It offers a way to continue developing one's academic discipline or field of knowledge. It propels a person into a lifelong learning path of reading, writing, and thinking as well as opportunities to act on important social and academic issues.

Every day in teaching is a new experience in which you will use and expand your knowledge of subjects, adolescents, and schools. Together, you and your students create the future through your responses to the present. To further your thinking about teaching as a career that matters, we turn next to a discussion of how the learning and teaching of adolescents happens in places called middle and high schools.

NOTES

1. Richard Hofstadter, *Anti-intellectualism in American Life* (New York: Vintage Books, 1963).

2. U.S. Department of Education Initiative on Teaching, *Ensuring a Talented, Dedicated and Well-Prepared Teacher in Every Classroom* (Washington, D.C.: U.S. Department of Education, 1997), 5.

3. Debra E. Gerald and William J. Hussar, *Projections of Education Statistics to 2005* (Washington, D.C.: U.S. Department of Education, 1995), 65.

4. "U.S. School Population Will Hit a Record," *USA Today*, 22 August 1997, 3A.

5. U.S. Department of Education, *Community Update*, no. 38 (Washington, D.C.: U.S. Department of Education, August 1996).

6. Western Interstate Commission for Higher Education, *Knocking at the College Door: Projections of High School Graduates by Race/Ethnicity 1996–2012* (Boulder, CO: Western Interstate Commission for Higher Education, 1998).

7. Beth Daley, "City Faces New Shortage of Teachers," *The Boston Globe*, 23 March 1998, A1, B10.

8. Jacques Steinberg, "Help Wanted in New York: 3,000 Teachers (Or Maybe 9,000)," *New York Times*, 10 August 1997, 29–30.

9. "Survey Reveals Teaching Shortages in Many of Nation's Largest Cities," *The Recorder*, 22 May 1996, 7.

10. National Commission on Teaching & America's Future, *What Matters Most: Teaching and America's Future* (Washington, D.C.: National Commission on Teaching & America's Future, 1996), 15, 16.

11. "Teachers Who Have the Knowledge and Skills to Teach to Higher Standards," *Education Week*, 8 January 1998, 83.

12. Richard A. LaFleur, "Latina Resurgens: Classical Language Enrollments in American Schools and Colleges," *The Classical Outlook*, Summer 1997, 125.

13. Gilbert W. Lawall, "Graduate Latin Teacher Preparation Programs," in *Latin for the 21st Century: From Concept to Classroom*, edited by Richard A. LaFleur (Menlo Park, CA: Scott Foresman–Addison Wesley, 1997), 216.

14. G. Cannella and J. Reif, "Preparing Teachers for Cultural Diversity: Constructivist Orientations," *Action in Teacher Education* 26, no. 3 (1994), 37–45.

15. Sonia Nieto, "We Speak in Many Tongues: Language Diversity and Multicultural Education," in *Multicultural Education for the 21st Century*, edited by Carlos Diaz (Washington, D.C.: NEA Professional Library, 1992), 112–136.

16. National Center for Education Statistics, *America's Teachers: Profile of a Profession, 1993–94* (Washington, D.C.: U.S. Department of Education, 1997), 10.

17. David and Myra Sadkar, *Failing at Fairness: How America's Schools Cheat Girls* (New York: C. Scribner's Sons, 1994).

18. David Tyack and Elizabeth Hansot, *Learning Together: A History of Coeducation in American Public Schools* (New York: Russell Sage Foundation, 1992).

19. C. Emily Feistritzer, "The Truth Behind the 'Teacher Shortage.' " *The Wall Street Journal*, 28 January, 1998, A18.

20. David Berliner and Bruce J. Biddle, *The Manufactured Crisis: Myths, Fraud, and the Attack on America's Public Schools* (Reading, MA: Addison-Wesley, 1995).

21. Dale Ballou and Stephanie Soler, *Addressing the Looming Teacher Crunch: The Issue Is Quality* (Washington, D.C.: Progressive Policy Institute, February, 1998).

22. Linda Darling-Hammond, "The Current Status of Teaching and Teacher Development in the United States," *Educational Research Association Invitational Conference on Teacher Development*, May 6–8, 1996.

23. American Association for Employment in Education, *1998 Job Search Handbook for Educators* (Evanston, IL: American Association for Employment in Education, 1998), 13.

24. Susan P. Choy, *Teachers' Working Conditions: Findings from The Condition of Education, 1996*, no. 7 (Washington, D.C.: U.S. Government Printing Office, 1996), 5–7.

25. Darling-Hammond, "Current Status," 8.

2

Teaching in Schools Today

The introductory course in our Secondary Teacher Education Program starts with a discussion of what motivates students to enter a career in teaching. One semester, near the end of the first class, an older student explained that he had been training to become an air traffic controller, but decided not to pursue that occupation because he did not want to deal with the pressures of the job. He suggested, and the other students agreed, that teaching could not possibly be as stressful as directing the arrival and departure of airplanes.

Teaching, the instructor replied, is itself a high-intensity, high-demand occupation. There are hundreds of different students to instruct, constant interpersonal interactions to manage, simultaneous levels of awareness to maintain, and discordant interruptions of the public address system to endure.[1] While not having an immediate life and death impact, classroom educators make 150 critical instructional decisions every day, any one of which may have profound long-range implications for students, their learning, and their motivation to succeed in school.[2] The members of the class listened carefully, but the instructor saw that they were not fully convinced by this description and analysis of the teaching role.

While we agree that teaching may not be the most stressful work there is, prospective educators need a realistic sense of the pressures and possibilities they will face in "a place called school."[3] Our goal is to describe teaching as ultimately one of the most meaningful ways to earn a living, but also one of the most complex with its own tensions and demands. In this chapter, we invite you into the teacher's role for a brief time. Reading about teaching does not substitute for actual experience, but it may help you to recognize key aspects of the job so that you can be more reflective and realistic in your decision making and more broadly aware of the field.

VIEWS OF TEACHING AND LEARNING

Early in their teacher education program, we ask our students to pick an idea or concept in their subject area that they think is significant and teach it to a small group of their peers in a seven-minute mini-lesson. Almost to a person, the students teach their lesson by lecturing. Their initial concept of teaching is one of "telling."[4]

Since most of their ideas about being a teacher are autobiographical, their first teaching is an unwitting commentary on the prevailing type of education many of them experienced in elementary and secondary school as well as in college. They see teachers as knowledgeable individuals straightforwardly presenting information (and ways to understand that information) using words, numbers, pictures, and diagrams. Students are expected to remember the information and concepts they have been told, and recall or reconstruct it accurately on subsequent tests and essays.

It is true that a lecture can be an effective way of teaching. A well-crafted, engaging verbal presentation is a delight. It organizes and structures complex information; conveys large blocks of material to large numbers of learners; introduces new, unfamiliar concepts; and summarizes assigned reading from the textbook.

But in middle or high school classrooms, lectures day after day may deaden the heart, mind, and soul of students. Try as they might to be active listeners, the structure of a lecture eventually leads students to become passive and disengaged. They become accustomed to seeing themselves as recipients and teachers as dispensers of information. Many of our prospective teachers have experienced this method so repeatedly in their own education, that when it is their turn to teach, they almost instinctively assume the role of teller, master of the field, lecturing to the uninitiated. Even if many of them were critical of the way they had been taught in school, at the beginning of their teacher education program, they tend to teach the way they had been taught.

Teaching as telling also supports a popular view that many new teachers have about the act of teaching itself. They assume that a good teacher is someone who can present information in a convincing, engaging style. Teaching becomes defined as a form of verbal entertainment: The best performer is the best teacher. All focus is placed on the teacher; the students are receivers of information. Left out of this conception is the idea of the teacher assisting students to discover ideas and information for themselves, or relinquishing control of portions of the class so that the students might learn from each other.

Teaching as Banking

Teaching as telling is closely associated with the idea that the school system is like a banking system. The student is a long-term account into which teachers deposit valuable information on a regular basis. As knowledge accrues, the account grows in value and pays dividends on the investment when the student moves from school to society as a productive worker and citizen. The teacher is the source of information and understanding; the student must receive and store all that the teacher has to offer.

Educator and philosopher, Paulo Freire, among others, has sharply criticized a banking view of teaching. While most educators agree that there is essential information and skills that students need to have in order to function and contribute to society, Freire argues that everyone must be active learners rather than passive recipients in the educational process. It is true, he notes, that prospective educators get information about teaching in their teacher education programs, but they actually "learn how to teach as they teach something that is relearned as it is being taught."[5]

Freire cautioned against teacher domination of classrooms. In his view, "*teaching* cannot be a process of transference of knowledge from the one teacher to the learner." A teacher's role is not to cover but to uncover the material through conversations and dialog with students. For example, many of our prospective teachers, realizing that it is important to get students involved, start their lessons by asking them a question. But when the students do not give the expected answer right away, the teacher promptly provides it, sometimes disregarding what students may have said as though they had never spoken it.

To work with students in the way Freire suggests, teachers must continually study, read, and write so they can "become involved in their students' curiosity and in the paths and streams it takes them through." Teachers teach, "not as *bureaucrats of the mind* but by reconstituting the steps of their curiosity" in a dynamic relationship between educator and student.[6]

Teaching as Judging

Some beginning teachers come into our program with a view of teaching as a process somewhat like cooking or gardening. It implies a master chef blending the ingredients of academic information and intellectual skills. The student is essentially the product of the quality of the ingredients and the chef's good acts. In the garden analogy, the teacher supports the growth of students by systematically attending to the needs of individual learners as well as the quality of the overall environment of learning. By carefully tending the soil, air, and water of education, the educator makes it possible for all of the students to flourish.

One of the basic problems with this approach to teaching is that it interacts with another major assumption many of our students bring to teacher education. They view some kids as more intelligent than others, and unwittingly use such words as "smart," "bright," "dumb," or "slow." By assessing their students in the same way a chef or a gardener might evaluate their stock or plants, these certification candidates assume that if the quality is not good in the first place, those natural ingredients should be improved or used in another way.

Like many of us, these beginning teachers consistently confuse the academic and social performance of their students with an individual's innate capacities. If the student does not perform well, the teacher defines the individual as less smart, less talented, less capable. The tracking system that prevails in many schools sustains this confusion between ability and performance. Students are grouped according to what is called their "ability," another word that masks the distinction between innate capacity and daily performance. Because many beginning teachers have themselves been products of a tracking system in school, it is natural for them to categorize students in the language of natural inborn abilities such as intelligence, capacity, and competence, rather than in the more complicated language of performance.[7]

Teaching as Coaching

Some beginning teachers conceive of teaching as coaching. Many of us remember a special mentor who guided us in sports, music, art, or dance by stressing the fundamentals of the activity and supporting our novice performances. The coaching metaphor recognizes that performance is a developmental process that needs to be supported and facilitated. The new learner is continually trying out the skills and strategies the coach is teaching while also putting her or his own ideas into the process. The coach does not try to mass produce results by giving the same information to everyone, but attempts to individualize the instruction (as much as possible) to meet the needs of, and bring out the best in, each performer.

In *The Paideia Program* education reformer Mortimer J. Adler equated good teaching with good coaching.[8] A teacher/coach engages in "lively conversation" with students about their skills; focuses on a student's work; gives immediate feedback; offers "shrewd criticism"; concentrates on how students use their minds; and promotes practice to develop "error-free habits." This view of coaching blends "telling" and "questioning" with an "artful blend of information, challenge, drill, . . . and encouragement." As the teacher/coach evaluates and responds to each student's performance, the student develops the knowledge and understanding that the school wants to teach.

Of course, coaches can also be dictatorial individuals who yell and scream at mistakes. This notion of coaching as teaching is "Do it right, or you are benched!" Such coaches assume one right way to perform and often create a fear of failure rather than a desire for excellence and accomplishment. Coaching styles are not inherently or necessarily cooperative or authoritarian; it depends on the mindset of the coach, the novice, and the interactions between them.

A Constructivist Perspective

Of the many images that beginning teachers tend to have about education, a constructivist view is perhaps the least likely because it places the responsibility for learning on the interactions that occur between students and teachers; students and students; and students, teachers, and academic subjects. Constructivism sees knowledge and understanding not as previously known information, but as the product of learners constantly grappling with ideas and concepts. In this view, what is taught in school is not something inert that can be produced, stored, and then communicated to a class by a teacher. Rather, a subject must be reconstructed each time as students work with a topic of inquiry.

Constructivists envision the classroom as a well-equipped studio where minds-on, hands-on activities support thinking and discovering. In such an active environment, "students 'write' history through inquiry into varied sources and rearranging a narrative," or they " 'discover' science by manipulating wires, batteries and light bulbs."[9] Teachers strive to make knowledge accessible to students as conductors of experience—structuring situations, providing materials, and encouraging individuals in many different ways to build new understandings and refine existing ones. Accordingly, constructivist teachers are always considering when to lead, when to follow, and when to get out of the way of their students' activities.

Constructivist teachers also necessarily challenge established meanings, believing that learning happens when contradictions, puzzles, and anomalies force individuals to reconsider their taken-for-granted assumptions. Teachers ask students to think differently about what they think they know: who is doing what; why things exist as we know them; why some individuals' views are different; how systems and practices might change. Learners construct their understandings anew when long-held ideas are called into question. Some students may object to efforts to analyze and reassess their views of the world. To get adolescents to reconsider established meanings is hard work, and it takes time for individuals to build increasingly complex viewpoints about self, others, and society.

Some beginning teachers are slow to embrace a constructivist approach to teaching, first because they have had little experience with these concepts in their own education. Second, constructivism seems to demean established bodies of information including names, dates, facts, and concepts that critics like E. D. Hirsch believe everyone in the society must share if the culture is to be sustained.[10] They fear the personal experiences of individuals will become more important than scientifically established research. Third, some find constructivist teaching difficult to conceptualize and to do well, and with all the other things to learn about education (classroom management, writing objectives, calculating grades), why add more complexity?

There may be a post-constructivist synthesis developing in education where constructivists and their critics are trying to find common ground that corresponds with the realities of a changing economy and society. As economists Richard Murname and Frank Levy suggest, students need "new basic skills" for the future, including the ability to read and do math; solve semistructured problems; work in groups with diverse people; communicate effectively; and use personal computers.[11] To teach these skills to students, educators will need a repertoire of teaching metaphors (including telling, coaching, and constructing knowledge together) and ways to move easily among them.

The Intellectual Work of Teachers

There is no one right way to teach. Probably any method or combinations of methods that is carried out with passion and humor by a teacher will be more effective than any theoretically sound approach delivered in a mechanistic, formulaic manner.

Good teaching requires going beyond one's own personal history and the assumptions about education that it generates. It depends on thoughtful reflection about the complexities of how people learn. It requires making sense of pedagogical issues, like:

What do I think knowledge really is?

How is it attained by different people?

What is the difference between knowledge and understanding?

What is an idea?

How does thinking differ from sensing?

Teaching also requires understanding all the complexities that affect a student's performance and addressing them without using the shortcut of categorizing someone as smart, average, or dumb. It is demanding intellectual work.

To become an excellent teacher, one must integrate teaching methods that respect and ask questions about the knowledge that already exists; affirm the centrality of students being actively engaged with old and new ideas; assess students' learning from developmental perspectives; and understand that a student's performance in class is affected in many ways by his or her life outside of school.

The complicated threads that a teacher must keep track of and skillfully interweave every day may not appear as complicated as the air-controller's radar screen, with its ever-changing scene of moving planes converging on a limited space. But as you examine the roles of a teacher, the daunting complexities of the job will emerge. Many of our students want to enter teaching because they have enjoyed school, know they love learning, and hope to continue working with a subject field they find compelling. As beginners, they confront the enormous amounts of preparation and planning that an excellent teacher does before entering the classroom. As they continue teaching, they strive to keep their passion for learning despite the complexities of schooling.

A LOOK AT THE STUDENTS YOU WILL TEACH

When we ask our prospective teachers to visit and observe in schools, many see a formerly familiar place from a different point of view. Some go back, for the first time since they graduated, to the schools they attended as adolescents. Others visit schools that are new to them. They walk through the classrooms and corridors seeing middle and high school kids from a future teacher's perspective.

They may enter the student bathroom and be appalled by behavior they once accepted as part of the scenery, or overhear conversation in the teacher's lounge that intrigues or bothers them. They may talk with a teacher and think how different he or she seems when thought of as a potential colleague. If they themselves are college-age undergraduates, they may be the object of curious stares or unwanted and unwelcome remarks as they walk between classes.

As they spend more time in the school, they will see students consumed with how they look. They may be troubled by the public displays of touching, kissing, and flirting that many youngsters experience whether they want that sort of attention or not. If the subject comes up in a classroom they are observing, they are likely to hear the most virulent homophobic comments as the realities of sexual identity become confused by the stereotyped bravado of some youngsters. If they are relatively unobtrusive, they may overhear plans for weekend parties, binge drinking, and drug use that occurs among some teenagers. If they are keen observers, they will recognize hints of same sex relationships that are usually deeply camouflaged in secondary schools and seldom discussed. They may find a kid high on marijuana or a student asleep in the back of the room. They may learn about a student who recently committed suicide, was killed in a car crash, or, most unthinkable until recently, was shot by a classmate.

At the same time, if they turn their attention away from subcultures of youth, our observers will also see the enormous "positive potentials" of adolescents.[12] In every in-school class or after-school event, they will find exciting learning happening as middle and high schoolers read and respond to literature; write creative stories; solve mathematical and scientific problems; learn a new language; perform drama; create art; conduct experiments; play sports; analyze social issues; get involved in the community; influence school and public policy; and engage in many other learning activities that show just how much these young individuals can accomplish. Viewed in these terms, the possibilities for what students and teachers can learn together seem almost limitless.

Dimensions of Adolescent Experience

The currents beneath the surface in the lives of students carry all the complexities of the broader society and are made even more complicated by the adolescent stage of human development. For example, you are going to see few schools that are genuinely integrated. The overwhelming majority of students of color go to schools where minorities predominate.[13] Looking more closely, you may find tracked advanced classes in those urban schools that are predominantly White despite the fact that students of European heritage are in the minority in the school. Entering the cafeteria, except in the most unusual school, you will see African American kids sitting with African Americans, Latinos sitting with Latinos, Asians sitting with Asians, and European American students sitting among themselves. Many African American youngsters, notes psychologist Beverly Daniel Tatum, find that other Black youth provide them with more understandable answers to the questions "What does it mean to be a young Black person?" and "How should I act?"[14]

The fact is that our society is becoming more and more diverse. Students of color comprise more than 30 percent of the national student body, and that percentage will continue to rise, signaling the emergence of what Carlos E. Cortes calls America's "demographically multicultural future."[15] By 2007/08, for example, White non-Latino students will be only 50 percent of the high school graduates in the nation's western states.[16] Yet our teacher candidates are predominantly of European American descent, and most of the teachers they will observe will be as well. The enormous complexities of ethnic diversity, group stereotyping, and racial bias that take place in the wider society get played out every-day in the microcosm of schools.

Inside schools, many female students seemingly disappear in class-rooms while aggressive boys dominate the discussion. Studies indicate girls lose confidence in themselves academically and personally from ages ten to sixteen, especially in science and math courses.[17] They are at greater risk of depression and suicide attempts and "more vulnerable than boys of the same age to eating disorders, substance abuse, and dropping out of school."[18] By contrast, boys get more complex questions, are allowed more time for answers, and rewarded with praise more often by teachers. They are evaluated disproportionately for advanced place-ment in mathematics and science; but the same holds true for placement in special education programs as well. Both genders encounter "hostile hallways" with unwanted sexual touching and innuendo.[19]

Depending on the part of the country where you are thinking of teach-ing, many of the students in the school may not speak English as their first language. There are, for example, 109 different languages spoken in the Washington, D.C., metropolitan area. In 1996, at Everett High School outside of Boston, students spoke Vietnamese, Chinese, Hindi, Cape Ver-dian, Korean, Italian, Polish, Creole, Somali, Spanish, Bengali, Albanian, Fanit, Turkish, Thai, French, Arabic, German, Czech, Polish, Portuguese, and Cambodian. Just a decade ago, only eight languages were spoken by students at the school.[20]

Nationwide nearly three million students are learning to speak English as a new language. Most of these students are Spanish speakers (74 per-cent) while Vietnamese is the next largest percentage group at 3.9 per-cent.[21] These bilingual students find themselves in the middle of intense political and educational debates. In California, a state with 1.4 million bilingual students, voters recently passed Proposition 227 which threat-ens to reduce drastically bilingual education in the state's schools and substitute immersion programs in English. In other states, some districts have implemented English-only teaching mandates. By contrast, other schools are focusing on two-way bilingual programs that emphasize crit-ical thinking skills and cooperative interactions between bilingual stu-dents and native English speakers. In these programs, good teaching and a respect for diverse languages are keys to success for all students.

If you look carefully in the halls between classes, you may catch sight of children in wheelchairs or on crutches, or with awkward walks being led by teachers and aides quietly through the halls from a classroom to the cafeteria. Nationwide, 11 percent of the students are physically chal-lenged, speech or language impaired, mentally retarded, emotionally disturbed, autistic, or face other special learning needs.[22] Since the Amer-icans with Disabilities Act was passed in 1991, and the notion of inclusion has taken hold in schools, many of these students are "mainstreamed" in the classroom. Special education teachers and aides work directly with the students and their regular education teachers. The opportunities for mutual growth among "regular" and "special" education students and teachers are enormous. But, if you speak with teachers you will hear strong views for and against the notion of inclusion. Nevertheless, the energy for inclusion is significant and future teachers are likely to face that added degree of complexity and possibility in their jobs.

Although you may remember doing your homework regularly when you were in school, you are likely to be teaching classes in which four out of five students hold part-time jobs, either because the family needs the money or the student is saving for school or supporting a car, a hobby, or a wardrobe. Other students may be caring for younger siblings or they may be parents themselves. For them, the demands of family life will compete directly with the time needed to do school work. For some youngsters facing abuse or neglect at home, school is the safest place in their daily lives.

Connecting with Students

Adolescent students must make "fateful choices" about their lives.[23] For many youth, school is a crossroads between establishing positive directions or unhealthy lifestyles, and the choice can remain unsettled for some time. As a prospective secondary educator, you will have your hands, heart, and mind full as you try to figure out what influence you can have on the paths your future students will take. It is different, but equally as challenging and complicated as the flight controller's job, and in the long run, it is as significant.

The heterogeneity of adolescent experience is without question one of the realities of schools today. Responding to that heterogeneity as an educator can push the individual teacher to his or her limit. It is not easy to be patient with and attentive to a range of demands that may go beyond your own personal experience. Each teacher brings his or her own autobiography into the classroom. Many of the education decisions that teachers make are quick and almost instinctive, and they most likely lean heavily on their own past experience. All of us in teaching are more or less comfortable with different students in our classrooms. The challenge is to broaden our experiences, to go beyond our personal histories to connect to the autobiographies our students bring to the classroom.

We ask our prospective teachers, "Do you like kids?" It seems to us that that is one of the essential issues every prospective teacher has to face. To succeed in secondary teaching, an educator needs to enjoy being in the company of adolescents. They must be able to look at the students in their classes and sense and engage all the potential that resides in each and every youngster. Is this the case for you? Are you interested in every student or just those who are easy to teach? How future teachers answer these inquiries is central to whether they will inspire success or failure within the range of needs, interests, and potentials of the students they teach.

MIDDLE SCHOOL OR HIGH SCHOOL: WHERE DO YOU WANT TO TEACH?

The question "Do you like kids?" often takes an unexpected turn when we ask prospective teachers if they are interested in teaching in middle schools. Most states offer secondary certification for grades 7–12. Some, responding to the argument that middle-school-age youth present different challenges than high-school-age students, have established two levels of certification in the secondary range. In these states, prospective secondary teachers must choose between middle or high school certification, although it is possible to prepare for both levels.

The overwhelming majority of prospective teachers in our program begin their teacher education courses wanting to get certified for high school. They dismiss or reject the notion of teaching in middle schools. To examine their assumptions, we ask them to observe a high school and middle school and to report their observations. Reading their field reports in class, we list the salient characteristics that they observe in both places.

Our college students are surprised by the middle school students, especially the range and the differences between sixth and eighth or ninth graders. Some youngsters have nearly reached their adult physiques while others are only beginning their adolescent changes. Many kids are giggly, antsy, loud, and their attention spans are hard to direct. Others appear excited by ideas, are eager to participate in discussions and projects, and seek learning enthusiastically. Some of our students see one class and conclude that early adolescents are nothing more than a set of raging hormones. Others see a group working with a different adult and realize that how middle schoolers attend to learning depends a great deal on the teacher.

On balance, however, when we ask our students why they choose not to teach in middle schools, many answer that they want to teach their subject matter at a "higher level." They do not see teaching the more basic foundations of their field as intellectually satisfying. They picture high school teaching allowing them to delve more deeply into their subject, perhaps akin to what they did in their college experience. In fact, if we asked what level they would really like to teach if they could, many say college.

You, too, will face decisions about what grade level you want to teach. As you consider middle school and high school, there are significant teaching opportunities at each level. Some basic points about each follow.

Looking at High Schools

As the pinnacle of K–12 public education, high schools represent the crucial transition point for students between going to school and participating in adult society. A widely recognized goal of high school is to prepare adolescents for productive roles as workers and as citizens. Ideally, notes educator Theodore Sizer in *Horace's Compromise*, students learn academic knowledge, career skills, citizenship, moral values, how to get along with one another, an appreciation of the arts, good health practices, and acceptance of diverse cultures.[24] In fact, most high schools struggle to achieve even parts of the overwhelming mission society has set for them.

To graduate from high school, students must complete a prescribed core curriculum that includes English, mathematics, science, social studies, and health/physical education. In most states, the board of education or legislature sets the parameters for high school requirements; local school districts then adjust their policies to meet community standards. Many districts choose to mandate world languages and fine arts. Four states—North Carolina, Delaware, Texas, and Mississippi—have created computer literacy/technology requirements for those who will graduate in the twenty-first century.[25]

High schools are generally large, sometimes impersonal places enrolling between one and five thousand older adolescents in grades 9 or 10 through 12. Size alone determines some of what happens to students and teachers. The demands of trying to manage education for hundreds and hundreds of youngsters often creates complex bureaucratic structures with separate academic departments and relatively independent grade levels. The work of every two teachers is supported by the efforts of one other school employee: administrators, counselors, nurses, janitors, bus drivers, coaches, security personnel, media staff, and human service providers. Tying it all together can be a problem. Some schools are moving to smaller learning communities within the school building to encourage more flexibility for teachers while providing group support for students.

Yet, as Theodore Sizer noted, for many youngsters, high school days pass with a remarkable sameness. There are classes on poetry followed by algebraic formulas followed by the Civil War, often with little sense of personal relevance.[26] Ever present is the friction between too little time and too much curriculum. While our prospective teachers think about teaching subjects in "advanced" ways, they sometimes note, but perhaps do not fully understand, the boredom and lethargy of many high school students.

Inherent in high school teaching is an ongoing tension between teaching subject matter and making that subject matter relevant so students can understand it thoughtfully. It is a powerful challenge, and one of the great rewards of upper grades teaching. As a high school teacher, you can go beyond academic information by exploring its implications and applications for society. You have the opportunity to build students' interests in important questions, work with them to create alternative solutions to those issues, and set the stage for them to carry on problem-solving activities in college or career.

A Middle Grades View

Traditionally, the education of young adolescents has taken place in junior high schools. As the name suggests, junior high is a scaled-down version of high school. Students move from class to class to be taught by subject field specialists. There are graduation requirements as well as elective courses, and the student is expected to take increasing responsibility for her or his school performance. The academic content of most junior high classes mirrors the content of high school subjects at less advanced levels. In some fields, the goal is to provide the foundation for later work; for instance, students learn algebra in order to take geometry, calculus, and other higher mathematics in high school. In other cases, teachers focus on specific topics within a broad field of knowledge, such as world history and geography or important works in American literature.

In the past two decades, middle schools have begun replacing junior high schools, spurred on by the 1990 *Turning Points* report from the Carnegie Council on Adolescent Development. The report challenged much of the conventional wisdom about how to educate young adolescents. Sadly, the authors noted, many schools were "large, impersonal institutions" that ill-served at least one in four young adolescents. Students moved from class to class, but "the subject matter of one class typically has nothing to do with the next, creating a fragmented learning experience for students."[27]

In contrast, one of the significant changes in the transformation of junior highs to middle schools is the creation of cohorts of students placed in teams or houses as a way to retain interpersonal bonds among the students and between the students and the teachers. As Cynthia S. Mee concluded after conducting extensive interviews with two thousand ten- to fourteen-year-olds in six states, middle schoolers give uppermost importance to issues of "care and caring," and they want their teachers to listen to them. Mee urged teachers to slow down, relax, and "demonstrate that you care about your students and enjoy just being with them."[28]

If you are like the students who enter our program, you may have an initial bias against teaching at the middle school level. But, the intellectual challenge of teaching your subject matter in a way that is foundational and relevant to young students' lives, along with their unbridled, enthusiastic responsiveness to caring adults, may eventually change your mind. Moreover, groups of middle school students are often taught by an interdisciplinary team of teachers who are given planning time to integrate their approaches to subject matter and to be reflective about the progress students are making in their classes. Team teaching offers opportunities for collegiality and cooperation among faculty which are not common at the high school level.

Another reality of the educational marketplace contributes to reconsidering the choice between middle school and high school. As positions become available, they are almost always posted internally first. Therefore, if a high school position is open, someone in the district's middle school may apply for it and be given preference over someone from outside the system. The district fills the opening by moving the middle school applicant to the high school and then advertising the vacated middle school position. Often this results in more middle school than high school jobs available to new teachers.

THE DIALECTICS OF SECONDARY TEACHING

No matter whether you choose to teach at the middle or high school level, your task will be enormously complex and subject to contradictions. Typically our students experience what we have come to call the "dialectics of teaching." They set forth considerable energy in their preparation, planning, and teaching. The school, the society, and even the students themselves provide counterbalances or antitheses to that energy. The teacher struggles with the complexities of the interactions, and, together with his or her students, tries to come to a creative synthesis or resolution.

It is important to see that within the vast array of activities that are part of a secondary teacher's work—instructing, advising, supporting, and nurturing adolescents along their developmental path in complex school organizations—there are constant processes of action and reaction where teachers create syntheses that are meaningful to themselves and their students. Four key dialectics follow.

Individuals and Groups

One of the consistent tensions that teachers face flows from an accepted practice in United States education: meeting with groups of students at regularly scheduled meeting times in situations called classes. You will most likely teach four or five classes a day and be responsible for between 100 and 125 students. Note that some school systems are moving to block schedules in which teachers meet with fewer classes for longer periods of time. During class time teachers are expected to keep the entire group focused on the required curriculum.

At the same time, teachers are also responsible for each individual student in the class. They want every student to understand and learn, but motivating groups and inspiring individuals is not necessarily the same process. Teaching to the group as a whole often leaves some individuals lagging behind or feeling unable to push ahead. Teaching individuals at their own pace is often logistically difficult when there is one teacher and twenty students. Many days, teaching seems like a search for a mythical middle ground where educators can make sure that each individual student succeeds while the entire class continues to move forward.

Although it is not always easy to think in these terms, a "teacher operates out of a kind of blind faith" that by consistently providing individuals and groups with compelling experiences in and out of the classroom they will learn.[29] This view builds on the assumption that human learning does not happen solely through predictable processes of stimulus and response. Students in school learn in non-linear ways as they try out new ideas and activities. Adolescent growth and development involves taking action, making mistakes, trying again, imitating others, and exploring (with adult guidance) issues that concern them and their communities.

What makes all this simultaneously interesting and perplexing is multiplying the complexities of each individual's learning processes by the number of students in the classes. Looking at a roomful of students you will see a mosaic of learning potentials. Some individuals always learn at a different pace than the others. They make connections quickly, mentally vaulting from plateaus of understanding to peaks of learning to plateaus again. Others move more slowly. Both need different combinations of experiences to forge new understandings.

As a teacher, an important part of your job is to arrange and set in motion the opportunities for students to build connections that lead to learning. At the same time, there is no way to avoid the tension between covering the curriculum and making sure everyone understands it. It is easy to worry about doing everything right for every student. Sometimes you must make uncomfortable compromises between individuals and groups. If you are lucky and creative, and are a member of a department or team that is thoughtful about such matters, these dynamics will lead to new learning and teaching approaches that create success for everyone in the class.

Subjects and Students

Another powerful tension exists between teaching subjects and teaching students. Most elementary teachers would not hesitate to answer the question, "Do you teach a subject or do you teach kids?" by saying "I teach kids." Middle and high school teachers, specializing in a subject matter, have less obvious responses. Most secondary teachers have a strong commitment to their subject matter. They see themselves teaching an academic field of knowledge that is well established and widely known. The pressures of school reform are lending even more weight to the idea of teaching subjects. Thirty-eight states have adopted curriculum standards in the core academic subjects.[30] Teachers are under pressure to prepare students to do well on standardized tests keyed to these frameworks.

Yet, as committed as teachers may be to their subject area, many soon find that unless they can connect school work to daily life, they lose their students' interest. To make academic subjects more relevant to adolescents, teachers find themselves relating to students beyond "lecturer" and "grader." As one educator noted, a teacher is called upon to be a psychologist, parent, friend, judge, trail guide, and cheerleader.[31] Teachers play instructional and developmental roles. It is not simply a matter of what they teach to students, it is also a matter of how they relate interpersonally to adolescents and motivate them to develop their skills, interests, talents, and potentials.

Playing a positive developmental role requires an optimistic attitude. A teacher cannot afford to be cynical about life when students are trying to develop their own. You must have confidence, integrity, and trust the potential of your students.[32] These are difficult requirements for any prospective teacher.

Many teachers have found ways to balance the tension between subjects and students. "It is all about building relationships," one first-year mathematics teacher told us. The key is "establishing positive connections with kids, maintaining them, and repairing them when necessary." He was an older new teacher, age forty-five, starting a second career after working in private business. He began with the idea that his job was to teach math, and only math. Soon he discovered that he could use all his daily interactions with adolescents to create a climate in which students would support his teaching rather than oppose it. Positive relationships did not mean being buddies with students, "hanging" with kids, or giving them whatever they want. It meant establishing high expectations for learning, communicating optimistically yet honestly, implementing rules fairly, and respecting students as individuals.

Isolation and Support

One of the aspects of teaching that prospective teachers seem to understand least is the strange notion that in the midst of a busy school with constant interactions between students, colleagues, and administrators, a teacher can feel isolated. The pace of school is so quick that there is little time for reflective conversation or sharing ideas with colleagues. Some student teachers quickly learn to stay out of the faculty coffee room, for the teachers that inhabit it seem to be those who are most bitter about their work and their students. Because curriculum is delivered through a series of separate classes, there is often little time for discussion among high school departments or middle school teams about curricular and instructional issues or broader educational goals.

School-wide faculty meetings can be equally frustrating. Many secondary schools in this country are fashioned on an industrial model with teachers being the equivalent of workers, and principals and superintendents being the equivalent of forepersons and chief executive officers.[33] This top-down organizational model is essentially undemocratic. It is the outstanding principal who knows how to engage his or her faculty in a collaborative, collegial manner work toward shared goals with a sense of equitable voice for all. Faculty meetings in schools can unfortunately lead to more, rather than less, alienation among teachers.

Sexism and gender inequality in schools not only affects students, it structures how many teachers relate to the work of teaching. Ann Lieberman and Lynne Miller suggest that historically a "male culture" has prevailed in many high schools. Male teachers think about advancing to administrative or other leadership roles. Women teachers, although there have been some changes recently, tend to view classroom teaching as their life's work.[34] In a recent study, one researcher found a significant discrepancy between the talent, insight, and wisdom embedded in the experience of mature female teachers in school and the opportunities they have for leadership in schools which still seem to be run like old boys' clubs.[35] Women remain frustrated by a "glass ceiling" that has severely limited the number of female school leaders at the secondary level.

Spending most of their days with adolescents, having little time and little encouragement to team with colleagues, and being subject to a leadership style designed for a factory in the early twentieth century, teachers can feel isolated and lonely in a crowded building. In the face of these realities, some teachers remain alone, creating a sense of themselves against the system. Others identify with subgroups within the faculty: the coffee room complainers, the weekend golfers, those who dedicate themselves to the students by supporting extracurricular activities.

Other teachers follow a different route. They join other like-minded teachers in urging curricular reform, attending professional conferences, and participating in decision making as much as the school culture allows and supports. They attend courses during the summer and in the process interact with teachers from other schools who share their enthusiasm for learning. Through their involvement in professional development, they recapture a sense of the possibilities of teaching which attracted them to the work in the first place.

Rewards and Satisfactions

Like anyone who works for a living, teachers need positive rewards and a sense of satisfaction in their work. Many of you reading this book may be well aware of the frustrations of being unhappy at work; some of you may be thinking of going into teaching for that very reason. You want a job that integrates personal interests and professional choices.

Most workers say that reward and satisfaction on the job is part monetary, part psychological. They not only want to make a living from their work, they also want that work to be meaningful. It is ironic that you are thinking about entering teaching at a time when the job opportunity is better than it has been since the 1960s, but it is also a time when public education is under almost constant attack. Public respect and support for teaching seems, at least according to the media, to be wavering. Some appear so unhappy with public education that they seem intent on destroying it as we know it to substitute a privatized system. Others are working to save public education, but they are demanding reforms.

Education is an easy target for critics. Politicians seem uninterested or impotent in the face of the underlying problems of schooling, namely, a country in which the distribution of wealth is becoming more and more inequitable, and in which there are "savage inequalities" in the opportunities for an education afforded our students depending on the social class into which they were born.[36] Politicians seem ready to pass legislation to reform schools unmindful that they are dealing mostly with symptoms rather than underlying causes.

Despite the political attacks and the sense of being on the defensive, there are few jobs that offer the intellectual, spiritual, and psychological meaningfulness that can be yours in teaching. You create and set in motion opportunities for students to build new connections that can lead to a wonderful sense of the excitement of learning. It is true that you may worry about doing everything right for each of your students, and you may take negative responses from individuals very personally. Virtually no other job hinges success on your making every conversation, every lesson, and every action have meaning and significance.

Connecting a sense of accomplishment as a teacher to your students' performance, however, is risky business. Some days you see results right away. There is a sense of electricity in the classroom air. Students are excited by the material, ask penetrating questions, finish great projects, and do well on the exams. At these times teaching seems like the best job of all because you are succeeding in promoting learning. Other days you get a mixed set of responses. Everyone seems tired or bored, time is crawling by, and little progress is being made. Teaching becomes a long, grinding way to spend the day.

We repeatedly explain to certification candidates that their students will walk out of the classroom at the end of the year and they may or may not say thank you. Occasionally a student will send you a note or say something that acknowledges the positive impact you have had on her or his life. At this developmental stage, adolescents have other things on their minds and many other demands to meet. Acknowledging a teacher is not usually central to their attention. Teachers touch many lives, but seldom hear from students again after graduation.

A grateful student does sometimes write a "nice note" to express appreciation for what a teacher has done. On these rare occasions, expressions of thanks do buoy a teacher. Some teachers say, upon receiving such a note, "This is what it is all about." While compliments from students are wonderful to receive, on a practical level, even for the best of teachers, they arrive too infrequently to rest a career on. A flight controller knows that he or she has succeeded when the plane lands or takes off safely. There is tangible, immediate evidence of a successful job. For a teacher, the evidence is intangible, delayed by years, and often hidden from view.

The intangibility of rewards means a teacher must create his or her sense of satisfaction from an inner measure of doing good work. How do you do that? If, after a year in school, teaching is still intellectually exciting to you and you still like kids, then you are probably doing good work. A need for an internalized sense of accomplishment is one of the complexities of a teaching career that prospective educators must face. A successful resolution allows the old saying, "Those who can, do; those who can't, teach," to be replaced by "Those who can, do and do and do and do; those who understand, teach."

NOTES

1. Philip W. Jackson, *Life in Classrooms* (New York: Holt, Rinehart and Winston, 1968).
2. C. M. Clark and P. L. Peterson, "Teachers' Thought Processes," in *Handbook*

of Research on Teaching, 3rd ed., edited by M. C. Wittrock (New York: Macmillan, 1986), 255–296.

3. John I. Goodlad, *A Place Called School: Prospects for the Future* (New York: McGraw Hill, 1984).

4. Mary Ann Bowman, "Metaphors We Teach By: Understanding Ourselves as Teachers and Learners," *Teaching Excellence* 8, no. 3 (1996–1997), 1–2.

5. Paulo Freire, *Teachers as Cultural Workers: Letters to Those Who Dare Teach*, translated by Donaldo Macedo, Dale Koike, and Alexandre Oliverira (Boulder, CO: Westview Press, 1998), 17.

6. Ibid., 22.

7. Noam Chomsky, *Language and Mind* (New York: Harcourt Brace Jovanovich, 1972).

8. Mortimer J. Adler, ed., *The Paideia Program: An Educational Syllabus* (New York: Macmillan, 1984), 33–46.

9. Byrd L. Jones and Robert W. Maloy, *Schools for an Information Age* (Westport, CT: Praeger, 1996), 82.

10. E. D. Hirsch Jr., *Cultural Literacy: What Every American Needs to Know* (Boston: Houghton Mifflin, 1987).

11. R. J. Murname and Frank Levy, *Teaching the New Basic Skills: Principles for Educating Children to Thrive in a Changing Economy* (New York: Free Press, 1996).

12. Yolanda Yugar, "The Positive Potential of Middle School Students," *National Dropout Prevention Newsletter* 10, no. 4 (Fall 1997), 8.

13. G. Orfield with S. Schley, D. Glass, and S. Reardon, *The Growth of Segregation in American Schools: Changing Patterns of Separation and Poverty Since 1968* (Washington, D.C.: National School Boards Association, 1993).

14. Beverly Daniel Tatum, *"Why Are All the Black Kids Sitting Together in the Cafeteria?" and Other Conversations About Race* (New York: BasicBooks, 1997), 60.

15. Carlos Cortes, "Beyond Affirmative Action," *MLE Alumni Bulletin*, June 1996, 1–5.

16. Western Interstate Commission for Higher Education, *Knocking at the College Door: Projections of High School Graduates by Race/Ethnicity 1996–2012* (Boulder, CO: Western Interstate Commission for Higher Education, 1998), 6.

17. American Association of University Women, *How Schools Shortchange Girls* (Washington, D.C.: American Association of University Women, 1992).

18. Joan Jacobs Brumberg, *The Body Project: An Intimate History of American Girls* (New York: Random House, 1997), xxiii–xxiv.

19. American Association of University Women, *Hostile Hallways: The AAUW Survey on Sexual Harassment in America's Schools* (Washington, D.C.: American Association of University Women, 1993).

20. Dick Lehr, "Classroom Buzz," *The Boston Globe*, 11 February 1997, E1, E6.

21. Laurel Shaper Walters, "The Bilingual Education Debate," *The Harvard Education Letter* 14, no. 3 (May/June 1998), 1–2.

22. Tamar Levin, "Where All Doors Are Open for Disabled Students," *New York Times*, 28 December 1997, 1, 20.

23. Fred Hechinger, *Fateful Choices: Healthy Youth for the 21st Century* (New York: Hill & Wang, 1992).

24. Theodore R. Sizer, *Horace's Compromise: The Dilemma of the American High School* (Boston: Houghton Mifflin, 1985).

25. Dennis McCafferty, "Master Your Computer—or Flunk," *USA Weekend*, 6–8 February 1998, 28.

26. Sizer, *Horace's Compromise*, 81.

27. Carnegie Council on Adolescent Development, *Turning Points: Preparing American Youth for the 21st Century—Abridged Version* (New York: Carnegie Council on Adolescent Development, 1990), 10.

28. Cynthia S. Mee, *2,000 Voices: Young Adolescents' Perceptions & Curriculum Implications* (Columbus, OH: National Middle School Association, 1997), 57.

29. Ann Lieberman and Lynne Miller, *Teachers, Their World, and Their Work: Implications for School Improvement* (Alexandria, VA: Association for Supervision and Curriculum Development, 1984), 3.

30. "High Standards for All Children and Assessment Aligned with Those Standards," *Education Week*, 8 January 1998, 80.

31. David Maloof, "A Teacher's Repertoire of Roles," *Boston Sunday Globe*, 1 February 1998, C5–C7.

32. Shirley F. Heck and C. Ray Williams, *The Complex Roles of the Teacher* (New York: Teachers College Press, 1984).

33. Raymond E. Callahan, *Education and the Cult of Efficiency: A Study of the Social Forces That Have Shaped the Administration of the Public Schools* (Chicago: University of Chicago Press, 1962).

34. Lieberman and Miller, *Teachers, Their World, and Their Work*, 49.

35. Susan R. Clarke, *Taking Care: Women High School Teachers at Midlife and Midcareer* (Unpublished Ed. D. diss., University of Massachusetts–Amherst, 1998).

36. Jonathan Kozol, *Savage Inequalities: Children in America's Schools* (New York: HarperPerennial, 1991).

3

Navigating the Certification Maze

Teacher certification may be broadly defined as a license to teach. It is granted by a state to an individual teacher for a specified period of time. Certification says, in the eyes of the state granting the certificate, that you have demonstrated command of subject matter, knowledge of learning and teaching, and personal integrity and moral character necessary to teach in public schools.

Why do states certify teachers? The goal is to protect the public from unqualified, uninformed, and unethical individuals teaching children. As a result, in most states most of the time, you must be certified to teach in a middle or high school. In this respect, teacher certification is like other licenses whereby appropriately prepared individuals are allowed to drive a car, offer counseling services, sell real estate, remove asbestos, do electrical wiring, or provide medical care in emergency situations. In each of these cases, the state's licensure seeks to ensure a certain standard of quality work.

In the past, states offered lifetime teaching certificates. Today almost every state has implemented at least a two-tier system of certification. The first or initial certificate is meant to be probationary. It allows you to begin teaching while your performance is reviewed by experienced teachers and administrators. This review, along with additional coursework, sets the stage for your second or advanced level certificate. In most states, advanced certificates must be renewed periodically. First gaining, and then maintaining certification is something you will be doing throughout your teaching career.

This chapter is our effort to sort out the complex procedures and policies that make up what we call the "teacher certification and licensing maze." There is no single national teaching certificate, so you must be aware of fifty different credentialing systems. Information is spread out in many different places and is always changing. There is a vocabulary of terms to learn including "subject area and grade level," "academic majors," "professional preparation courses," "student teaching," "two-tiered certification systems," "teacher tests," "reciprocity agreements," and "national board certification," to name a few.

We offer specific information about how to transform your background or interests in mathematics, English, the sciences, history/social studies, world languages, or other subjects generally taught in secondary schools into a teaching license. We examine the essential stages of earning teacher certification, and we answer some frequently asked questions about the licensing process including whether to get certified as an undergraduate or graduate student and whether to specialize at the middle or high school levels.

So far we have been using the terms certification and licensing interchangeably. However, there is a move across the country to distinguish between certification and licensure. The National Board for Professional Teaching Standards is sponsoring a certificate for experienced teachers. This organization, along with other reformers, wants states to grant licenses that assure at least minimal competencies to teach. Professional teaching organizations would then issue certifications of advanced levels of performance.[1] At the moment some states use the terminology of certification, others use licensure, and some use both as though there were no distinction between the two.

STEPS TO CERTIFICATION

Approximately nine out of ten new teachers become certified to teach by entering a college- or university-based program designed to prepare individuals for licensure and entry into the job market. The remaining future educators seek alternative routes to certification that are school-district-based rather than conducted by colleges or universities. (We discuss the advantages and disadvantages of alternative paths to certification in Chapter 4.) Whether you seek certification through a college or university program or a school system alternative, the overall requirements for your license are basically the same:

- An arts and sciences bachelor's degree from an accredited college or university
- An academic major or its equivalent in a subject area corresponding to courses and subjects taught in middle and high schools

- Professional preparation courses focusing on teaching methods and philosophies
- School-based field experiences and student teaching
- Teacher tests (in forty-five states)

If you pursue a college- or university-based path toward certification, you will generally follow five essential teacher licensing steps in sequential order (see Figure 3.1). The first two steps represent your college education, including an undergraduate arts and sciences degree with a recognized academic major in the area you intend to teach. The next two steps are your professional preparation courses and school-based teaching experiences. Finally, depending on your state, you may be required to pass teacher tests in order to enter the profession.

In many college- and university-based teacher education programs, these five steps are combined within the coursework of your undergraduate degree. At other schools, you may need a fifth undergraduate year to complete them, or they might be done as part of a combined master's degree/teacher certification graduate program. Or you may choose to complete the steps as a postbaccalaureate, certification-only student.

If you pursue certification through an alternative school district path (see Figure 3.2), you already will have completed your college degree and subject field coursework, and you are able to start teaching in a school setting. As you teach, you must still meet the state's certification requirements by taking professional development courses on site in your school district or at a nearby college or university. Alternative certification candidates must also pass state-mandated teacher tests.

To review more fully the requirements for certification, we discuss each step in detail.

An Arts and Sciences Degree

Every state requires that you earn at least a baccalaureate degree from an accredited college or university with a minimum overall grade point average (GPA), usually 2.5 or better on a 4.0 scale. As part of your undergraduate program of study, you are expected to have at least passing grades in general education courses in the following areas:

- *Arts and Humanities* (choosing from among art, music, languages, philosophy, literature, classics, western and non-western cultures, theater, drama)
- *English* (including literature, writing—with grammar and composition—and communications)

Figure 3.1
A Certification Ladder

MIDDLE OR HIGH SCHOOL
TEACHING POSITION

5)Teacher Tests

4) Field Experiences
and Student Teaching

3) Professional Preparation
Courses

2) Academic Major or
its Equivalent in a
Teaching Area

1) Bachelor's Degree in an
Arts and Sciences Field

Figure 3.2
An Alternative Certification Ladder

5)Teacher Tests

4) Professional Development Courses

3) MIDDLE OR HIGH SCHOOL
TEACHING POSITION

2) Academic Major or
its Equivalent in a
Teaching Area

1) Bachelor's Degree in an
Arts and Sciences Field

- *Social Studies/Social Sciences* (choosing from among U.S. history, government, geography, economics, sociology, anthropology, psychology)
- *Natural Sciences* (choosing from among biological and physical sciences with courses that include laboratory experiences)
- *Mathematics* (including algebra and calculus, or its equivalent)
- *World Languages* (a working knowledge of a language other than English)

At least eighteen states offer specific outlines for the general education courses you must take as part of your undergraduate education.[2] This includes minimum credit hour totals ranging from as few as thirty-nine to as many as seventy-one. Rest assured, however, that if your teacher education program is accredited by the state in which it resides, the general education distribution that you take in your college or university will meet the state's requirements for general education. In the thirty-two states that do not specifically mandate general education credits, your bachelor of arts and sciences degree from an accredited college or university is generally sufficient to meet this requirement for teacher certification. Look closely at your general education courses, and make sure that you have completed or are taking courses in all the areas listed in your state's certification guidelines.

An Academic Major and a Teaching Area

Academic majors and teaching areas are one of the most complex aspects of the licensing process. As part of your undergraduate degree you must complete an academic major in one of the liberal arts or sciences offered at your school. As part of a teacher preparation program, you must earn a specific secondary level teaching area certificate. Not all majors are equivalent to certification areas, so you may need to make some choices about how to organize your undergraduate program of study. Here are key points to keep in mind.

Every certified teacher earns some type of subject area and grade level certification. "Area" is the academic subject you are certified to teach. It is also known as your "teaching field." "Level" refers to the grades which you are approved to teach. As a middle and high school teacher, you are certified in a particular subject area *and* for a specific grade level span.

Many secondary teaching areas are equivalent to an individual's academic major in college. For example, an English major establishes the basis for English certification, a physics major for physics certification, a Spanish major for Spanish language certification, and so on. In the cases of social studies and general science, the teaching area represents an interdisciplinary collection of subjects rather than a single college major.

Thirty-two states require a major in the certification area you intend to teach.[3] Other states allow something less than a major in a certification field, and this is the subject of criticism by many observers. When your major does not correspond to your teaching area, there is extra work to do. For example, a prospective English teacher who is majoring in journalism will need to take additional courses to create the equivalent of an English major. An economics major who wants to teach biology will basically need a second major in the sciences to meet the requirements for biology. Second career adults often need some additional courses to make their former college major match up with current certification area requirements. We discuss subject area preparation more fully in Chapters 5 and 6.

Almost half the states now specify the number of hours a teacher certification candidate needs to complete in a teaching subject area.[4] Thirty hours in a given field is the most common number found among the states, but the minimums do vary greatly within teaching fields and across states. Fortunately, at many colleges, the minimums for a college major often exceed the minimums required by the states, so you are likely to be ahead of the requirements, not behind them. Compare your school's requirements with the expectations of the states where you think you want to teach.

Note that a college major outside of the arts and sciences is not accepted for teacher certification in many states. In these cases, a major in accounting, marketing, hotel and restaurant management, or nursing is not sufficient to meet the arts and sciences requirement for teacher certification. Each is considered a professional field of study leading to employment in those areas only.

Some states, including California, Connecticut, and Massachusetts, will not permit you to major only in education at the baccalaureate level, even though you are planning to teach. Education, too, is not an arts and sciences field. If you have a college major in a non-arts-and-sciences field of study, you will almost certainly need to take additional courses to complete the equivalent of an arts and sciences course distribution before being certified to teach.

Selecting a Certification Area

Listed in various state licensing materials, you will find single subject and a few interdisciplinary secondary certification areas. Most states also use the term "endorsement" as a way of indicating the specific subject area(s) a person is approved to teach. Figure 3.3 lists the most common middle and high school teaching certificates or endorsements. Some cer-

Figure 3.3
Common Middle and High School Certification Areas

English/Language Arts

History

Social Studies

Mathematics

Sciences (Physics, Biology, Chemistry, Earth/Space Science)

Technology & Computers

World Languages

tifications, such as mathematics and English, are found in every state. Others vary from state to state. It is possible, for example, to be certified in history in one state but not in another.

While Figure 3.3 provides an overview of the common secondary certificates, it does not fully describe the range of certificates available within different states:

English. The basic certification for English teachers is English/Language Arts; however, depending on the state, it is possible to earn a related certification in one of the following humanities areas: journalism; communications; drama/theater; debate; and literature.

History/Social Studies. History teachers earn history certification while social studies teachers combine courses in history, government, economics, and geography in one certificate. Depending on the state, it is possible to earn separate certifications for history, social studies, or one of the social science fields of political science/government; psychology; sociology; geography; anthropology; American studies; and economics. Lakota Studies is an option in South Dakota. Some states offer certification in the related fields of classics or philosophy.

Sciences. Science certification is subdivided among the specific science fields normally taught in middle and high schools. Commonly, there are separate certificates for chemistry, physics, earth/space science or geoscience, biology, zoology, or botany. In some states, the science certificates are designed more broadly, so that a candidate earns certification in natural science, biological science, or physical science. Like social studies, there is an interdisciplinary certificate called general science that combines work in the fields of biology, chemistry, physics, and geosciences.

Mathematics and Technology. Mathematics is a common certificate in all the states. By contrast, technology has many different certificates depending on the state, including computer/technology education, computer science, or educational media and computer information systems.

World Languages. World or foreign language certification enables an educator to teach a language other than English in middle or high school classrooms. It verifies not only competency in the language, but readiness to teach about communication, culture, and connections to other disciplines. Most states offer certificates in French, Spanish, German, and Latin as well as the languages used by significant cultural groups in the state. California, for example, in addition to the above languages, offers certificates in Japanese, Mandarin, Russian, Punjabi, and Vietnamese.

In addition to the above secondary subject areas, most states grant teaching certificates in more than thirty-five other areas. There are Early Childhood Education certificates for pre-kindergartens through grade 3, and Elementary certificates for teachers in schools that define themselves as elementary. Other common certification areas include:

Arts certificates in art, music, dance, visual arts, photography, and other performance areas.

Vocational certificates in agriculture, health, marketing, business, industrial arts, culinary arts, home economics/consumer studies, and other world of work areas.

Special Education certificates in learning disabilities, speech and hearing, moderate special needs, severe handicaps, gifted and talented education, and other areas related to the physical and emotional development of youngsters.

Specialist certificates in bilingual education, English as Second Language (ESL), guidance, school psychology, reading, physical education, and other services to students.

Administrative certificates include Supervisor, Director of Special Education, Principal, Vice Principal, Assistant Superintendent, and Superintendent of Schools.

Depending on the state, certification in vocational, special education, specialist, and administrative areas requires an academic major and professional training in an appropriate field. Many are second-level licenses that include an elementary or secondary teaching certificate and advanced graduate coursework.

Keep in mind that just because a state offers a certification area does not mean there are excellent job prospects for you in that field. Facing an increase in the number of students, and the public's reluctance to increase taxes to support education, many systems focus on a basic curriculum of English, social studies, mathematics, the sciences, world languages, art, music, special education, and physical education while reducing the electives they offer. For example, photography may be a certification area in the state where you hope to teach, but the number of job openings is likely quite small. Speech is a common certification area in many states, but fewer schools now offer speech courses separate from English classes. Psychology is listed in some states, but only a few school systems offer courses in this area.

To understood how your academic major and teaching area relate to job prospects, consider the organization of a typical comprehensive high school serving two thousand students. It has separate departments consisting of five to six English, social studies, science, and mathematics teachers because every student must take courses in these areas. Each department may offer fifteen to twenty different courses in their area. It may also have a large bilingual and special education staff. This same school will have only one or two instructors in the technical, commercial, vocational, and elective subjects. Sometimes teachers in the arts may do double duty in more than one area such as music and dance. Even then, the school may not offer courses in all the sciences or in each of the social studies and language arts specialty areas.

Selecting a teaching area may depend on balancing several factors: your interest in a subject field, your ability to successfully teach key ideas from that field to adolescents, the state where you are planning to teach, and the likelihood that schools in that state will have certifications and job openings in your specialization. Investigate the middle and high schools in the region where you plan to teach to find out what courses they offer. Consider which certification areas give you the best chance to combine your intellectual/academic interests with realistic job prospects. Then you are on your way to choosing the teaching area that is right for you.

Professional Preparation Courses

You must complete a sequence of professional preparation courses in order to receive a middle or high school certificate from a college or university. Depending on the program, you may begin your professional studies while you are earning a baccalaureate degree or after graduation as part of a master's degree or postbaccalaureate teacher certification program. Your education courses are intended to develop and refine the competencies and talents you will need to teach your subject and adolescents effectively in middle and high school classrooms. They also build on the academic foundation and subject specialty created by your general education courses and your academic major.

Every state has certain basic professional competencies that every prospective teacher must meet, and often, a minimum number of course or credit hours that must be earned in those areas. Candidates either complete an approved teacher education program that incorporates these requirements or satisfies them individually before applying for a license. Even those individuals hired under an emergency-need certificate complete coursework in these required areas before gaining full certification.

Nationwide, most professional preparation programs require you to take courses in the following areas:

Human growth and development, usually met through one or more courses in adolescent growth and development, adolescent psychology, or educational psychology, and covering such topics as the physical, social, emotional, and intellectual development of children; self esteem and identity; impacts of class, race, and gender on learning; and problems of substance abuse and family disruptions.

Social and historical foundations of education, usually covering the history, philosophy, sociology, and politics of education; school financing; work lives of middle and high school teachers; schools as organizational cultures; legal rights of students and teachers; contemporary social issues and educational problems; and the role of public education in American society.

Curriculum and Instruction, including essential teaching methods and strategies; learning theories; communication strategies; classroom management techniques; and student evaluation and assessment. This requirement may include a specialized methods course related to teaching specific fields, entitled, for example, "Teaching Mathematics in Middle and High Schools."

Some states also require coursework in specialized teaching skills such as reading, assessment and evaluation, classroom management, multicultural education, education of gifted children and/or children with special needs, or computers and other educational technologies. In Arizona, Texas, and California, for instance, there are specific requirements related to the history and culture of the state and the nation while most other states include historical knowledge in the general education courses taken by all certification candidates.

Across the country, the average for professional education courses is twenty-two credits.[5] Many colleges and universities require more as part of their certification program. In general, if you intend to get certified for both middle and high schools, plan on closer to thirty education credits (including student teaching).

Figure 3.4
Teacher Certification Levels

High School (Grades 7-12)

Middle School (Grades 5-9)

Elementary (Grades 1-6)

Early Childhood (Pre-Kindergarten-Grade 3)

Certification Levels

As part of their professional studies, every prospective teacher faces a decision about what certification grade level to pursue within their teacher education program. There are four basic classroom teacher certification levels: early childhood, elementary, middle, and secondary (see Figure 3.4).

Early childhood and elementary educators may teach any of the grades covered by their certification span; their certification area is also their certification level. Commonly, they instruct kids in a generalized curriculum of reading, writing, mathematics, social studies, science, and in some schools, arts, music, computers, physical education, and health as well. Some elementary educators further specialize as an upper elementary grade or lower elementary grade teacher.

Commonly, as a secondary teacher, you will be eligible to teach in grades 7 to 12. Some states ask you to choose between middle school (junior high) and high school, while others allow you to be certified at both levels. Some teachers prefer to teach at the high school or the middle school level, and the 7 to 12 grade range allows them to do both. Others try different levels at different times in their teaching careers. As you gain experience in teaching, you may decide that you prefer one level over the other.

State to state, the grade spans for the different certification levels vary considerably. The elementary level ranges from pre-kindergarten to grade 9. Middle school includes grades 5–9 in Massachusetts and Florida, grades 5–8 in Delaware and Illinois, and grades 6–8 in Virginia. Many states certify single subject secondary teachers for grades 7–12 inclusively, but not all include the option of a middle grades certificate. The various specialist, special services, and administrative certifications have their own grade level ranges, either K–12 or 6–12. It is important to know the grade spans for the certification level(s) you are seeking in your state.

Field Experiences and Student Teaching

Most teacher preparation programs require prospective educators to practice teach in schools before they are certified. This is called student teaching or the teaching practicum. As a student teacher, you work in the role of a regular classroom teacher for a specified number of hours (state-approved program requirements range from 5 to 12 credit hours) under the guidance of a cooperating teacher and college program supervisor.[6] Although you do some observing, most of your time is spent preparing and teaching classes and working with students in your certification area.

Prior to student teaching, most states require certification candidates to observe experienced teachers, tutor and work with small groups of students, learn the basic structure of the school, teach supervised microteaching and mini-lessons, and develop lesson plans and curriculum units. A common term for this stage of teacher education is the prepracticum, meaning the courses and practice one gets before the student teaching practicum. In most cases, college or university personnel and their school partners will review your prepracticum performance and determine whether or not you are ready to student teach.

In many student teaching placements, you will start out teaching one class in your subject and then increase your responsibilities to additional classes (sometimes in more than one course). A social studies student teacher, for example, might teach two 10th grade world history classes, and one 12th grade contemporary problems course. A mathematics student teacher at the same school might do three sections of algebra I. At another school, the arrangement could be different; for example, multiple sections of world history for a social studies teacher, and sections of algebra I and II or calculus for a math intern.

As you student teach, you are guided by a cooperating teacher and a university supervisor. A cooperating teacher is an experienced public school educator who, in most cases, is certified in your subject area. It is this person's classes you teach during the practicum. A university supervisor is the representative from your college or university program who observes you in the school. Together, your cooperating teacher and university supervisor work with you to improve your performance while also evaluating what you do in terms of state requirements for a teaching license. Generally, both must sign the paperwork that verifies that you have successfully completed the experience. We will discuss the dynamics and complexities of student teaching more fully in Chapter 6.

TESTS FOR TEACHERS

Tests for teachers are one of the new realities of your professional life. In 1983 only eighteen states mandated some form of testing for teacher certification.[7] As of 1999, the situation had changed dramatically. Only Idaho, Iowa, South Dakota, Utah, and Vermont did not require some form of teacher test as part of their certification process.[8] In most of the forty-five states with tests, teacher candidates are expected to pass a test of basic skills, subject matter knowledge, and, in a few cases, principles of teaching and learning, after graduating from a teacher education program but before being awarded certification. In some states, colleges and universities preparing teachers require a test of prospective students' basic skills as a condition of entry into a certification program. In several states, future teachers must pass tests both at the point of admission to and exit from certification programs. (See Part II for state-by-state teacher test requirements for earning a license to teach.)

An even more recent development is that some states like New York and Texas (and soon, most likely, Massachusetts) will require institutions of higher education that prepare teachers to have at least 70 or 80 percent of their graduates pass the state teacher test in order for that school to continue preparing teachers. Some states will likely prepare and publish listings of the pass rates of the graduates of different colleges and universities on the teacher tests. While the complexities involved in such success rates are very significant, it is in your interest to attend a college or university teacher education program whose graduates pass the required tests at a high rate of success.

The web of motivations for the move toward greater teacher testing is tied in part to the attempt to professionalize teaching and teacher education. Some reformers, concerned about the status of teachers, argue that education must have greater quality control over who enters the profession. They point out that other respected fields require new professionals to pass tests before they are granted licensure and allowed to practice. If teaching is to become a profession with the status of law and medicine, the argument goes, it must prove that its standards are equally rigorous by testing its candidates before they are placed in charge of a classroom. Others agree that testing is a first step in establishing higher standards for teachers and a key to better schools.

The Manufacturing of Tests

It is important to point out that while the adoption of testing as a major strategy to improve the quality of our teaching force imitates professions such as medicine, law, and architecture, the tests in those fields are developed by the professional organizations particular to each field.

In education the tests are manufactured by testing companies vying to have their product accepted by various state legislatures and boards of education.[9]

The field of teacher testing is currently dominated by two corporations: Educational Testing Service (ETS) of Princeton, New Jersey, and National Evaluation Systems, Inc. (NES) of Amherst, Massachusetts. ETS, reports the *New York Times*, is the largest testing company in the world. In 1996 its revenues were more than $400 million.[10] Comparable figures for NES, a privately held company, are not available.

ETS designs and administers the well-known SAT test for college entrance as well as the AP (Advanced Placement Program), GRE (Graduate Record Exam), GMAT (Graduate Management Admission Test), and TOEFL (Test of English as a Foreign Language). The company reports that of the forty-five states requiring some form of teacher testing for certification, thirty-six use ETS designed and administered tests.

For the teacher testing market, ETS has developed the Praxis I, II, and III series of standardized tests. The predecessor of Praxis was known as the National Teacher Exam (NTE). ETS administers all or parts of this series in the states with whom they hold the contract. Although the series is designed to be given nationwide, it is adjusted in some instances to the specifications of individual states.

The Praxis I and Praxis II series are designed for the beginning teacher seeking initial licensure. Praxis I is a test of academic basic skills in reading, writing, and mathematics. Praxis II consists of Core Battery tests in the areas of General Knowledge, Communication Skills, and Professional Knowledge. Each area is comprised of the following:

- The General Knowledge section consists of thirty questions in social studies; twenty-five questions in mathematics; thirty-five questions in literature and fine arts; and thirty questions in science.
- The Communication Skills section contains forty listening questions; thirty reading questions; forty-five writing questions; and an essay.
- The Professional Knowledge part of the test features six subsections: planning instruction (twelve questions); implementing instruction (twenty-three questions); evaluating instruction (sixteen questions); managing instructional environments (nineteen questions); professional foundations (twenty-three questions); and professional functions (twelve questions).[11]

Praxis II also includes:

- Subject Assessments/Specialty Area Tests
- Multiple Subjects Assessments developed specifically for California
- Principles of Teaching and Learning Tests

Praxis III is directed at the person who has taught for a few years and is seeking the second or advanced level certification in his or her state. This test is designed to be conducted in the teacher's own classroom and is based on actual observation.

National Evaluation Systems currently designs and administers the tests for ten states, including some of the largest ones: Arizona, California, New York, New Mexico, Texas (two different tests), Oklahoma, Illinois, Michigan, Massachusetts, and Colorado. (This distribution can change regularly since ETS and NES are in intense competition to gain the contract for teacher tests in individual states). The NES approach to the teacher testing market appears different from that of ETS. Rather than developing a series of tests to market nationwide, NES seeks to customize individual tests to the specifications of each state for whose contract they are bidding. Individual states using NES generally specify a different range of testing objectives, so that the test in Texas may be different from the test in Colorado.

In general, NES covers the same test territory as that offered by ETS. In a state using an NES-developed exam, you can expect to have to pass a test in anywhere from one to four areas:

- General education skills of writing, reading, mathematical computation, and communication
- General knowledge consistent with a liberal arts education at the Bachelor of Arts level
- Subject matter competency in the field and for the level at which you wish to teach
- Pedagogical knowledge, that is, professional knowledge and judgment about issues in learning and teaching

What does this mean for you, a person thinking about becoming a middle or high school teacher? First, since ETS and NES dominate the field of teacher testing, most prospective teachers in states requiring a teacher test will likely take a test designed and administered by one of these two organizations.

Second, the test(s) you must take will depend on the state where you take it. In some states and in some teacher preparation programs, you might have to take only one or two of the tests before you become licensed to teach.

Third, the test will be criterion referenced, not norm referenced. In a criterion-referenced format, test takers are evaluated against a pre-established set of standards rather than against each other as in the case of many of the exams you take in your college courses. To pass the exam, you must reach a set qualifying score. It does not matter how many individuals reach the passing score each time the exam is given, or whether you pass by one or twenty points. You either pass or you must take the test again.

Check with the certification office of the state department of education in which you want to be licensed or with the teacher education programs in which you might be interested, to determine specifically which test is required and at what point you will be expected to take the test. If a teacher education program requires one of these tests for admission or completion, we assume that it will say so clearly in its admission materials.

Costs of Teacher Tests

The cost of taking these tests is not absorbed by the states that require them, it is passed on directly to you, the prospective teacher. Taking just the Praxis II core battery General Knowledge, Communication Skills, and Professional Knowledge tests costs $60 each, or $180 for the series. Each subject matter test costs $65. Costs are subject to change. If the state in which you hope to gain licensure requires the core battery tests and a subject matter test, you will pay $245 to take the test. (Most states also charge a fee for applying for a license to teach.) The fees charged for NES tests are comparable. Both NES and ETS provide its tests at pre-set announced times. ETS administers its tests at testing centers throughout the country; at this time, NES offers its tests only at sites within the state for which you are taking the test. This means if you live in New York State and want to take the NES-administered test for Texas, you must travel to Texas to do so.

In a recent development, ETS has contracted with the Sylvan Learning Centers to offer a computerized version of their Praxis I test. If your state requires the Praxis I test, you may take it at a Sylvan Learning Center at any time by making an appointment with them. Sylvan charges $70 for each test. Like other merchandisers, it offers a discount if you purchase or register for more than one of its products: $90 if you sign up for two at the time of registration, or a discount price of $110 if you register for all three tests at once. (Since teacher exams are high stakes tests, you should be cautious about trying to save money by taking communication, literacy and subject area tests on the same day.) Both NES and ETS charge late fees if you register for a test after the posted deadline for registration.

Issues in Teacher Testing

The forerunner of the ETS Praxis series was the National Teacher Exam (NTE). ETS inherited the National Teacher Exam from an organization called the Cooperative Test Service and began to administer it in 1951.[12] During its lifetime, the National Teacher Exam was mired in controversy:

- There were a number of court challenges of the NTE test on the basis of alleged racial bias.
- Testing experts continually cited its lack of predictive validity.
- There was no standard national cut-off score for passing the test. This meant that while in one state you had to score at a certain level in order to pass the test, another state using the same test had established a different score for passing.
- The cut-off points have little relationship to the reality of teaching. That is, there is no way to have confidence in a judgment that if you were to score below a certain cut-off, you would not be a good teacher, or that if you were to score above a certain cut-off, you would be a good teacher.[13]

Evaluators pointed out that the NTE test had never been screened for its relationship to what actually occurs in classrooms; therefore, the connection between a person's test score and his or her likely performance as a teacher in a classroom was basically unpredictable. As with any multiple choice test, the NTE was not easy to contextualize. Much of what might be considered best practice in teaching depends on the interaction of the specifics of a setting. A question on any test that does not take into account the nature of the school and community, the students, and the particular situation in which the teacher finds him or herself cannot accurately assess the thinking of a prospective teacher taking the test.

There also is the issue that test questions often seem to reflect more the opinion of the test writers than grounded knowledge from the field. Reviewers found NTE questions were ambiguous, open to misinterpretation, and had more than one right answer, especially in the professional section of the test.[14] Some scholars thought that it was possible that in response to certain pedagogical questions, the more you might know about teaching and learning the more complicated you might find it to answer a question.[15] Here again, the situational realities of schools are not easily reproduced in questions on a test. Good teachers might use one strategy one time and another strategy the next time, depending on the day and the children involved. Choosing only one strategy out of several on a test is inconsistent with how teachers teach.

The criticism and challenges must have been very severe because ETS dropped the National Teacher Exam, which had a command of the market, and developed its new Praxis series of tests. In so doing, it gave up the market recognition of the name, National Teacher Exam.

To build a second generation of tests, test makers at ETS and NES are devising new approaches to assessing the readiness of teachers to enter the classroom. They may present a narrative of a situation, much like a case study, and ask the test-taker to respond to multiple answer questions. In one sample test of English which we have seen, a writing sample from a student is presented. The test-taker is asked to write a comment to the student acknowledging the strengths of the writing sample and giving directions for improvement.

In another question the test-taker is asked to read a short passage and to identify the figure of speech embedded in the material. While these more contextualized approaches seem like improvements, certain sample questions had more than one reasonable response among the multiple-choice answers. While it appears that the test designers have tried to meet the criticisms, it is too early to say how successful they have been.

The growth of the testing industry raises another important teacher testing issue. That ETS, a non-profit corporation, is now linked with Sylvan Learning Systems Inc., a decidedly for-profit business, is an explicit sign that major corporations are developing a vested interest in teacher education policy across the country. Indirectly, they could be part of the business community urging the reform of education through testing.

ETS has, since its beginning in 1947, cultivated a professional image in which the welfare of its clients is its highest priority. It promotes a disinterested, professional regard for testing expertise.[16] The same may be said of NES. Now, in their earnest competition, both organizations may be beginning to lose some of the allure of their professional and academic image at exactly the time that their products are being used even more widely. You can learn more about issues in teacher testing by contacting the National Center for Fair & Open Testing in Cambridge, Massachusetts (see Part II).

So Where Does This Leave Us?

The political pressure for educational reform, the popular recourse to testing teachers, and the fact that a great deal of money is now involved in the teacher testing industry all contribute to the momentum for teacher testing despite serious questions about its efficacy. The complexities of the situation make this subject especially difficult for us to comment about. On the one hand, it is hard to argue against any method that promises to improve the quality of the teaching force. On the other hand, the contradictions, criticisms, and professional illusions inherent in teacher testing cannot be overlooked.

We do not want our discussion to undermine your will to take the tests or your confidence to perform well and to pass the exams. To be fair to the test makers, Praxis II is a second generation teacher test, and

NES is constantly designing new tests and redeveloping older ones to meet the criticism of testing experts and the specifications of states. Although the independent reviews are not in yet, the current tests are probably better tests than the originals were.

The reality of testing means that you must learn about the testing requirements in your state and face the task of paying for and taking tests that some in the field strongly support and others ardently criticize. On the other hand, you should know that the general knowledge tests attempt to ascertain whether you can read, write, and do basic math calculations. As students, you have already taken tests similar to these in which you are asked to read a passage and perhaps identify a problem in usage, or note the main idea, or provide a writing sample that shows that you can organize and support your views. The subject matter tests supposedly test comprehension of a teaching area which you have studied in some depth at the college level.

We hope that with time the design, administration, and the commitment to teacher testing will catch up with the serious criticism that has been levied against it. We think there are wiser processes for reassuring the public that the qualities of people like you, if you are anything like the students with whom we work, are on the whole admirable. In the meantime, hopefully this discussion will offer a heightened awareness of the implications of testing for you and the students you teach.

SOME FREQUENTLY ASKED QUESTIONS ABOUT CERTIFICATION

What Is Middle School Certification?

In recent years, communities all across the country have created middle schools as alternatives to junior high schools, their goal being to focus directly on the developmental and educational needs of early adolescents. Given the rise of middle schools, many school districts are now looking for well-prepared teachers who know how to promote academic learning, critical thinking, and healthy lifestyle choices among middle-school-age youth. Many states, too, have joined the move toward middle school education and created a distinct middle school certification. The two basic types of middle school certifications are the middle school subject area certificate and the middle school generalist certificate.

Subject area certificates at the middle level are similar to the secondary subject area certificates offered by the states. You are approved as an English/language arts, mathematics, science, social studies, or world languages teacher for the middle grades; that is, you are a subject area specialist with a focus on younger adolescents. By contrast, the middle school generalist certificate is structured more like an elementary teaching credential. A generalist is someone who knows enough about all of the subject fields to teach any of them within a team or interdisciplinary instructional model. Accordingly, there is an emphasis on a range of coursework covering all the major subject fields taught at the middle grades.

As you weigh your certification choices, think seriously about becoming a specialist in the education of early adolescents. Take courses in the growth and development of ten to fifteen year-olds so you understand the needs and pressures facing this age group. Learn about subject area curriculum that offers younger students ways to become actively involved in learning while forging connections between the classroom and the outside-of-school environments they encounter in their daily lives. Three more points to keep in mind when thinking about pursuing middle grade certification follow.

First, jobs often appear in the middle grades since expanding student populations reach this level first, creating openings for more teachers. As we have noted, another less obvious reason for middle grade openings is that when a school system has a high school position, it is often first advertised internally, and veteran teachers take this opportunity to change grade levels. A move in the other direction—from high school to middle school—is less common, thus creating more middle-level openings. Take a look at the hiring trends in the area where you plan to teach. The likelihood of job openings may be a good reason to add middle school certification to your professional résumé.

Second, many of our students facing the choice between middle school and high school initially think that they want to teach at the high school level because it will let them explore their subject more extensively. When they realize through their observations in the schools that early adolescents have an enormous enthusiasm for learning and are inspired by teachers who offer them a sense of the most important basic ideas in their field, they reconsider their initial stance. You may be one of those who commit themselves to middle school teaching with good reason. Since fewer teachers focus their preparation on the middle grades, you will have an area of competence that many school districts say they need.

Third, in some states, the academic requirements for coursework in a middle school subject field are fewer than those required for high school certification. Be careful if you choose middle school on the basis of reduced course requirements. You may later find you want to teach at a higher grade level, but your subject coursework in college is not sufficient. At a time when many school districts are emphasizing the academic preparedness of teachers, you may want to complete more than the minimum requirements in your area as a way of establishing expertise in your subject field.

What Is Reciprocity?

"If I am licensed to teach in New York, can I teach in California?" This question arises regularly as new teachers negotiate their way through the teacher certification and licensing maze. Teacher preparation programs offer you courses and field experiences leading to licensure in the state where the program is geographically located. For example, if you complete a teacher preparation program at a college in Arizona, you will be prepared to gain certification in Arizona.

At this time there is no national system of initial licensing for teachers. The process of gaining licensure in a state different from the one in which you did your teacher preparation depends on reciprocity. Reciprocity is a process by which a state recognizes and accepts the teaching license you earned in another state. To make it easier for teachers to move across state lines, forty states, the District of Columbia, Guam, and the Commonwealth of Puerto Rico have entered into an Interstate Certification Contract agreement (ICC) which is sponsored by the NASDTEC (National Association of State Directors of Teacher Education and Certification). NASDTEC is an organization which has a great deal of influence over the lives of new teachers, but to most, it is relatively unknown. Every two years they publish a "Manual on Certification." Meant for professionals in the field of teacher education, it is a good source of information about licensing issues throughout the nation.

Here is how the ICC reciprocity agreement works: If you earned licensure in a state which has signed the interstate agreement and you want to teach in another state which has signed the same agreement, the process will be greatly facilitated. By signing, states are indicating that they recognize the education and licensure requirements of the other signing states as equivalent to their own. You still have to apply for a license in the new state and meet any other state-specific requirements, for example, its teaching test. But in general, you will find the overall process of gaining certification much less complex.

The states currently participating in the ICC are:[17]

Alabama	Florida
Arizona	Georgia
Arkansas	Hawaii
California	Idaho
Colorado	Illinois
Connecticut	Indiana
Delaware	Kentucky
District of Columbia	

Maine	Oklahoma
Maryland	Oregon
Massachusetts	Pennsylvania
Michigan	Rhode Island
Mississippi	South Carolina
Montana	Tennessee
Nevada	Texas
New Hampshire	Utah
New Jersey	Vermont
New Mexico	Virginia
New York	Washington
North Carolina	West Virginia
Ohio	Wyoming

What if a state does not participate in the interstate agreement? Your out-of-state teaching license may still be recognized. Alaska, Arizona, Mississippi, Montana, New Mexico, and Oklahoma are non-ICC-signing states who will offer you a license if you have graduated from a teacher education program at a college or university accredited by the National Council of Accreditation for Teacher Education (NCATE). Investigate carefully the rules surrounding certification and reciprocity. A state that has signed the Interstate Certification Contract, and recognizes graduates of programs approved by NCATE, offers the widest possibility for accepting a candidate for teacher licensure from another state. If that is not the case, then you will need to work within whatever rules prevail in the state in which you wish to teach.

Certification as an Undergraduate or Graduate Student

Many prospective teachers wonder which is more advantageous for landing a job: becoming certified as an undergraduate or a graduate student. Some have heard that they might be at a disadvantage if they have a master's degree because they would be more expensive to hire than a candidate who has certification with only a bachelor's degree. Others wonder if they will even get an interview if they do not have a graduate credential. In fact, at some institutions, teacher preparation is offered only at the graduate level, reflecting a view that the demands of becoming a teacher are too great to be accomplished within a normal four-year undergraduate program.[18] As you assess different viewpoints, be careful about evaluating certification options as an either-or, undergraduate-versus-graduate, proposition. This is not usually the best way to compare your choices.

It is hard to predict the market situation in the school district where you might seek employment. Either the undergraduate or graduate scenarios may have an advantage in different school districts at different times. You may get some idea by talking with a department head or a principal and straightforwardly asking whether the school prefers candidates with master's or bachelor's degrees. Our experience has been that if jobs are tight and school systems have high academic standards and strong community support, then a graduate degree is preferred. In addition, more and more states are making a master's degree a requirement for the second level of advanced certification.

It is sensible to make the decision to pursue certification when it fits best with the rest of your academic and personal goals. The trend is toward getting certified at the graduate level. You will be well served by concentrating on a four-year degree in your subject field and obtaining your certification as part of as master's degree program. (We describe some graduate level certification program options in Chapter 4.)

If you feel truly compelled to begin working in schools directly after college, pursue certification as an undergraduate. Being already certified, you can seek a master's degree in your subject matter area later. Given the higher status of subject field degrees in relation to education degrees, this option might serve your job prospects well in the long run. If you are an older individual and decide to do teacher preparation through a master's program, find one that allows you to combine study in your subject-matter field with work in teacher preparation. It will let you present up-to-date evidence of your academic and instructional readiness to teach.

What Is Performance-Based Licensing?

It should be noted that there is a move toward performance-based licensing being promoted by the Interstate New Assessment and Support Consortium (INTASC), the National Board for Professional Teaching Standards, NCATE, and others. Performance-based systems "describe what teachers should know, be like, and be able to do rather than listing courses that teachers should take in order to be awarded a license."[19] The idea is that new teachers need to demonstrate that they can use what they know in the classroom to promote learning for students. Performance-based approaches also implicitly criticize college and university-based programs that focus on competencies measured by the successful completion of courses.

Candidates for a license under the INTASC standards are expected to submit evidence that they meet the standards which might include not only courses taken, but a portfolio showing skills and knowledge and performance assessments of their teaching in schools. You may well become part of a program that is using some form of performance-based assessments. If so, the development of a professional portfolio and the focus on assessment will be consistent with what many school systems are looking for when they hire new teachers.

NOTES

1. Robert A. Roth, "Standards for Certification, Licensure, and Accreditation," in *Handbook of Research on Teacher Education*, 2d ed., edited by John Sikula (New York: Macmillan, 1996), 244.

2. Christopher J. Lucas, *Teacher Education in America: Reform Agendas for the Twenty-First Century* (New York: St. Martin's Press, 1997), 185.

3. "Teachers Who Have the Knowledge and Skills to Teach to Higher Standards," *Education Week*, 8 January 1998, 83.

4. Ibid., 186.

5. Ibid., 189.

6. Ibid., 190.

7. Marlene Pugach and James D. Raths, "Testing Teachers: Analysis and Recommendations," *Journal of Teacher Education* 34, no. 1 (January/February 1983), 34–37.

8. Theodore E. Andrews, ed., *The NASDTEC Manual on the Preparation and Certification of Educational Personnel 1998–1999* (Dubuque, IA: Kendall/Hunt, 1998), G-2.

9. Linda Darling-Hammond, Arthur E. Wise and Stephen P. Klein, *A License to Teach* (Boulder, CO: Westview Press, 1995), 11.

10. Douglas Frantz and Jon Nordheimer, "Giant of Exam Business Keeps Quiet on Cheating." *New York Times* (Northeast edition), 28 September 1997:32.

11. Cornelia Cocke, *Cracking the Praxis II: NTE*, 2d ed. (New York: Random House, 1997).

12. Walter Haney, George Madaus, and Amelia Kreitzer, "Charms Talismanic: Testing Teachers for the Improvement of American Education," in *Review of Research in Education* 14, edited by Ernst Z. Rothkopf (Washington, D.C.: American Educational Research Association, 1987), 180.

13. Ibid., 169–238. See also Linda Darling-Hammond, *The Right to Learn: A Blueprint for Schools That Work* (San Francisco: Jossey Bass, 1997), 301.

14. Darling-Hammond, *A License to Teach*, 57–67.

15. Ibid., 50–53.

16. Frantz and Nordheimer, p. 32.

17. Andrews, ed., *NASDTEC Manual 1998–1999*, H-2–H-16.

18. Lucas, *Teacher Education*.

19. Interstate New Teacher Assessment and Support Consortium, "Next Steps: Moving Toward Performance-Based Licensing in Teaching" (Washington, D.C.: Council of Chief State School Officers, 1995), 6.

4

Finding a Program That's Right for You

Making sense of your options when you look at the different teacher education programs available across the country seems like a monumental job. Collecting information from a small sample of the 1363 institutions of higher education that prepare teachers takes weeks. Then, after locating interesting places, you may find that some of them have more than one type of certification program within their teacher education department. (See Part II for a state-by-state list of all colleges and universities offering programs for secondary certification.) In addition, there are a growing number of state or district-level alternative programs that place people directly into the classroom without their first taking education courses or doing supervised student teaching.

Small wonder many prospective teachers narrow their choices to one or two colleges or universities, often those nearby or with which they are familiar from prior experiences. Or they reject the idea of teacher education altogether in favor of an alternative program approach. They may assume, "Certification is certification; all I need is the credential to teach." There is a fundamental problem with this assumption—not all routes into teaching are the same. Philosophical and programmatic differences exist at all levels. It makes good sense to evaluate carefully all your options before deciding.

To assist you in understanding the different types of teacher preparation programs, we have divided this chapter into two parts. Because approximately nine out of ten new teachers complete an approved program at an accredited college or university, we first look closely at four basic philosophies of teacher education. We go inside the structure of programs so you can be thoughtful about curriculum, faculty, relationships with public schools, and other key features. We assess the importance of reputation and accreditation in choosing a program, and we then discuss some new models for preparing teachers. Second, we explain the advantages and disadvantages of alternative certification programs as a way to enter the profession.

PHILOSOPHIES OF TEACHER EDUCATION

Since teacher education is still a developing field and there is no wide consensus on how best to prepare teachers, different programs adopt different philosophical approaches.[1] Some take a "scientific" stance. They tend to concentrate on the skills and techniques of teaching which the program organizers feel are based on firmly grounded research in the field. They may adopt a behaviorist emphasis to their notion of teaching, learning, and teacher education. They emphasize key skills they believe all new teachers need to know.

Other programs take a "teaching as a craft" approach, arguing that teaching is not a science and there is no technology of teaching for which you can be trained. They see teaching as a blend of personal creativity and expression in the classroom, as well as what you can learn from reflecting on your experiences working with students. Such programs try to create opportunities for you to observe the craft of teaching, practice it, and reflect on your practice in reasonably supportive settings. They regard the teacher preparation program as the first step in a continuing endeavor to develop your craft as a teacher.

Some programs stress that a prospective teacher "build on his or her own biography." They see the task of becoming a teacher as one in which a candidate gains experience by working with teachers and students while studying the larger social context of schools and the society in which the schools reside. The task of the program is to work with its students to make meaning from their experience and study, and in so doing, to acquire a personal understanding of themselves as educators.

A fourth approach might be called "developmental." It concentrates more on the potential of the future teacher than any of the other approaches. A developmental model assumes that individuals have the talent and competence to become excellent teachers. The program seeks the best ways to facilitate a person's development and performance in the classroom. It will allow you to progress at your own speed, build in a series of coursework and experiences that are progressively more and more complex, and it will support you as you refine your sense of competence and self-understanding as a teacher.

It is unlikely that the programs you are considering will profess one pure philosophical stance. Programs often adapt an eclectic philosophical foundation by borrowing and blending from each of the above positions.

You can explore different philosophical assumptions by asking faculty about their rationales for teacher education. A good program will reflect the thought processes and assumptions which undergird its course of study and experience, and the faculty explanation of the program will reflect these as well.

DIFFERENT PROGRAMS/DIFFERENT APPROACHES

Understanding the design and operation of a college or university teacher education program is essential to choosing one that is right for you. By "design and operation" we mean everything from a school's overall mission statement to the nuts and bolts of day-to-day activities. Each in its own way impacts significantly on how you learn to become a teacher.

A teacher education institution's mission statement is important because it tells you about the program's core values and long-term commitments. Excellence, equity, creativity, change, diversity, anti-racism, gender fairness, and inclusion are more than just words. They are signposts of what an institution is striving to achieve in its education program activities. The challenge is for the school (and for you as a student at that school) to translate ideals into action as a professional educator. It makes sense to choose a school that articulates a clear, forceful educational mission. Without core beliefs and ideals, it is difficult for a program to sustain itself organizationally or intellectually. Be sure to request mission statements from each of your prospective schools, and compare what they have to say. At the same time, recognize that programs must have more than good rhetoric.

The nuts and bolts of a program are also key indicators of the kind of experiences you are going to have at a teacher preparation institution. The details of course registration, faculty office hours, advising arrangements, staff friendliness, certification forms, financial aid awards, library resources, computer access, textbook availability, and career guidance services all have a great influence on your day-to-day experiences as a student. Pay attention to how the routine parts of a professional program are organized at the schools you are considering.

Besides the mission statement and day-to-day routines, here are nine other areas to examine as you choose a teacher education program: program of study, faculty, advising, classmates, relationships to schools, student assessment and evaluation, support for graduates, and economics of time and money.

Program of Study

To select a professional preparation program, one of your first questions should be, "What is my program of study?" The curriculum you take to prepare for teaching certification generally includes required courses and field experiences. Find out if there is a clearly written sequence of what you will take along with a description of why the program is arranged the way it is. You should be able to tell how long it will take you to go through the program, when you are expected to take the different parts of the curriculum, and when you will finish.

Once you know the proposed program of study, it is important to find out if all the required courses are offered on a regular basis. Ask that question directly and expect to receive an answer that you can understand. Uncertainty on the part of the college about when courses are going to be available is usually a sign of larger organizational issues related to faculty availability and budgetary problems.

Another reasonable question is whether any previous education or education-related experiences can be counted in your program. Some programs will allow you to waive certain requirements because you fulfilled them previously with equivalent courses or experiences. Other programs will allow you to test out of certain requirements. The best situation is not necessarily a program that is extremely flexible and liberal about waivers or testing out processes, but one that has considered the issue and has a clearly defined process stating what is and is not possible.

Considerable research indicates that it is desirable to combine fieldwork with academic study at each level of the program. Inquire if there are field experiences integrated into the beginning, middle, and culmination of your course of study. Such an arrangement will place you in classrooms throughout your professional education program. Some programs lump together in-school experiences at the end of the program. While this creates intensive involvement for a short period of time, it may not allow you to gradually increase your familiarity with kids and schools, change your plans about which grade level to teach, or try out different instructional methods.

How are the required field experiences scheduled? Does the program expect you to "go out and get some experience in schools," or does it serve as a resource in placing you in a range of educational settings where you will observe many different instructional approaches? While some students prefer to make their own arrangements, it is generally better to do your field experiences at schools where teachers have agreed in advance to welcome your participation in their classes.

Probably the most pressing issue facing United States public education is how to provide equity and excellence to a diverse student body. NCATE and many states expect teacher educators to prepare future teachers for multicultural and mainstreamed classrooms. Ask faculty in programs you are considering if they offer courses dealing with racial and gender equity as well as the mainstreaming of students with special educational needs. Find out if you will do field work in schools where students from diverse backgrounds and cultures are learning together.

Student teaching is an essential component of your program (see Chapter 6). Before choosing a program, find out how student teaching is organized. Here are some questions to ask:

• How long is the practicum?
• Are you expected to spend the entire day in a school?
• How many classes and how many preparations will you have?
• Do you find your own school placement?
• Who will supervise you and how many times will you be observed?
• How is your cooperating teacher selected?
• Will you have the opportunity to teach in middle and high schools?

While there is no one right answer to any of these questions, the information you receive will tell you whether the program is thoughtful and organized about these issues.

Faculty

Arguably, the most important aspect of your teacher education program is the faculty with whom you will work. The interactions and relationships you form with your teachers are important to the kind of educator you will become. Teacher education faculty provide essential knowledge, helpful role models, and inside information about your new profession. While it is very difficult to assess faculty from a distance, you can make some inroads by finding out not only the reputation of the faculty, but also the role they play in preparing teachers.

In many schools and departments of education in large universities, teacher preparation programs are coordinated by faculty but staffed and taught by doctoral students acting as teaching assistants. These doctoral students are usually capable professionals, generally chosen because they have had experience teaching in the public schools and are interested in a career in teacher education. Still, if a program is rated highly for the quality of its faculty but most of the courses are offered by doctoral students, you might think twice and ask more questions.

At many smaller colleges, two or three faculty teach the entire teacher education curriculum supported by part-time and adjunct instructors. These supplemental faculty are often professionals in the area's public schools. Adjunct and part-time faculty frequently change every few years. It is reasonable to ask who actually teaches the courses you will take as well as how the instructors are chosen and evaluated over time.

Since teaching in middle and high schools is subject-matter oriented, you will want to ask about the nature of faculty support in your academic field. University-based teacher education programs and larger state college programs usually have subject-matter-content specialists in the areas of English, mathematics, history and social studies, the sciences, and world languages on the program faculty. Such programs offer subject-matter-based courses in principles and methods of teaching in these specific subject areas.

Smaller state college programs and small teacher education programs in liberal arts colleges may not have such subject matter specialists on their faculty. At these schools education professors offer general cross-discipline principles and methods courses. They may also invite subject matter specialists from the arts and sciences to become involved in the preparation of teachers. Such involvement can range anywhere from an English, history, math, science, or world language professor teaching a methods course in their field to making supervisory visits when students in their area are student teaching.

Both models of faculty involvement in your subject area can work well. On one hand, a generic, cross-disciplinary course on the principles and methods of teaching has the advantage of highlighting approaches and issues common to any subject matter area. On the other hand, access to both a subject matter specialty course in your subject area and the participation of arts and sciences faculty offers opportunities that will minimize the dichotomy between content and methodology. Any effective principles and methods course will explore the pedagogical knowledge that comes from knowing the logic and method of your subject matter deeply and knowing how to communicate it successfully to students.

Advisors and Advising

The accessibility of faculty as academic advisors is another important factor to consider when choosing a program. Think twice about attending a school where the faculty treat appointments with students as what seems like an imposition. To research this issue, you might call the school that you are interested in to make an appointment with the faculty advisor in your area, and see how easy or difficult it is to find a time that is mutually convenient.

Faculty are not the only source of essential information and good advice. Ask if the program offers non-faculty sources of advising support. Does it have a peer advising program? Does it have a full-, or part-time person whose primary job it is to advise teacher education candidates? It is important to find out not only who does the advising but what type of advising you will receive.

Good advising includes the written material you receive about the program. Assess the quality of the materials and note whether the responses to your requests are timely and informative. Advising also involves the quality of the telephone or e-mail messages you have with program representatives. You want a program that is responsive to your inquiries.

In addition to written materials, find out if there are group orientations and developmentally based advising meetings. It is one thing for a program to advise at the beginning about the course of study you will be required to take, and it is another to provide advising as you continue making important decisions about where and at what level to do field experiences and student teaching. A thoughtfully designed program provides advising support throughout your progress, including post-certification and as you begin your teaching career.

Classmates

The quality of your experience in teacher preparation depends to some extent on your classmates. These individuals will be your professional colleagues and work associates throughout the program. You will take courses, develop curriculum, work on projects, and have many discussions together. If you call the school to make an appointment with a faculty member, ask if you can meet some students as well. If you are unable to visit the school, see if they have the e-mail or postal address of current students or recent graduates who are willing to be contacted about their experiences in the program.

Ask whether future classmates are primarily from the local area or are from the region, or are recruited nationally. Are they traditional-age undergraduate or master's degree students, or is there a mix of older, non-traditional certification candidates? How much and what kind of diversity is there among the teacher education student body? Ideally, you will find other teacher education students who will support you by working collaboratively and productively on projects of mutual value and challenge you by presenting differing perspectives and ideas for you to consider. In good programs, group support, diversity, and intellectual challenge are cornerstones of individual success.

Relationships with Public Schools

Perhaps the most revealing aspect of a teacher education program is how it relates to public schools. More and more emphasis is being placed on partnerships between schools and higher education in the preparation of teachers. Many reformers recommend that school personnel be directly involved in all aspects of the licensing process, from admission to approval of certification. You are going to spend considerable time in the schools, so the degree of collaboration between them and your program is directly important to the quality of your experience.

Ask about the relationships between the program you are interested in and the schools with which it works. Find out if the program has a "clinical site" or "professional development school" partnership with any of these schools. A clinical site is a school or district with whom a teacher education program cooperates in the placement and supervision of a cohort of student teachers. A professional development school is a partnership between a school and a college or university that focuses not only on preparing new teachers but on increasing veteran teachers' skills and competencies as well. (We will discuss these arrangements later in the chapter.)

The involvement of teachers and administrators in teaching or co-teaching education courses is another way to assess the relationship between teacher education programs and public schools. Excellent teacher preparation programs include school personnel in course planning and delivery. Teachers and administrators, immersed in the day-to-day operation of schools, know what works with kids, and they can often identify the practical strengths and shortcomings of popular educational methods. They bring a sense of immediacy and passion to their teaching about teaching.

At the same time, immersion in school cultures does not always allow teachers and administrators time and energy outside their day-to-day experiences to reflect about the best educational practices. College faculty, who are outsiders, may be able to sort through the conflicting images and situations of classroom life to generate useful analyses. More to the point, courses that are co-taught by school and college faculty offer opportunities to combine insider and outsider points of view for multiple perspectives on learning and teaching. As you investigate programs, be sure to ask what roles public school faculty play in teacher education at both school sites and on campus.

Evaluation

Quite naturally, students are concerned about how they will be evaluated in their teacher education program. They want to know what is expected of them and how they are doing at each stage of the process. It is important that you understand the assessment and evaluation policies of the program you are planning to attend. The consequences of your performance in teacher education are significant for all concerned. You will affect the lives of many students when you graduate, and a program must assess your readiness to teach in terms of that fact. Funding, reputation, and academic viability rest in part on how well a program's graduates do as teachers.

Evaluation can be designed not only to judge whether you are ready to seek a teaching position but also to help you learn more about yourself as a teacher as you proceed through the program of study. Find out what grading system your program uses, and ask how your performance in each course is assessed. Ask if the program uses only a mid-term and final evaluation or if are there ongoing opportunities to demonstrate your learning, gain feedback, and diagnose what you have to do to succeed. It is a good idea to find out if your evaluations will be based primarily on the judgments of others, or if your self assessments will be part of the process.

Multiple sources of evaluation are being encouraged at all education levels. A portfolio that you develop over the course of your program is a way of tracing your educational development and growing levels of accomplishment as a teacher. Portfolios right now are in fashion, and like all fashionable items, they can easily become mass produced and imitative. Find out if the program uses portfolios for new teachers, and if not, why? If they do, how are portfolios organized, reviewed, and presented to help you grow as a teacher and find a job in the field? (We explain portfolios as part of the job search process in Chapter 7.)

Finally, evaluation is always an issue of power. College faculty have the responsibility of saying to a state licensing board, "This student is ready (or not ready) to teach." How that power is exercised is crucial. As a prospective student you need to get a sense of whether or not program faculty are thoughtful about evaluation issues and whether or not that thoughtfulness creates a process of fair-minded assessments of your development as a teacher. Do faculty depend mainly on the power of grades to motivate students to do good work? Does more than one faculty member have a say in whether a student has met the requirements of the program? What role do you play in evaluation? A good program teaches about the equitable use of power in grading by how it goes about evaluating prospective teachers.

Job Placement Support

Most teacher education programs have a system of job placement support. At a minimum, they provide access to a college or university's career placement office where you will find job listings from around the state, region, and nation, plus assistance in writing résumés and preparing for interviews. Beyond that, a program may maintain contact with professional organizations and school districts which inform them when job openings are going to occur.

A thoughtfully designed program will hold workshops on how to prepare your materials for presentation to prospective school districts. It may hold mock interviews to assist graduating students to feel more comfortable presenting themselves professionally to school personnel. Program alumni are another important source of job information and placement support. Many districts prefer interviewing candidates from a teacher preparation program that has provided them with successful hires in the past.

While you are looking at the job placement record of schools, pay attention to an important, though often unrecognized, factor in the job placement support process. Are those who know your work in the teacher education program willing to take the time to write recommendations as you approach graduation? Ask recent graduates what it was like to get recommendations from their faculty and supervisors. In a program that supports its students, the faculty, cooperating teachers, and supervisors know the students well and consider it part of their job to write thoughtful, substantive letters of recommendation.

Teaching can be a lonely profession, particularly for new educators who get hired in districts far away from family and friends. To support new teachers, some forward-looking teacher education programs are creating Internet and e-mail contacts with their graduates. The idea is to build electronic learning communities among new and experienced educators. Networking with like-minded practitioners, educators can share everyday successes and perplexing issues with colleagues. Individual problem-solving is enhanced by the ideas of teachers in different communities. Find out if the program stays in contact with its graduates electronically or otherwise. Remaining linked with your program can be a wonderful professional resource.

Program Costs

We put the question of program cost last because deciding how much to spend on your professional education is best assessed in light of other factors. For example, getting a teaching credential as an undergraduate may limit the expense of going to another school for certification, but it may also shortchange you in overall college experience. Many students find there is simply not enough time in four years to complete an academic major and minor, work a job to support yourself in school, let alone spend a junior year abroad, learn a second (or third) language, play a collegiate sport, become active in community organizations, and earn teacher certification.

Combining certification with a master's degree earns you a higher starting salary, but it increases your overall educational expense and potentially the amount of loans you must pay back after graduation. With the current average annual cost of a four-year degree at public institutions at $10,759 and at private institutions $20,003,[2] another year or two of college is a significant investment. A master's degree has considerable value in terms of academic and professional preparedness. Cost, then, is always related to what it is you want to do academically and personally in higher education.

Is there a reasonable amount of expense that one might incur in becoming certified to teach? It is possible to estimate how many years it will take you to cover or recover the cost of your teacher preparation program once you get a job. If you go to a school that costs you $5,000 to become certified, and your beginning salary of $28,000 allows you to save $2,000 per year, it will take you a minimum of two and one half years to pay for your teacher preparation and certification program. If your teacher certification program costs you $20,000 per year, and your beginning salary of $28,000 allows you to save $2,000 a year, it will take you ten years to cover or recover the cost of your teacher preparation.

These numbers may seem to argue for the less expensive routes to certification. After all, the money you make as a teacher rises very slowly as your years in the profession and professional development activities increase. In some systems, top salaries barely double entry ones. So while the costs of your program are a matter of personal finances and what you are willing to pay, it is fair to ask, "What do I get for my money at a school?" Program costs are in part related to program quality, and some less expensive schools lack the resources—excellent faculty, access to technology, extensive libraries, partnerships with public schools—to provide the kind of experiences you need to become an effective teacher. Yet some expensive schools place no more resources in teacher education than less elite institutions.

View the school you attend not just as a teacher preparation institution but also as a career-development process. Some schools may do a better job than others of getting you ready for the job market of the future. Some offer prestige as well as academics, and that high reputation opens leadership opportunities in many different organizations. Less-well-known schools may provide good preparation and have outstanding local reputations where you want to get a job. Your learning experiences, academic credentials, and career opportunities must all be considered as you make decisions about the cost of teacher education.

RATING THE PROGRAMS

When many prospective teachers apply to a school, they have some notion of how it is perceived by other students, teachers, parents, the schools that will be their future employers, and the public at large. They want to go to a place that is regarded positively by others. Reputation may be not be the sole reason for choosing a school and its teacher education program, but it is an important factor. At the same time, reputation can be more—or less—than it seems.

For example, a college may have famous alumni, you may know a former graduate personally, or its image may make it appealing to attend. Such informal sources of reputation, while interesting, are not reliable. You need far more concrete information about courses, faculty, connections to local schools, and opportunities for graduates to make an informed decision.

Local school personnel can often provide a practical guide to how well a college or university is regarded in the area. A "good" reputation probably means that schools have hired and been pleased with the college's or university's graduates as teachers. Sometimes a college or university has been part of a professional education partnership with a school district, or its faculty have done workshops for teachers in the schools. When these associations are successful, the result is respect for the college or university as a place that successfully prepares individuals for the realities of teaching.

There are also national reputations to consider. Since 1995, *U.S. News & World Report* has published its yearly ranking of top fifty graduate programs in education (see Part II). (They also rate leading schools in law, medicine, engineering, business, public administration, and liberal arts Ph.D. programs). The list purports to show the "best of the best" among 188 graduate-level education schools that grant Ph.D. or Ed.D. degrees. Five basic criteria are used: selectivity in choosing students; ratio of faculty to full-time doctoral and master's degree candidates; research by professors; reputation of the school among education school deans and top faculty; and reputation among school superintendents in districts enrolling more than five thousand students. A complex formula of weighted rankings is used to place every program from first to last in each category, and then to rate the institutions.[3]

The list is hardly surprising. Elite colleges and large public and private universities dominate. Hundreds of schools that do teacher preparation but do not have doctoral programs are not part of the survey. In addition, some well-known private schools are not on the list because they do not offer teacher education as part of their undergraduate or graduate programs.

A close look at the rankings reveals some unusual features. First, it is fairly easy for institutions to move up and down the list—or even on or off the chart. A change in just one of the criteria can mean a change of many points on the rating scale. Harvard moved from first place in 1995 to fourth in 1997. Boston College dropped from sixteenth to twenty-eigth in three years, while the University of Texas at Austin jumped from twenty-seventh to twelfth and UCLA moved from tenth to fifth in the same time period. The year 1997 also marked the first appearances of Virginia Tech and the University of Oklahoma in the top fifty; in 1998

San Diego State and the University of California–Riverside joined the list.

Second, rankings offer little guidance about how personal needs and interests are met by a particular program. There is no mention of a school's theoretical approach to teacher education, or how much academic content or field experiences are stressed in the program. Lists provide little guidance about accessibility of faculty, quality of advising, substance of courses, job-related supports offered to graduates, or whether an East Coast student will enjoy a West Coast school or whether an individual from an urban background will be comfortable in a more rural campus setting.

Finally, the rankings assign considerable significance to the research activities of faculty at the institutions on the list. The rankings do not tell you whether these same faculty members are going to be your teachers in the graduate education program you choose to attend. At many elite colleges and large universities, teacher preparation is not the primary mission of its graduate school of education. These schools see their role as influencing public policy, generating research, and redefining theoretical approaches to curriculum and instruction, not preparing teachers for the classroom.

It is true that an educational researcher who is an active writer, grantsperson, and speaker has much to teach prospective teachers. At the same time, there is a question as to whether you will ever take courses with these individuals as part of your certification program. Many research faculty are not directly involved in the teacher education side of the institution. As a result, you need to look closely at the faculty in the teacher education program you are planning to attend. Ideally, you will find teachers who combine research and scholarship with a commitment to effective teacher education.

ACCREDITATION

When you choose your teacher education program, it would seem obvious and smart to choose a program in a college or university that is accredited. But what does accreditation actually mean? Most colleges and universities and the programs within them are constantly evaluating themselves. But the accreditation process adds an external perspective to the process of constant self-evaluation. It asks an institution or a program within it to evaluate itself not only in terms of its own standards, but also in terms of standards held by other comparable institutions or professional organizations.

Furthermore, to avoid self-interested bias, the accreditation process asks outside visiting teams to develop their own independent judgment as to whether the institution or program is truly meeting its objectives with a high degree of quality.[4] If an institution or program is accredited, you are assured that some external agency has reviewed the institution or program and says it has the requisite physical and intellectual resources to do the job of preparing teachers at a credible standard of excellence.

There are at least three levels of accreditation in teacher education.

Level One

In the United States a system of regional accreditation governs all institutions of higher education. Every college, university, or technical institute is required to submit itself to review by one of the following regional accreditation associations: New England Association of Schools and Colleges, Middle States Association of Colleges and Schools, North Central Association of Colleges and Schools, Southern Association of Colleges and Schools, Northwest Association of Schools and Colleges, and Western Association of Schools and Colleges.[5]

These regional accrediting bodies serve to ensure the public that the institution's purposes are sound and that they have the resources to carry them out in intelligently designed programs. This level of accreditation provides a baseline of assurance that the school which you are considering for your teacher education program has the characteristics most reasonable people would deem necessary for an institution to call itself a college or university in the United States.[6] Most of you will simply assume that your prospective school is accredited by the appropriate regional organization. While that is a reasonable assumption, if you are considering a small, private, and perhaps entrepreneurial institution, it is a good idea to ask about its accreditation status.

Level Two

In all fifty states, if you are to achieve state certification or licensure through a college or university teacher education program, that program must be approved by the state's department of education or the state's professional board of standards in education. Avoid a teacher education program that claims to prepare teachers for state licensure but is not approved by the appropriate state agency. At the end of your program, you will have trouble gaining the license you need to teach.

Level Three

It is clear that you should pick an institution that is accredited by one of the regional associations and a program that is accredited by the appropriate state agency. A more complicated question is whether you should choose a program that is accredited by the National Council for Accreditation of Teacher Education (NCATE).

NCATE is an accreditation agency which administers a voluntary accreditation process for colleges and universities offering teacher education programs. Colleges and universities with teacher education programs are not required by statute to seek NCATE accreditation. Of the 1,363 institutions which offer teacher education programs in this country, only 493 are accredited by NCATE.[7] Of the 870 institutions offering teacher education that are not NCATE accredited, some were unable to pass NCATE accreditation standards, but many did not seek it. (We list all NCATE–accredited institutions by state in Part II.)

So how important is it to you whether the program you are considering is in an institution accredited by NCATE? In NCATE's view, as well as the perspectives of many educators, it is crucial. They regard the state level of accreditation as assuring that basic standards are met; NCATE's review is seen as the center of a major effort to improve standards in teacher education and to professionalize the field.[8]

If you choose a program accredited by NCATE, you can be sure that:

1. It has been subjected to external scrutiny by educators outside the college or university.

2. It has tried to be responsive to standards that many in the field see as central to the pursuit of excellence in teacher education.

3. It is in line with initial efforts by NCATE and the educational unions that sit on its board to encourage school districts to hire only graduates of NCATE–accredited institutions.

4. It is more likely that the license you earn in one state will be treated reciprocally by another state.

5. It has chosen to meet the highest current national standards in the field of teacher education.

While most new teacher candidates graduate from NCATE–accredited institutions, the majority of institutions that prepare teachers are not accredited. Furthermore, some of the most prestigious colleges and universities that offer teacher education programs are not accredited by NCATE. Of the top fifty graduate programs in education listed in the 1999 *U.S. News & World Report* rankings, only twenty-four had NCATE accreditation.

As a prospective teacher, you should know that there is a debate in the field over NCATE's approach to improving teacher education. There are some who question whether a knowledge base for teachers central to the notion of professionalization urged by NCATE has been achieved or is achievable.[9] Others argue that NCATE's goal of professionalizing teacher education is ill conceived and inconsistent with a democratic notion of education.[10] Still others contend that there is not enough evidence to assert that a program accredited by NCATE produces better teachers than one that is not and that the organization itself does not yet have a good enough sense of what is involved in controlling quality through accreditation.[11] NCATE counters by pointing out developing research that indicates graduates from their approved programs will be better prepared for the realities of teaching.

At the time of this writing, NCATE is the only national accrediting agency for teacher education, but an alternative process is being developed under the auspices of the Teacher Education Accreditation Council (TEAC). The existence of TEAC may confound the situation even more, or it may offer an alternative accreditation process that, by its very competitiveness, will lead to improvements.

If the program you are considering is not in a NCATE–accredited institution, ask why not. Did it try to be accredited and not succeed? That would be a serious drawback. Did it choose not to submit to NCATE review? If that is the case, what was the reasoning for that decision? Was it based on thoughtful disagreement with NCATE's philosophy? Perhaps it was not expedient to seek NCATE approval, or the program was not ready to be reviewed, or adequate resources had not been dedicated to teacher education. Each reason may reveal partial information about an institution's credibility as a preparer of teachers.

NEW DEVELOPMENTS IN TEACHER EDUCATION

A 1997 report by the National Commission on Teaching & America's Future offered a broad criticism of the way in which many colleges and universities go about preparing teachers. It cited inadequate undergraduate programs, fragmented efforts, uninspired teaching methods, superficial curriculum, and a traditional view of schooling.[12] Eight recommendations for reorganizing teacher education in higher education included:

1. Stronger disciplinary preparation
2. Greater focus on learning and development
3. More knowledge about curriculum and assessment design
4. Greater understanding of how to help special-needs students
5. Multicultural competence
6. Preparation for collaboration

7. Technological skills

8. Strong emphasis on reflection and inquiry

Many veteran teachers also have little good to say about the teacher education they received in college. When surveyed by the Council for Basic Education, some six hundred award-winning educators urged higher subject area standards, including averages of B or better and passing scores on content-knowledge exams; professional education courses co-developed and co-taught by college faculty and classroom teachers; and more time spent in schools by prospective educators as tutors, mentors, aides, and student teachers. One teacher in the survey spoke for many in stating that, even after numerous education courses, "I was totally unprepared for the impact of teaching itself."[13]

In response to calls for change, colleges and universities across the country are implementing an array of new approaches within their teacher education programs. Three new models are five-year combined undergraduate/graduate programs, professional development schools (PDS), and extended internship and immersions.

Five-Year Combined Undergraduate/Graduate Programs

In typical four-year undergraduate programs, students take professional preparation courses during their sophomore, junior, and the first part of their senior year. Undergraduate degree work as well as certification culminates with student teaching. Critics contend such arrangements shortchange a new educator's academic study and teacher preparation. While teaching in schools, students may not concentrate fully on demanding arts and sciences content courses. Packing everything into four years means that new teachers do not spend enough time developing curriculum, and interacting with kids.

In five-year combined programs, certification candidates take an extra year to complete general education courses, an academic major, professional studies, and student teaching, while earning a bachelor's and master's degree. Typically, students devote the fifth year to education courses and work in schools so they have the time and space to pursue their liberal arts degree and their preparation without crowding or shortchanging either. In a few five-year programs, prospective teachers earn two undergraduate degrees—one in their subject field and one in education.

Professional Development Schools (PDS)

Professional development schools (PDS) are one of the most popular new developments in teacher education today. Noting that more than two hundred schools of education now have professional development school partnerships, the National Commission on Teaching & America's Future straightforwardly recommends that every new teacher be part of a year-long internship in a PDS setting. Comparable to teaching hospitals in medicine, professional development schools provide new recruits with sites for intensively supervised internships where they can experience state-of-the-art practice that is linked to their coursework.[14] The movement is so widespread that NCATE has issued draft standards for identifying and supporting quality professional development school partnerships.

In a PDS model, public schools agree to welcome and support certification candidates from a college or university teacher preparation program. Often, a group of prospective teachers do their practicums simultaneously at the school site. Many members of a school staff are directly involved in the education of new teachers, co-teaching courses, and interacting with the candidates on a regular basis. In some cases, entire high school departments or middle school instructional teams serve as mentors and supporters.

In return the college or university supports public school personnel with graduate course waivers, in-service workshops and in some instances, financial support. There is a stated commitment to the professional development of veteran educators as well as to the preparation of new teachers. The partners also agree to conduct joint action research projects to improve student learning and to support broader school improvement and educational reform goals. To learn more about PDS partnerships, contact the Professional Development School Network (see Part II).

Extended Internships and Immersions

Extended internships and school-based immersion programs at the master's level are a sharp new departure from traditional teacher preparation arrangements. In such programs certification candidates teach for an extended period of time, in many cases a full year, at a school site. On-site graduate coursework in education is integrated with their teaching experience. Extended internships and immersions seek a blended or seamless teacher education process that minimizes the split between campus and classroom found in many programs.

Year-long immersion in a school allows for greater collegial support among new teachers and more focused supervision by school and college or university personnel. It also means added teaching resources for middle school teams and high school departments. For schools, this "overstaffing" element is one of the most important parts of the model. Since certification candidates are in the building for the entire year, co-teaching arrangements become workable. Each adult in the room can focus on groups of students, or the student teacher can take over classes of veteran teachers, freeing them to develop new curriculum or do other projects of value for the school. At the completion of the year's intensive teaching and study, the candidate receives a master's degree and recommendation for certification.

When thinking about any new model, remember: change is a positive development, but change for the sake of change is not. Give serious consideration to a school that is implementing new models of teacher preparation for thoughtful reasons. Such a school will be able to clearly explain how new models will prepare you to be successful in present and future classrooms. Look twice at a program that offers rhetoric about innovation but cannot show evidence for the substance of those approaches.

Being part of a new program model may give you a competitive edge when you walk into a job interview; you will likely have a different set of experiences to build upon when you enter the classroom full time. New models often incorporate the best of what is known about how to get novices ready for the classroom and provide the skills and insights beginners need to succeed as first- and second-year teachers. Many seek to make individual best practices the hallmarks of their approach to teacher preparation. If you are interested in constructivist approaches, educational technology, community service learning, cooperative group-work, or another innovative idea, then choose a program that emphasizes them.

Despite the advantages of new models, brand-new or recently established programs, while offering departures from traditional practices, require significant planning and development. They typically go through a "shakedown" time, when many program features are not yet in place and activities are often changing. As a participant in one of these projects, you will need to have a tolerance for ambiguity and a willingness to be flexible. Such programs offer exciting opportunities, but they can be frustrating as well.

ALTERNATIVE PATHS TO CERTIFICATION

While one reaction to criticisms aimed at teacher preparation has been the development of new models within institutions of higher education, another approach has been to establish alternative routes to certification. As non-college or non-university-based systems, these alternative routes may appeal to those of you who want to enter teaching as quickly as possible. For many reasons—such as time, money, or considerable work experience in a professional field—you may have no desire to enroll in a college- or university-based program.

School-Based Certification Programs

Each state requires that teachers in public schools be certified, and each state determines its requirements for licensure. Historically, when states have faced teacher shortages in various curriculum areas, they have issued emergency certifications. While such certificates allow individuals to begin teaching in a particular field before being fully certified, the state's requirement is that the candidate become certified as soon as possible.

School-based certification programs originated with the notion of emergency certification, but their use expanded significantly in the 1980s. New Jersey, Texas, and Connecticut as well as Chicago and Los Angeles led the development of these alternative paths for four basic reasons:

- To provide ways for talented individuals who might have lost their jobs to corporate and military downsizing to enter teaching easily
- To find a way to attract minority teachers to the field
- To deregulate the preparation of teachers outside the context of colleges and universities
- To operate certification efforts at less state expense than campus-based teacher education programs.[15]

Ironically, states relaxed requirements for alternative programs while instituting even more rigorous demands on colleges and universities to raise standards.

Almost all states now have school-based certification programs with the following features:

- A candidate must already possess a bachelor's degree in a relevant subject matter area.
- The program is primarily based in schools: a candidate is either hired as an intern or a full-time first-year teacher and placed in a full-time or nearly full-time teaching situation (often in the most demanding situations).
- Ideally, the new teacher is teamed with an experienced master teacher whose role it is to serve as mentor to the first-year teacher.
- Various arrangements are made to provide the coursework normally associated with teacher certification. The school district might be approved to offer some of the courses themselves. Or, as is more often the case, the school district will seek the cooperation of a local university or college to offer evening and summer courses, sometimes on a condensed or intensive basis.

In many alternative programs, candidates are placed in classrooms and given full teaching responsibilities almost immediately. If they are to survive, they must quickly learn to teach. They learn by doing and, ideally, with the support of an experienced mentor. Courses about teaching, students, schools, and society come later, either in the school district or at nearby colleges and universities. Students in college- or university-based programs take courses, visit schools, and student teach in a step-by-step process culminating in student teaching. The best comprehensive guide to alternative programs is *Alternative Teacher Certification: A State by State Analysis* by Emily Feistritzer and David Chester of the National Center for Education Information.

Teach For America

Teach For America is one of the most appealing alternative paths to becoming a teacher. Wendy Kopp founded the organization in 1989 as a senior honors project at Princeton University. It capitalized on the idealism and desire to serve on the part of many liberal arts graduates as well as a growing skepticism among policymakers and reformers regarding the need and value of any extended college teacher-preparation program. The program quickly gained funding support from corporate America.

Teach For America offers a short summer preparation program, work in some of the most challenging inner-city and rural-area teaching situations in the country, and ongoing support and reflection on practice through small groups that meet regularly. Admission to the program is selective with about one out of six applicants being admitted and placed. Teach For America's path to certification is not as clear as it might be. Their promotional literature states: "Corps members may or may not be certified at the end of two years depending on their own initiative and on the requirements of the state in which they teach. State regulations usually require that individuals complete education course work and other in-service activities to become certified, and the cost and length of study vary by district and university."

At this time, Teach For America is energetically pursuing the authorization to be a full teacher-certifying agency by having the states where it places teachers recognize it as an approved alternative path. Maryland already accepts Teach For America experience for its certification requirements. Other states allow individuals to use their experience in the program to fulfill some teacher education requirements.

Complexities of Alternative Paths

Every system, no matter how good, needs a way around itself. Alternative certification pathways provide a useful safety valve to campus-based teacher education programs. Yet concerns about alternative paths are significant. Some critics argue that states are using alternative paths to certification as a way of continuing to meet the need for teachers as cheaply as possible. Instead of raising salaries for teachers, for the purpose of attracting additional qualified people to the field, states are expanding the pool of potential teachers and keeping salaries down by encouraging alternative routes toward teaching.[16]

Linda Darling-Hammond, among others, sharply criticizes alternative paths, particularly Teach For America. She cites research showing that candidates entering teaching through alternative routes are less highly rated, less successful with students, and tend to stay in teaching for fewer years than teachers prepared in more traditional campus-based programs.[17] Instead of constructing alternative routes, Darling-Hammond urges raising standards for educators through a professionalization of teaching. In her view, there is a body of knowledge about learning and teaching that all teachers should know. Alternative paths to certification that allow local districts to determine requirements for entrance to the field do not assure a common base of knowledge and competency among new teachers.

Clearly, as authors and educators, we believe in alternatives and options, and we recognize that some of those provided by the states might be worthwhile for you. Because you have observed teaching more than any other professional occupation, your familiarity with it may make preparing to teach seem relatively simple.[18] Becoming a teacher, however, is a developmental, social, and cognitive process that requires careful shaping and guidance in order for the prospective teacher to develop into the best teacher he or she is capable of being—the kind needed by the schools. Teaching is intellectual work. The path to becoming a teacher should prepare you for that work in more ways than just studying your subject matter.

Teaching is also a process that requires that teacher and student make meaning of what they do together. To make that meaning, teachers need a chance to reflect on their preparation, experiences in the classroom, responses of students, and the work of other teachers. An alternative program that can support that process and allow you to develop your skills fully may be the right one for you.

Check with the state's department of education to see how clearly defined the alternative process is in that state and whether or not you understand it. Are there clear beginning and ending points? Does it place you in classrooms where even more experienced teachers would fear to tread, or does it place you in situations in which you are most likely to succeed? Does it offer the consistent involvement of a mentor who is not only a master teacher but also one who knows how to coach and support a novice? Or, as we have seen in a number of instances, is the language of mentoring more rhetoric than actuality? We advise you to ask the same questions of a campus-based program.

In essence, what every prospective educator needs is excellent preparation to teach. Whether the program is established or experimental, traditional or innovative, campus based or school based, it must prepare graduates to be comfortable with, interested in, and ready to teach a wide range of students in many different educational settings. It must incorporate the realities of how students learn and how schools work in its approaches to teacher education. It must give you a chance to develop your talents and succeed as a teacher.

NOTES

1. Lucas, *Teacher Education*.

2. William H. Honan, "The Ivory Tower Under Siege," *New York Times Education Life*, 4 January 1998, 44.

3. "America's Best Graduate Schools," (Washington, D.C.: U.S. News & World Report, 1999), 108–111.

4. Kenneth Young, Charles M. Chambers, H. R. Kells and associates with assistance from Ruth Cargo, *Understanding Accreditation: Contemporary Perspectives on Issues and Practices in Evaluation of Educational Quality* (San Francisco: Jossey-Bass, 1983).

5. Ibid.

6. Ibid.

7. National Council for Accreditation of Teacher Education, *A List of Professionally Accredited Schools, Colleges, and Departments of Education* (Washington, D.C.: National Council for Accreditation of Teacher Education, November, 1997).

8. American Association of Colleges for Teacher Education, *Capturing the Vision: Reflection on NCATE's Redesign Five Years Later* (Washington, D.C.: American Association of Colleges for Teacher Education, February, 1993).

9. Arthur Wise and Jane Leibbrand, "Accreditation and the Creation of a Profession of Teaching," *Phi Delta Kappan* 75, no. 2 (October 1993), 133–157.

10. David F. Labaree, "Power, Knowledge, and the Rationalization of Teaching: A Genealogy of the Movement to Professionalize Teaching," *Harvard Educational Review* 62, no. 2 (1992), 123–154.

11. Gary D. Fenstermacher, "Controlling Quality and Creating Community: Separate Purposes for Separate Organizations," *Journal of Teacher Education* 45, no. 5 (1994), 329–336.

12. National Commission on Teaching & America's Future, *What Matters Most*, 76–77.

13. Diana Wyllie Rigden, "How Teachers Would Change Teacher Education" *Education Week on the Web*, 11 December 1996, 1.

14. National Commission on Teaching & America's Future, *What Matters Most*, 80.

15. Robert A. Roth, "The University Can't Train Teachers? Transformation of a Profession," *Journal of Teacher Education* 45, no. 4 (September–October, 1994),

261–268. Also see Linda Darling-Hammond, "Teaching and Knowledge: Policy Issues Posed by Alternate Certification for Teachers," *Peabody Journal of Education* 67, no. 3 (Spring, 1990), 123–154; and Christopher Lucas, *Teacher Education*.

16. Darling-Hammond, "Teaching and Knowledge."

17. Linda Darling-Hammond, "Who Will Speak for the Children? How 'Teach For America' Hurts Urban Schools and Students," *Phi Delta Kappan* 76, no. 1 (1994), 21–34.

18. Pamela I. Grossman, "Learning to Teach without Teacher Education," *Teachers College Record* 91, no. 2 (Winter, 1989), 191–208.

5

Getting Accepted into the Program of Your Choice

To gain entry to most college or university teacher education programs, you must be accepted by an admissions committee which reviews applications against the school's established admissions criteria. Depending on the school, application reviewers assign different degrees of importance to certain factors. In theory, admissions is a selective process. In practice, some programs are hard to get into while others tend to admit many of those who apply. In this chapter, we describe the criteria many select programs use for admissions. We also discuss the mechanics of preparing your application, including: writing your personal statement, organizing letters of recommendation, and submitting college transcripts.

ADMISSION TO TEACHER EDUCATION

In reviewing applications, most admissions committees pay close attention to the following four areas: subject matter preparation, experience with children or adolescents, commitment to diversity and equity, and leadership activities. If you understand the logic of these areas and their importance to successful teaching, you can prepare a thoughtful, focused application that best presents how your background, motivations, and talents meet the criteria for admission.

Subject Matter Preparation

To be admitted to a teacher education program, you will need evidence of a strong background in your subject matter field. Prospective middle and high school teachers do not major in education; instead they major in their teaching field or in a closely related academic subject. Many of the widely recognized academic majors for the common middle and high school teacher certifications are listed in Figure 5.1.

Note that, in a few institutions, the academic major for secondary teacher certification is not located in the arts and sciences but in a department, school, or college of education. Teacher candidates major in English education, social studies education, mathematics education, science education, or foreign language education. In such cases substantial coursework outside of education in arts and sciences departments related to the teaching field is also required.

As an undergraduate, choose your major because of your love for and interest in that subject. Doing so usually translates into the good grades and solid preparation that teacher education programs look for in prospective applicants. Remember that if the major you choose does not correspond to what is taught in the middle or high schools, you may need additional coursework once you enter the certification process.

Perhaps you are already out of college and have become interested in teaching but lack a major in the subject you want to teach. You do not have to become an undergraduate again. Many major universities and colleges have divisions of continuing education or other non-degree, special student programs that encourage and facilitate older students returning to college to meet the subject matter requirements for certification. Advisors in continuing education programs will meet with you to analyze the transcripts of your past work and tell you how many additional courses you will need to meet subject matter requirements. Knowledge of your subject matter is basic to becoming a middle or high school teacher. By planning ahead, or by being willing to do additional coursework, you can take charge of your preparation in this crucial area.

Having a high grade point average (GPA) is a plus. It shows you have excellent intellectual, analytical, and communication skills. Most programs have minimum GPA requirements. But if your GPA is not quite as high as you might wish, don't give up. You may be able to demonstrate those skills through your performance in extracurricular activities, volunteer or paid employment, or a portfolio of your past work that you think best shows your potential to be a great teacher.

Ideally, admissions committees look for evidence that you are committed to learning. If you are currently an undergraduate thinking of teaching, now is the time to make sure you have the strongest record possible. If you graduated college with less than a stellar GPA, return to school as a part-time, non-degree or continuing education student, and work toward higher grades. By doing this you will show an admissions committee that your past record does not speak sufficiently to your present level of motivation, willingness to work hard to succeed, and who

Figure 5.1
Common Certification Areas and Academic Majors

Area of Certification	Academic Major
English	English
History	History
Social Studies	History
	Political Science
	Economics
	Anthropology
	African American Studies
	Women's Studies
	Sociology
Mathematics	Mathematics
Biology	Biology
	Biochemistry
	Botany
	Zoology
Chemistry	Chemistry
	Biochemistry
	Chemical Engineering
Earth Science	Geology
	Astronomy
	Civil Engineering
General Science	Biochemistry
	Biology
	Chemistry
	Geology
	Physics
	Zoology
Physics	Physics
	Mechanical Engineering
	Electrical Engineering
Communications & Performing Arts	Communications
World or Foreign Languages	
French	French
Spanish	Spanish
Portuguese	Portuguese
German	German
Chinese	Chinese
Japanese	Japanese

Figure 5.2
Ways to Gain Experience Working with Kids

Consider paid or volunteer jobs:	Consider working with kids through:
Baby-sitter	Peer education programs
Camp counselor	Community service projects
Coach	Big Brother/Big Sister
Lifeguard	Local YWCA/YMCA
Parent	Church, Synagogue, or Mosque groups
Tutor in schools	Recreational clubs
Substitute teacher	Girl Scouts/Boy Scouts

you are as a person and a potential teacher. This new evidence, in addition to your professional and community experiences, can be persuasive.

Experience with Children or Youth

Teacher education admissions committees tend to ask the question: Does this candidate have any experience with children or adolescents that would indicate commitment to, and a talent for, teaching? The personal and professional experiences you describe in your application can reveal your readiness to teach middle and high school age students. It can show that you care about and respect young people while understanding the potentials and complexities of working with them.

Try to gain different kinds of experiences with middle and high school age youngsters by participating in children- or youth-oriented programs and activities (see Figure 5.2). Make an effort to work with a range of young people in different situations and settings. This is important not only to demonstrate to admissions committees that you are interested in middle and high school age groups, but it also will help you to determine whether you enjoy and respect young people. If after a variety of experiences across a reasonable span of time, you find your experience with adolescents aggravating and just not fun, you should think twice before trying to become a teacher.

Commitment to Diversity and Equity

Prospective teachers, regardless of their backgrounds, will be expected to teach students whose life experiences may be decidedly different from their own. They must do so with a commitment to equity and excellence. Children and adolescents come to school from many different socioeconomic and cultural backgrounds. An increasing number speak English as a second or even third language. Many individuals, who once would have been placed in special education classes because of physical, emotional, and intellectual challenges, are now being included in mainstream classrooms.

How an applicant presents his or her experience with, attitude toward, and interest in a diverse range of students will be highly significant to admissions committees of programs that are concerned with equity in education. Sophisticated admissions committees look for evidence that candidates recognize and respect differences and are also willing to build on what their students have in common. Some teacher education programs stress this area of concern, and institutions that are accredited by the National Council for Accreditation of Teacher Education (NCATE) are required to address this issue directly in their admissions processes.

Older candidates sometimes have life experiences that may have brought them in contact with people from diverse backgrounds. If that is the case for you, describe your experience in your personal statement or include a letter of recommendation from someone who can honestly assess your involvement with issues of equity and diversity. No matter where you are in your life history, it is important to you and to your potential teacher education program that your experience reflects your willingness to cross some of the boundaries that our society imposes between groups of people.

Admissions committees look not only at the experiences candidates describe but at the language they use to depict these experiences. Psycholinguist Lev Vygotsky said that our language is a microcosm of our consciousness.[1] Therefore, choose words that honestly and accurately reflect your thoughts without the possibility of being misconstrued. For example, one recent candidate to our program tried to show her appreciation and respect for a diverse range of students. However, in her writing she used the phrase "these people." That indication of separation and distance could make an admissions committee look even more closely at how a candidate thinks about her or his relationship to potential students.

Issues of equity and diversity are also factors in the demographics depicting who is coming into teaching. For a range of reasons, minorities are not entering teaching in numbers commensurate to their representation in the population. Many colleges and universities are actively recruiting African Americans, Native Americans, Asian Americans, Latino Americans, and other minorities to enter teacher preparation programs. If you are a student of color, find out whether the college or university of your choice offers scholarships or other forms of financial support designed to encourage you to pursue teaching as a career.

Leadership Experiences

Teaching is a multifaceted discipline, but among its most important aspects is leadership. Guiding groups of students toward becoming engaged, good humored yet serious communities of learners requires strong leadership skills on the part of the teacher. Teachers must also exercise leadership in their contact with administrators and parents. In fact, all of the teacher's roles—establishing goals and objectives, creating curriculum, and evaluating and assessing students' work—necessitate leadership qualities and skills. Many teacher education programs will look for evidence that you have had leadership experience, past and present.

Leadership skills can be gained and demonstrated in many ways. If, as an undergraduate, you seldom venture beyond your established routines of taking classes and socializing with peers, you may need to change your "job description" as a student in order to gain leadership experience. Seek out campus-based and non-campus-based extracurricular activities in which you have the chance to be a leader. If you are already out of school, do not overlook leadership opportunities on the job, in the community, or in your house of worship.

As a leader you play new roles in new settings—a key to personal growth and development, according to social psychologist Urie Bronfenbrenner.[2] You practice new responses to people and organizations including relationship-building with campus or community groups. This kind of experience will help you acquire the skills you will need to succeed as a teacher. You will encounter fresh perspectives about academics and adolescents that will make your teaching more effective and relevant to all your students.

As a leader you learn to take responsibility for program activities, explain concepts to others, build dialog rather than debate, facilitate small group discussions, engage in collaborative problem solving, communicate in varied organizational contexts, resolve issues through meetings with staff and clients, and create and support new programs. As one college student tutor at our campus noted, leadership comes from "the opportunity to help others, and taking initiatives on your own. Leadership cannot exist without the leader being able to empower others so they too can become leaders. . . . Leadership builds self-confidence and enables people to put plans and ideas into action." As a prospective applicant to a teacher education program, search out leadership activities and describe them thoughtfully to the admissions reviewers.

Issues in Admissions

Critics contend that current teacher education admissions processes are either too lax or too focused upon those who have typically pursued teaching careers. Those who feel admissions are too lax contend that teacher education admits a less talented, less academically prepared group of candidates as compared to other professions or even the college or university population as a whole. They urge more rigorous standards, particularly in the area of academic achievement, to make admissions to teacher education more selective.

Another group of reformers, seeking to recruit teachers for culturally diverse learners in urban poverty situations, approach the issue of admissions quite differently. They believe that traditional admissions criteria result in the underrepresentation of "nontraditional" applicants who are more likely to be successful in urban schools.[3] They reject the idea that successful teachers must always have had a high GPA or be someone who always wanted to teach. Rather, say these urban educators, effective future teachers are individuals who can more closely connect to the pressures faced by city youth because they themselves have had similar experiences.

In response to criticisms about who is going into teaching, many institutions of higher education are changing their approaches to admissions. Most have sought to strengthen traditional criteria: higher GPA, stronger references in your subject field, and, in some cases, passing scores on state-mandated teacher tests before entering teacher education. Accordingly, you will find both GPA and academic work in your subject field listed as key admissions factors at many of the schools you may be considering.

Other schools are using the traditional admissions criteria but applying them in less traditional ways in an effort to broaden their assessment of potential certification candidates. They look at additional characteristics such as prior coursework in multicultural education, interpersonal skills and small group interactions as shown in an interview, prior community service work, computer literacy, a preprofessional portfolio, or the page length of personal reference letters. Some are developing alternative admissions procedures to recruit and select a more diverse teaching force.

Across the country, traditional criteria remain dominant in the area of admissions. If you are a college undergraduate in your early twenties, you may find that the traditional criteria work well for you. If you are an older, second career candidate, you will still need to prepare your materials with traditional criteria in mind.

COMPONENTS OF A SUCCESSFUL APPLICATION

Undergraduate and graduate applications to most programs in teacher education have similar core components:

• A personal statement or written responses to specific questions asked on the application

Figure 5.3
Components of an Application

Personal Statement   Recommendations

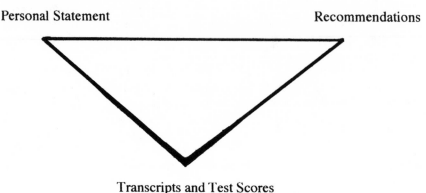

Transcripts and Test Scores

- A record of academic achievement usually represented in a transcript of your previous academic work in college
- An indication of academic knowledge as shown by your scores on national achievement tests and/or state-mandated tests for teachers—some schools require the Scholastic Aptitude Test (SAT) for undergraduates or the Graduate Record Examination (GRE) for graduate students
- Two or three letters of recommendation

Other elements that may be included in your application are a résumé and a portfolio reflecting relevant experience.

Successful candidates use the application to fully describe their motivations, experiences, and qualifications. Think of the application components as the sides of a triangle (see Figure 5.3). Each of the three sides must be solid and secure or the figure loses its shape and substance. Likewise, the components of your application must demonstrate how you meet the criteria for admission.

The Personal Statement

Most admissions committees place heavy emphasis on the personal statement; in some cases, it is first among equals in evaluating candidates for entry into a teacher education program. The importance of the personal statement comes from two seemingly obvious, but easily overlooked, factors. First, you are applying to become a teacher, and teachers make a living by making knowledge accessible to others. A personal statement is a great opportunity for you to demonstrate your communication skills and teaching potential. Do not be confined by the small space you will find on most application forms. Use one to three extra sheets of paper to articulate your reasons for attending the school to which you are applying and for wanting to become a teacher.

Second, this document is a *personal* statement, and admissions committees want to know who you are and why you want to teach. This is not an easy essay! Students continually tell us how hard it is to write about themselves; they feel unsure or confused by what they regard as "selling" themselves to an audience of unknown reviewers. Yet the personal statement is the one place in your application where you can describe yourself in your own voice. It is an opportunity to introduce yourself, make a positive impression, and invite the admissions committee to learn more about you as a potential student in their program.

What do admissions committees look for when reading a personal statement? First and foremost, it must convey as concretely as possible a sense of who you are now and what you have done in the past that leads you to the point of applying to a teacher education program. What experiences have prepared you to consider being a teacher? What is the source and substance of your passion for your subject and for teaching? How have you acted on that passion up to this point?

Here are some key points to remember when writing your personal statement:

Give concrete, specific reasons for wanting to teach. Avoid using broad statements or often-made generalizations that detract from rather than add to your personal statement. Instead, give specific reasons or real-life examples of why you want to pursue teaching at this time. Perhaps your parents or former teachers have influenced you to think about a career in education or human services or maybe a significant set of life experiences—joining the Peace Corps, tutoring in schools, working for a company or small business—have facilitated the realization that teaching is the right career for you at this time. Whatever the circumstances are, explain how they have influenced you.

Blend your experiences with the ideas and insights you have gained from them. Many personal statements read like a chronology or travelogue of a student's life. They straightforwardly present the writer's years of schooling, dates of graduation, work employment, and special events. While this is useful and important information to share with an admissions committee, you also want to tell readers what you have learned from your educational, work, and cultural experiences. For example, if you spent a year studying abroad, share the nuances of the trip and how it influenced you. Or, if you worked your way through college paying your own tuition and housing, explain how this experience affected your views about education. Effective personal statements weave together the facts of your experience with the impact they have made on your thinking about yourself, your education, and your career decisions.

Comment on specific, meaningful issues that relate to your reasons for entering teaching. Some applicants feel compelled to comment about the overall state of education in their personal statement. They characterize issues and trends as all one thing or another, failing to recognize nuance and complexity. In preparing a teacher education program admissions essay, be sure to discuss specific aspects of education that are personally meaningful, and explain why they are important to you.

For example, an applicant who was placed in either high classes or low classes in high school might comment on how tracking in schools affects a student's chances to go to college. Similarly, a student from a low-income community might discuss how educational opportunity is linked to economic opportunity, a woman might analyze her experiences in a male-dominated major like engineering, or a newcomer to American society might examine cultural differences and learning styles. In each case, these applicants are connecting examples from their own lives to their reasons for becoming a teacher.

Other things to keep in mind while writing your personal statement:

- Use language that is concrete, specific, and reflects a sense of energy and life.
- Describe your love of your subject matter, how it developed, and what keeps it alive.
- Present any experience that you have had with children or youth and what you have taken from it.
- Indicate your awareness of issues of equity in teaching and learning. Discuss your engagement with a diverse range of students and commitment to community service.
- Refer to reading you have done or teaching experiences that contribute to a more equitable society.
- Offer evidence of leadership.

Depending upon where you are in your life history, you may be able to emphasize one or another of these components. Although admissions committees may prefer an even emphasis across all profile areas, they will also take into consideration exceptional strengths in one or two areas that a candidate is able to communicate compellingly.

Transcripts

What do admission committees look for in transcripts? Transcripts and the grades on them are a shortcut to understanding the level of accomplishment you have reached. Ideally, admissions committees will look at your transcripts to see if they offer evidence of your commitment to learning. In reality, most admissions committees first look for academic achievement that meets at least their minimum grade point average standard.

Clearly, the higher your GPA above the minimum that the program has established, the better. It is usually courses outside a student's major that tend to draw an average down. So committees may place special emphasis on the average you have earned in your major. If there is a significant difference between your grade point average in your major and that outside your major, you should explain it to the committee.

Some students who do not have the best academic grades may try to ignore or sidestep the issue. Instead, it is most likely in your interest to discuss your academic performance in college whatever your grades— particularly if they are not the best. Explain the circumstances that may have negatively (or positively) affected your performance. Admissions committees may be more ready to deal with someone who is straightforward about her or his record than someone who trys to ignore poor grades in a personal statement.

Transcripts almost always tell a story. But the story is embedded and subject to misinterpretation because it is in shorthand. If a transcript is marginal, a good admissions committee may also look for development and improvement in the overall academic record. One positive initiative you can take is to write an accompanying explanation of your transcript.

For example, committees are well aware that the first semester or two on campus is often problematic for undergraduates, and they have seen many transcripts that tell the story of a rocky first year. In such cases, they look for evidence that the candidate settled down, became serious and engaged, and improved her or his accomplishment over the last years of study. Other students may have discovered that the major they first chose was not for them but not, unfortunately, until after earning some low grades. After changing to another field, the grades go up. If your grades improved after you switched majors, explain the changes to the admissions committee.

Erratic transcripts which go up and down from semester to semester call attention to themselves. If your transcript is inconsistent or if your GPA falls below the minimum required but you still want to apply, you should explain your record to the committee. Do not make excuses for yourself, but present any unusual mitigating factors.

If you do not have the required grade point average, you can sometimes successfully petition to take courses as a non-degree, special, or continuing education student in order to show the admissions committee what you are capable of achieving at this point in your life. You can use your record in these additional courses to support your reapplication to the program. Make the case that your performance in the courses you took most recently is a better indicator of your potential, especially if you have been out of school for a while.

Many programs have a category of admissions called "provisional admissions." This category is often used for applicants who have complicated transcripts. The admissions committee may recommend admissions on a provisional basis, the provision being that the candidate work up to a certain level in the program in his or her first semester or two, in order to be admitted to regular status. As a last resort, you might find out if the program in which you are interested has such a category of admission, and ask that you be considered for it.

Graduate Record Exam

If you already have a bachelor's degree, you may be applying to complete your teacher certification as part of a graduate master's degree program. In some cases, you will be required to take the Graduate Record Exam (GRE). While such standardized tests are being questioned by some educational reformers, many colleges require or strongly recommend them. There are general tests on verbal, mathematical, and logical aptitude, now offered only on computer through Sylvan Learning Centers. Appointments are scheduled on a first-come, first-served basis during most of the year. There are also pencil-and-paper subject matter specialty tests offered at selected times during the year. Most education master's programs do not require the subject matter specialty tests. Currently, the basic charge for each test is $96.

Some teacher education programs require that you achieve a minimum score on the GRE general tests in order to be accepted. Other programs may ask that you take the tests and submit the scores, but they do not weigh them as heavily in the admissions process. In fact, they may be interested in them for research purposes only. Some programs allow you to use the GRE results as supplemental information to compensate for an erratic undergraduate record. The requirements regarding the GREs are program specific, so you have to check with each program to which you are applying as to which ones insist on these tests.

Letters of Recommendation

Letters of recommendation are crucial to a successful application. If at all possible, ask the people who are writing references for you to address the reference specifically to the program to which you are applying. Given the widespread use of word processors, that is not an unreasonable request. The person writing your recommendation can create a basic letter and then adapt it to each program to which you are applying.

Sometimes candidates use recommendations that had been written for other, more generic educational or job-seeking purposes. If that is all you can get, such a recommendation is better than no recommendation at all. Remember, though, that the reference that speaks specifically to the fact that you are applying for a teacher education program works best. Letters included with your application must be up to date. In a competitive admissions round, a recommendation written a few years earlier may be discounted.

While no single recommendation may be able to speak to all the criteria that an admissions committee would use in its review, taken as a group, the letters should speak to most of them. Your recommendations should address your academic potential, your background in working with children, your experience with diverse groups, and your leadership experience. Admissions committees may also look to the letters for a sense of your character, your work ethic, your leadership experiences, and your ability to work cooperatively with other people in groups.

Ideally, one or more letters will come from a professor in your subject field who has taught you in a class. Many schools use this as further evidence of academic skills and knowledge. One of the dilemmas undergraduates in large universities face is the difficulty of finding faculty who know them well enough to write a recommendation. Most faculty will welcome your initiative to become better acquainted. Make an appointment with course instructors and discuss your interests and concerns. You want them to know more about you than they may be able to garner from reading your papers and exams.

Do not hesitate to use teaching assistants as references as well. Do not forget about advisors and heads of residence in your dormitories. They, too, know about your strengths and capabilities. It is less satisfactory for a college sophomore or junior to use a high school teacher as a reference, but if at the time you are applying to a program that is the most up-to-date reference you can get, use it.

For those of you who have been away from school for a while, past academic references should be supplemented by current references about your performance in your present and recent work. Take advantage of your experience by asking people who have worked with you professionally or who know you personally to write letters of recommendation.

You may wonder if recommendations based on part-time jobs, sometimes as waitstaff or salespeople, are relevant. Admissions committees may take significant stock in recommendations that speak to any work experience you have had, because they sense that your reliability and performance in such jobs are related to your ability to take responsibility in a classroom. When you later apply for student teaching positions, potential cooperating teachers prefer individuals who have had work experience. They want to know that the person with whom they are going to work can move from the much more individualistic role of the college student to the job of a teacher with responsibilities to individual students and a larger school community.

THE MECHANICS OF YOUR APPLICATION

Admissions committees try to keep their eyes on the substance of the application, but sometimes they are distracted by simple mechanical issues that a candidate can easily avoid. Typographical errors, misspellings, or other mechanical miscues can prejudice an admissions committee against an applicant.

At the risk of seeming simplistic, we suggest the following:

- Type or word process your applications. This may be more complicated than it seems. Some candidates hand write their applications because, although they have access to a word processor, they may not have ready access to a typewriter. It is hard to use a word processor on applications that have specific and limited spaces in which you are asked to respond. Try as they might to avoid doing so, members of admissions committees may unwittingly discount handwritten applications. Such applications may run the risk of indicating to the committee that the candidate was not serious enough to either type or word process the application.

- By the time this book is published, you may be able to submit your application to some programs electronically. In the meantime, one strategy to follow if you have access to a computer is to word process your responses on separate sheets of paper, cut and paste them into the appropriate sections of the application, and then copy the material for submission.

- Do not be afraid to take more space than the application allows. Write very clearly: "Please see additional material on separate page." Make sure you refer to the separate pages explicitly and clearly identify the section of the application to which you are responding. Don't forget to include your name on each extra page.

- Supply to people from whom you are requesting references stamped, addressed envelopes. This makes it easier for them, and you are taking more responsibility to see to it that the letters get sent to the correct places.

- Most institutions of higher education now give you the choice of being able to read your references or having them written without your having read them. The common wisdom is that admissions committees have more faith in recommendations that are written without your having access to them. You should not ask anyone to write a recommendation for you unless you are confident that it will be positive. If you are not sure, then check the option that would allow you to read the reference.

- Show your application statement to someone else before you submit it. Ask that person to read over your application for both its mechanics and its substance. An especially useful reviewer might be a person who is currently teaching.

- Before you submit your application, make complete copies of it for your records and in case the application is misplaced.

- Send your application in well before the application deadline. If you miss the deadline, see if there is a week or two of "wiggle room" between the due date and the time that an admissions committee begins to review applications. Most programs have a provision for reviewing late applications, although they may do so only after they have reviewed all those that have been submitted on time. The committee may defer it to the next admission round, in which case you should not have to pay a reapplication fee.

If at First You Don't Succeed, Reapply

What if you apply to a program and you do not get in? How can you analyze what went wrong and then what can you do about it? All programs have a professional responsibility to be fair in their admissions decisions. While it is not a perfect world and mistakes are made, assume that the admissions review committee has attempted to be equitable with your application. Begin by reassessing the application yourself. You may already be aware of how well you did or did not meet the program's admissions criteria. But you may also need the feedback of the program's admissions committee.

Look at what you presented in your application vis-à-vis the admissions criteria, procedures, and policies. Ask yourself and the head of the admissions committee how you could strengthen your application to gain admission. Try to uncover the reasons you were not admitted. Make clear that you are not arguing with the committee but, rather, trying to get information that will allow you to strengthen your application.

You should receive a fairly specific answer. It may be that the program had a great number of applicants and a limited number of slots. If that is the case, after your conversation, you should be able to understand where you fell short compared to those who were admitted. It may have been a weak academic record, inadequate experience with children or diversity, undemonstrated leadership skills, or falling short in other areas that led to your rejection.

If, after your initial conversation, it is still not clear to you what your application lacked or how it failed to compete against others, you should know that there are usually at least two levels of review in every admissions process. The second level of review usually verifies whether the primary reviewers followed a reasonable and equitable process. The secondary reviewers may not know your particular application, but they will be able to check the process and make sure that your application received a fair reading. If a second-level reviewer thinks that something went awry in the admissions process, this person may indicate that another assessment of your application is warranted. A reviewer at this second level may also be willing to go over your application with you and offer specific advice on how to strengthen it.

Admissions committees prefer anonymity and distance between themselves and applicants. They do not want to play favorites or operate under undue pressure to admit a particular person. But that distance and anonymity should not make the admissions process seem inscrutable to you as an applicant. A skillful admissions committee can use the application process as part of the initial advising the program might give to a prospective teacher. So do not let a rejection deter you from contacting faculty or administrators.

Accepting Admissions

If you are admitted to a program, you will probably be asked to indicate within a certain period of time whether you are accepting the admissions invitation. (This statement may be more pertinent to graduate programs than to undergraduate and continuing education programs, but the underlying principle is still important.) Before you decide, visit the program and the campus if you have not already done so. It is important to meet the faculty and students first hand, and reconfirm your sense that this is the program for you. Talk to your prospective faculty advisor and assess whether she or he promises to be a supportive and effective counselor and mentor. Your impressions of the school and program will help you decide whether you will accept their offer of admission.

NOTES

1. Lev Vygotsky, *Thought and Language*, translated by A. Kozulin (Cambridge, MA: MIT Press, 1987).

2. Urie Bronfenbrenner, *The Ecology of Human Development: Experiments by Nature and Design* (Cambridge: Harvard University Press, 1979).

3. Martin Haberman, "Selecting and Preparing Culturally Competent Teachers for Urban Schools," in *Handbook of Research on Teacher Education*, 2d ed., edited by John Sikula, Thomas J. Buttery, and Edith Guyton (New York: Macmillan, 1996), 755.

6

Succeeding as a Student of Teaching

Almost all middle and high school teacher education programs have three main components:

- Development of your teaching field or academic content area
- Professional preparation courses and field experiences
- Student teaching

In this chapter we describe some of the main issues you will face as you participate in a teacher education program. Becoming a student of teaching leads to a basic transformation in your identity from that of student to teacher, and it is crucial for you to play an active role in that transformation.

In a sense, to take full advantage of a teacher education program you must adopt a double consciousness. As you participate in classes and field experiences, you begin thinking not only as a student of teaching but also as a teacher of students. You will make choices about your academic specializations, teaching philosophies, instructional methods, and extracurricular activities with both of these roles in mind. These dual habits of mind, developed in your program, are an essential foundation for the way you will go about your work as a teacher in the future.

BUILDING YOUR FIELD OF KNOWLEDGE

In order to be prepared to teach, prospective middle or high school teachers must know their subject matter field. If you know your subject matter deeply, you understand its logic and organization. You begin to develop a conceptual sense of which ideas come first, which follow, and what must be understood at one level before someone can move to the next level within a field of knowledge. Based on these understandings, you can then determine what teaching strategies will best convey ideas and concepts to students.

The imperative of knowing one's subject matter as a basic prerequisite for teaching at the secondary level is the logic behind many states requiring prospective educators to have a major or its equivalent in the subject they are planning to teach. While some states require less than a major or its equivalent to teach a subject, most first-rate middle and high school teacher preparation programs will require that you have at least a major in your field. Some states, influenced by standards developed by professional organizations in many subject fields, may require even more courses than are normally included in a major.

One way of improving your footing in your subject matter area is to join the national organization in your field and make contact with its state-level chapter. Most have relatively inexpensive student memberships available. Each organization publishes one or more journals about teaching its subject matter, and reading them will help you stay more current in your field, obtain information about upcoming conferences, and receive professional development resources. Many have also issued voluntary national content standards for teaching the subject field in schools. Membership in a professional organization and attending its conferences also helps to alleviate some of the isolation that occurs in middle and high school teaching, and it allows you to have an active voice in the issues affecting education.

Several of the prominent professional organizations, their curriculum content standards, and journals for teachers are listed in Figure 6.1 and their addresses are available in Part II.

Graduate level teacher education programs may ask you to take additional coursework in order to ground your teaching in a solid understanding of your field. If you have not completed your major by the time you enter a teacher education program, you will spend part of your time in the program doing so. If you have completed your major and are in a Master of Education (M.Ed.) or Master of Arts in Teaching (M.A.T.) program, you probably will be asked to take additional graduate study in your field.

Developments in Fields of Study

In each of the major academic areas taught at the middle and high school level, significant changes are taking place regarding the content of each field of study. The canon of European and American literature

Figure 6.1
Professional Organizations for Middle and High School Teachers

Organization	Content Standards	Journals
National Council of Teachers of English (NCTE)	"Standards for the English Language Arts" (1996)	• *English Journal* • *Language Arts* • *Voices from the Middle*
National Council of Teachers of Mathematics (NCTM)	"Curriculum and Evaluation Standards for School Mathematics" (1989)	• *Mathematics Teaching in the Middle School* • *Mathematics Teacher* • *Journal for Research in Mathematics Education*
National Science Teachers Association (NSTA)	"National Science Education Standards" (1983)	• *Science Scope* • *The Science Teacher* • *Quantum*
National Council for the Social Studies (NCSS)	"Expectations of Excellence: Curriculum Standards for Social Studies" (1994)	• *Social Education*
American Council on Teaching of Foreign Languages (ACTFL)	"National Standards in Foreign Language Education: Preparing for the 21st Century" (1995)	• *Foreign Language Annals*
American Alliance for Health, Physical Recreation, and Dance (AAHPERD)	"Moving into the Future: National Standards for Physical Education, A Guide to Content and Assessment" (1995)	• *Journal of Physical Education, Recreation, and Dance (JOPERD)* • *Strategies: A Journal for Medical and Sport Educators*
International Society for Technology in Education (ISTE)	"National Educational Technology Standards for Students" (1997)	• *Learning and Leading with Technology*

is being challenged in the English curriculum by the inclusion of literature from diverse ethnic and racial groups as well as that of women writers. The process of analytic and creative writing is being emphasized; but you will also need to be prepared to teach your students how to produce mechanically correct writing and grammatically appropriate language.

In social studies and history, primary sources are increasingly being used to uncover the "herstories" and histories of people of color, women, the working classes, and other groups that have long been omitted from traditional textbooks. Teachers are challenged to "affirm diversity" while resisting racism and other forms of discrimination.[1] There is a growing emphasis on inquiry, analytical thinking, problem solving, and decision making as well as in-depth study of required topics. Still, many social studies educators contend that there is a foundational knowledge about democracy, the constitution, and citizenship that every student must learn.

In mathematics, educational reformers are stressing reasoning and understanding, but many in the business community counter that basic computational and numeric skills must be given priority. A strenuous debate on the appropriate role of technological tools like the calculator is dividing teachers of mathematics.[2] Some in the sciences are stressing the need to teach students the process of scientific inquiry and not just the product. They emphasize the importance of students asking questions, conducting research, and generating hypotheses based on data. In the area of languages, the switch from the term "foreign languages" to "world languages" indicates an effort to overcome an ethnocentric view of ourselves and to recognize the world community to which we all belong. Some teachers are using an emphasis on communicative language to challenge a grammatically based approach to learning a new language.

These issues provide both stress and excitement in each of the major academic fields taught in secondary schools. They require that prospective teachers expand and build upon their academic majors to develop their fields of knowledge not just to meet a state certification requirement, but to become a current, relevant teacher in today's middle or high schools.

Most of us associate majoring in a subject as synonymous with having the knowledge sufficient to teach it. There is, however, a problem embedded in that assumption. Studying English, math, science, social studies, or a world language at the college level is different from teaching those subjects at the middle or high school level. Teachers must translate what they have learned in their academic majors (and from their reading and other ongoing study) into concepts, skills, and attitudes accessible to adolescent students.

As a middle or high school teacher, your goal is to excite your students about the basic knowledge in your subject area. You want them to encounter the wonder of ideas and the love of learning that you came to appreciate in your own studies. You want your students to see how your subject matter reveals multiple dimensions of human experience or complex relationships within the physical and natural worlds. You want to give students information they can use to affect their own lives in positive ways. To accomplish all of this, it is essential to work with your students to build foundational literacy in your subject area.

What, then, is the relationship between what you learned in your college major and your role as a middle or high school teacher? Your major is a beginning. You must incorporate new developments in your field even if they have not yet taken hold in the major. You should also ask whether there are gaps or omissions in your study that you need to fill. For example, if you last took a course in a subject a decade or more ago, do you need some updating? Perhaps most important, as a student of teaching, you want to be able to go to the liberal arts essence of your major. That is, to continually recreate for yourself and your students the excitement of ideas and passion for a subject that originally led you to the field.

COURSES IN EDUCATION

In addition to your subject area coursework your teacher education program will ask you to take a series of professional preparation courses prior to student teaching. As outlined in Chapter 3, you will most likely have classes in an introduction to teaching, educational psychology, the history and sociology of education, teaching methods, and student assessment or tests and measurements.

Each of these courses have specific goals. The introduction to teaching and history or sociology of education course will offer you a context for your work in schools. It will attempt to develop your consciousness of where you stand in the history and structure of education and the role of teachers. The educational psychology course will introduce you to principles of learning theory, adolescent development, and specific areas such as that of students with special needs. The methods course, if it is subject area specific, will explore major issues in curriculum and teaching in your field. If it is a generic methods course, it will concentrate on methods of teaching that can be common to any area that you may teach. The assessment or tests and measurements course will concentrate on constructing and interpreting appropriate student evaluation strategies.

Of course, the teacher education program you enter may offer different courses, and the descriptions above cannot do full justice to all the courses in education for prospective teachers that are in the field. But one thing may be common to most education programs. Despite the variation of courses across the field and the range of quality of instructors from institution to institution, the reputation of these courses has suffered for many years.

Some of the criticisms aimed at education courses are well earned. You may enter your program with a skeptical attitude that says, "Prove to me that what I have heard about education courses is not true." But to heighten your understanding of the role of a teacher education student, you should know that there are aspects of the study of education that make it unusually vulnerable and subject to intense criticism.

First, teaching deals with what David Labaree calls stigmatized populations.[3] Those who enter the field are primarily women, and they are preparing to work with children. Men who teach become part of a "feminized" line of work. Since neither women nor children are associated with power and status in the United States, issues of gender and working with children make those who decide to become teachers or teacher educators easy targets for critics. Second, because teaching has traditionally been an occupation that allowed working class people to move into the middle class, the social status of students of teaching and professors of education is lower than that of students in such fields as law, engineering, and medicine.

Third, and perhaps most important, the field of education, according to Labaree, is inherently "soft." Teacher education is not a discipline. There is no beginning and end to the subject. It does not have its own unique method of inquiry.[4] Its boundaries are amorphous. It is an eclectic field that borrows from a range of academic areas. There is no science of pedagogy. Educational researchers are trying to develop a body of knowledge empirically tested that could form the basis of such a science, but to date the results are far from substantiating the claims that there is a knowledge base in education that everyone should know.[5]

Ultimately, to handle the criticisms, you have to be able to affirm your choice to become a teacher. One exercise we use in our introductory course is to ask students to tell a person whose respect they value highly that they are preparing to be a teacher. In that exercise, our students often meet head on the ambivalence around teaching and the scorn aimed at teacher education. In the face of both, a successful student of teaching must recognize the importance of the decision to teach and acknowledge the complexities and challenges of preparing to do so.

In part this means you cannot enter a teacher education program and expect to be taught all you need to know to be a successful teacher. You will gain ideas and understandings that can be brought to bear on the problems, issues, and opportunities of teaching; but there is no comprehensive, organized, cumulative body of knowledge in education that would be sufficient for you to become a teacher if you were to learn it. Rather than seeking to master a textbook of information about teaching, it is important to act in a teacher education program the way you would hope your students to act when you begin teaching: asking questions, thinking critically and creatively, and exploring multiple solutions to issues and problems.

Blending Theory and Practice

Students in teacher education must build a bridge between the college campus and the secondary schools and then cross it. In other words, they must make the study of education directly relevant to the teaching that occurs in schools. In reality, however, campus classrooms are separated from school classrooms by distance and time. Education courses are often held before students get into the classroom; sometimes this makes it difficult for certification candidates to see the relevance of the course content. Some reformers argue that the best time for teacher education courses is during, or even after, a student teaches, rather than before. This is the theory behind some of the latest alternative programs in teacher education.

Others believe that students preparing to teach should be immersed in the school setting, and that theoretically based courses delivered on site offer the best possible chance for integration between theory and practice. Still others argue that the time and space in which teacher education programs take place is not as important as the intellectual attitude of the teacher education instructors and students. Those instructors and students must always struggle to make connections in their minds between theory and practice and to transform what is learned in college courses so that it is relevant to the public schools in which they will teach.

Many education programs stress how-to activities, like constructing a lesson plan, writing behavioral objectives, developing multiple-choice tests, leading discussions, and responding to and managing difficult classroom situations. Some, however, view this approach to teacher education as vocational training inappropriate to the complexities of the role.[6] Rather than acquiring skills largely through imitation, recitation, and assimilation, these critics contend, prospective teachers should be making their own meaning of theory and basing their practice on that meaning-making process.

To further confound the issue, some veteran teachers who mentor student teachers urge them to leave behind everything they learned on campus as being impractical and idealistic. They contend that you do not really learn the realities of teaching until you enter the classroom. This split between what is taught in education classes and what is taught by practice in the schools is one of the main underlying arguments for increased collaboration in teacher education between school and college faculty.

Thus, teacher education happens in what Labaree calls the "mine field" on the border between theory and practice.[7] Most good teacher education programs try to combine theory and practice in their curriculum. In reality, learning to teach involves a complex, problematic, mixture of knowledge and understanding drawn from many fields and experience. We each bring unexamined and unchallenged theoretical assumptions to our teaching. These largely taken-for-granted ideas give rise to snap judgments, routine responses, and re-runs of prior educational experiences. Effective teaching practice emerges from a process of critically reflecting and building upon one's personal assumptions, academic studies, and school experiences.[8]

FIELD EXPERIENCES

In trying to bridge theory and practice, an effective teacher education program will build a sequence of field experiences into its curriculum. It will coordinate your time in schools so that you move from the relative passivity of an observer to a more active role in the classroom working with small groups, assisting the teacher, or perhaps tutoring or doing community service. The goal of these field experiences is to give you enough contact with schools, classrooms, teachers, and students so that when you begin your student teaching, you will not be surprised and overwhelmed by the task you face.

A well-planned program of observation will reintroduce you to middle and high schools. It will give you the opportunity to visit many schools and to reconsider, through reflection on your visits, the predisposition you may have to teach either at the middle or high school level. Try to observe a range of school and community settings, from suburban to rural to urban.

It is especially valuable to visit the type of schools you did not attend as a student, as your observations may dispel any stereotypes you may have acquired. Some students from the suburbs need to see urban schools that work well before they will give serious consideration to teaching in city communities. Similarly, some of those who grew up in cities and attended urban schools often find themselves uncomfortable being asked to think about teaching in a suburban or rural setting. Consider teaching at many types of schools, and use your field experiences to help you decide your preferences.

Best Practices

An effective teacher education program will ask its students to look for and get a sense of the "best practices" that are possible in the schools. During many in-school observations, prospective teachers may find approaches to teaching that seem strikingly familiar to what they remember as students. In some schools, the lecturing, class discussions, laboratory assignments, work at the blackboard, term papers, debates, drills, and in some subjects, the content, are much the same as they have been over the last fifty years.

It is not easy to generalize whether such long-in-use, familiar methods are automatically good or bad. A passionate teacher who knows and loves his or her subject, sets appropriate boundaries, expects a great deal of his or her students, and is firm but friendly can use the most traditional methods of teaching and the most traditional content and be a great teacher. Innovation in education is an overused term. It is sometimes mindlessly projected as the key to education reform. Often, however, what is promoted as an important change turns out to be a fad that has its brief moment as the current panacea for what ails schooling.

On the other hand, education reformers have been trying to develop a knowledge base for prospective teachers. Difficulty with this task has turned researchers to the notion of best practices as a way to build what they consider a sense of substance into the teacher preparation curriculum. The notion of best practices attempts to capture a broad consensus among teachers and reformers as to effective and exemplary ways to motivate and educate a broad range of children and adolescents.

One group of researchers reviewed the recommendations of several professional teaching organizations and concluded "best practices" means, among other things, that teachers of English, mathematics, science, social studies, and other subjects will have:[9]

LESS whole-class, teacher-directed instruction, e.g., lecturing	MORE experiential, inductive, hands-on learning
LESS student passivity: sitting, listening, receiving, and absorbing information	MORE active learning in the classroom, with all the attendant noise and movement of students doing, talking, and collaborating
LESS prizing and rewarding of silence in the classroom	MORE emphasis on higher-order thinking; learning a field's key concepts and principles
LESS classroom time devoted to fill-in-the-blank worksheets, dittos, workbooks, and other "seatwork"	MORE deep study of a smaller number of topics, so that students internalize the field's way of inquiry
LESS student time spent reading textbooks and basal readers	MORE time devoted to reading whole, original, real books and nonfiction materials
LESS rote memorization of facts and details	MORE choice for students; e.g., picking their own books, writing topics, team partners, research projects
LESS stress on competition and grades in school	MORE cooperative, collaborative activity; developing the classroom as an interdependent community

| LESS tracking or leveling students into "ability groups" | MORE heterogeneously grouped classrooms where individuals' needs are met through inherently individualized activities |
| LESS use of and reliance on standardized tests | MORE reliance on teachers' descriptive evaluation of student growth, including qualitative/anecdotal observations |

The notion of best practices is controversial. One problem is that what works best with one group of students in one particular context with one particular teacher may not work best in a different setting with different students and teachers. Nor will the best practices work at all if they are adopted as routine formulas or recipes for new teachers to follow. Many best practices are also widely criticized by conservative observers who favor returning to more traditional approaches as a way to improve schools. On the other hand, these notions of best practice are rooted in teachers' experiences, and as such offer something from which to learn.

As you pursue the observation assignments in your teacher education program, familiarize yourself with the notion of best practices. Are the classes you observe tracked? Do they depend on lecturing, reward silence, and rely on worksheets and workbooks? Do they stress memorization of facts and multiple-choice tests? Or is there active, experiential learning going on where thinking rather than memorization is stressed? Do students have choices and a sense of ownership of what they are doing? Whether the teacher is using what would be considered best practices or not, are the students actively engaged in what is going on in the classroom? Are they focused and moving toward a sense of accomplishment? Observe the dominant practices in the classroom and relate what you see to your own goals and plans as a teacher.

Tutoring in Schools

While observation will be an important part of your teacher preparation, an excellent program will also ask you to take on more direct responsibility with students before you student teach. Tutoring in schools or in community-sponsored organizations is one of the most important experiences you can have in order to prepare for teaching. If your program offers you the opportunity to tutor, do it; if it does not, seek opportunities for yourself. Tutoring involves your working directly with kids. If you are able to develop the very special one-to-one relationship that tutoring entails, you will come much closer to seeing how kids learn and how they think about school, themselves, and life in general. You will also discover just how much you enjoy working with kids.

Tutoring serves as an opportunity for prospective teachers to practice responses to almost every situation that may come up in a future classroom. In tutoring you will face students who do not understand their work, students who will say that they will not learn from you, and students who will vault ahead or lag behind depending on how the material is presented. You may face students who need a type of assistance and support more complex than that which you know how to provide. In addition to all that tutoring offers the prospective teacher, it also improves student learning. Studies show that youngsters who participate in peer, cross-age, small group, and individual tutoring show gains in academic performance, behavior in classes, attendance, attitudes toward school and self-esteem.[10]

You may have the opportunity to tutor in your subject matter or you may be asked to tutor across disciplines. You may be asked to help students improve study skills, organize notebooks, and manage the completion of homework. Besides assisting students academically, you also may become a role model for your tutee. As a person who has gone to college and someone to whom your pupil can relate, you may open up a new sense of the possibilities of learning for your students.

Tutoring is particularly valuable for younger prospective student teachers who do not have a lot of experience with kids, and it is also useful for older individuals who have been away from schools for a significant amount of time. Tutoring demonstrates to veteran teachers and to potential employers that you are committed enough to your teacher preparation to spend significant time working one on one with young people.

The self-reflection and self-learning dimensions of tutoring are an even more compelling reason to make it part of your teacher education program. Tutors tell us over and over again how the experience shifted their perspectives about teaching, learning, and kids and made them a different kind of teacher (see Figure 6.2).

We believe that tutoring can have a transformative effect on future teachers. It casts you into the middle of ongoing debates about how to make sense of education today and how better to respond to the needs of youngsters who are not succeeding academically or socially. It may bring you into direct contact with some of the harshest realities of schooling in the United States where many schools marginalize certain students. Tutors often deal one on one with youngsters who in their daily lives live out the "isms" our students talk about in campus classes. The students who are tutored are often outsiders who have been, for one reason or another, left behind educationally. Our students discover that terms like "underachiever," "language minority," "culturally deprived,"

Figure 6.2
Statements about Tutoring by College Students

"One of my expectations was that I would not know enough about the class or the material to be an effective tutor. However, I have been able to assist the students and I enjoy it."

"We conversed about China and Vietnam. The students told us about their experiences in their homelands."

"Tutoring enabled me to glimpse some of the realities of teaching."

"Sometimes you should talk and listen before tutoring. Students need to see you as a friend as well as a tutor."

"I encourage other children in the class to show the methods by which they solve the problems and either have the both of us work on the math, or have peer tutoring."

"I thought critically about my own cultural identity and how that has played a part in shaping me."

"There definitely is a tutor-tutee exchange as I am learning more from my tutees than they are learning from me."

and "slow learner" hide more than they reveal. They also learn that these words are potentially destructive because they locate the source of educational problems within the student. One infers that it is individuals, not the system, which must be changed.

Tutors get to know the kids that are labeled and learn the stories behind the label. They begin to understand that, while the students do have to take individual responsibility for themselves, the way the system is organized and the way students are taught in classes need change too. Our students tell us that tutoring has encouraged them to rethink their own ideas about teaching and learning in schools. They realize that the small events in their tutoring experience have the potential to touch a student's life. Tutoring serves to transform their sense of self and their sense of the potential and import of teaching as their chosen field of work.

Community Service Learning

The impact of tutoring on the prospective teacher's sense of possibility is rivaled by a new element that is beginning to play a significant part in some teacher education programs. More than 130 institutions of higher education are including service learning as part of methods and research courses for new and experienced teachers. Just as the middle and high school curriculum is beginning to be enriched by community service, so too is the teacher education curriculum. (For more information on service learning in K–12 schools, contact the National Service-Learning Clearinghouse listed in Part II.)

Community service learning (CSL) has been defined as a way of teaching academic content by involving students in service to their communities.[11] Serving others also has the power to transform how one sees and acts in the world. As psychiatrist Robert Coles observes in his book, *The Call of Service*, service projects place us "in situations where we straddle our 'regular' world and a world we 'visit.' "[12] Coles remembers Ruth Ann, a fourth grader he met while volunteering as a language arts teacher in a school in Cambridge, Massachusetts. "It's nice that some of you folks come here to volunteer," he quotes her as saying, "and we'll try to tell you everything we know."[13] Ruth Ann's message was abundantly clear: You may have something to teach me, but I have much to teach you too.

Coles was quite moved by the child's comment. Many times those providing service think in terms of the help they give to the less fortunate. Here was an eloquent reminder that service provides the chance to learn from and about people in the community. Participation in service need not stem from a "do gooder" mentality; it involves a commitment to reciprocity and mutuality in service learning relationships.

Other commentators stress the importance of students, teachers, and individuals in teacher education programs not only responding to pressing community problems, but also understanding the sources of those problems within existing social and economic systems. This is the idea of "critical community service."[14] A voter registration drive, for example, can extend participation in the electoral process to more citizens, but it may also demonstrate how money and media influence political decision-making. Similarly, working with seniors in an elderly housing facility can involve care for people and recognition of how many older Americans become isolated from the mainstream of social life.

As prospective teachers examine social, economic, and political issues more deeply in the context of service, they begin to rethink their own ideas and values in light of the experiences of others. Herein lies a key educational purpose of service: it challenges how students see the world while connecting them "to an active and change-oriented vision of education."[15] If you have the opportunity to take part in community service during your teacher education program, we urge that you take it. The goal, both personally and professionally, is to build an "ethic of care."[16] This attitude may transform your teaching in school classrooms by linking theories and experiences and showing the way to both individual and systemic change.

STUDENT TEACHING

The culmination of your certification program, not your development as a teacher, will be your student teaching. Much of the research says that, for better or worse, student teaching, or practice teaching as it is sometimes called, is a pivotal juncture in your learning to becoming a teacher. To some extent, how you handle the demands and challenges of student teaching previews your responses as a full-time teacher. The attitudes, behaviors, and patterns you adopt in student teaching carry over into your career.

Our students tell us that they have never worked harder than they did when they were student teaching. They also tell us that they have never learned more. Student teachers work almost full-time in a school without getting paid. They begin their teaching career in an ambiguous role, that of both student and teacher. They enter a school organization, with many unspoken norms, at or near the bottom of the school hierarchy. They are, basically, guests in the building. They must follow its rules, guidelines, and curriculum, and at the same time they must begin to develop their own identity in the classroom.

Student teachers begin to teach classes of students with diverse life stories and approaches to learning. They teach subjects that, up to now, most of them have only studied as students. The challenge of transforming what they know into what they teach—and hoping that their students learn—is awesome the first time around. Our students report spending so much time after school and into the night grading, preparing, and planning that it is difficult for many of them to have much of a life outside of school. Their lives are their student teaching.

Student teachers may well feel overwhelmed and consumed by the job, but the return for their hard work and commitment is deep learning about who they are as teachers. They learn how their sensitivities, tempers, and character play out in a classroom. As they grapple with the material they must teach, student teachers become even more connected to their subject matter. They engage students more regularly and personally than ever before, and they begin to experience the joy of working with kids whose stories have led them to being eager students. They also begin to face the sometimes frustrating dynamics of working with students whose painful life histories go beyond the boundaries of a student teacher's responsibility.

While working through who they are as educators, who their students are, and how to teach their subjects, student teachers also deal with the complexities of working under the guidance of a cooperating teacher and a college or university supervisor. The cooperating teacher gives up his or her class to allow the student teacher to learn to teach. Some cooperating teachers do that skillfully and diplomatically; others are possessive of their students and their "turf" and have difficulty allowing a student teacher the space he or she needs to learn by doing. A university or college supervisor can be a great "safety valve," mediating tensions that may develop between a cooperating teacher and a student teacher.

On occasion, through inexperience or inattention, the supervisor may put the student teacher in a difficult position between the expectations of the schools and those of the college or university.

While it is not possible to describe all the intricacies of this three-way relationship, it is important for the prospective student teacher to recognize that it is a power-laden triad. The student teacher is in a developmental situation overlaid by a significant amount of evaluation. While also serving as a coach and a resource, the cooperating teacher and university supervisor have the responsibility and the authority to evaluate the student's success in the classroom. Student teachers, therefore, must learn to negotiate the delicate balance among themselves, their cooperating teachers, and their college supervisor. They have to negotiate their way through sometimes conflicting perspectives, be tactful under pressure, and survive in a complex organization called school.

Models of Student Teaching

Virtually all college and university certification programs require a student teaching experience. Usually, but not always, it is the culmination of your program and occurs after you have fulfilled your subject matter and education course requirements. By contrast, individuals pursuing alternative paths to certification or hired under emergency certificates often do not have a student teaching experience in the conventional sense of the term. They are immersed almost immediately in full-time teaching, although many have a probationary job performance review period and, hopefully, the support of a skilled mentor.

The length and intensity of student teaching varies in different programs. In general, however, you must count on devoting anywhere from as few as six weeks to as much as a full semester to your work as a practice teacher. While student teaching, you most often take only courses related to your practicum; sometimes you take no other courses at all. Programs need to assure the schools in which you are placed that student teaching is your first priority. Often, there is a supervisory seminar that goes along with student teaching. You and other certification candidates will meet weekly, or perhaps twice a month, to process and reflect upon your classroom and school experiences.

As discussed in Chapter 4, a major new development in college and university departments and schools of education is the use of clinical site and professional development school (PDS) relationships with cooperating schools and districts. Before the development of the PDS, most colleges and universities placed a student teacher in a single school setting, as shown in the top third of Figure 6.3. In an individual placement model, the student teacher works with one cooperating teacher for a single semester.

Figure 6.3
Three Models for Student Teaching

Individual Placements	Single student teacher
	One cooperating teacher
	Single semester of teaching
Clinical Sites/Professional Development Schools	Cohort of student teachers at a school
	Several teachers working with interns
	Whole school welcomes student teachers
	Student teachers support each other
	Single semester of teaching
Immersion Programs	Cohort of student teachers at a school
	Several teachers working with interns
	Whole school welcomes student teachers
	Student teachers support each other
	Two semesters of teaching
	Sequence of increasing instructional responsibility

Clinical sites and professional development schools, the middle section of Figure 6.3, are based on relationships between colleges and districts in which schools commit to accepting a group of student teachers. Clinical sites and PDSs seek to transform student teachers into a cohort group that offers support to each other. There are usually on-site seminars, often co-taught by higher education faculty and public school teachers and administrators. In some cases, mentoring seminars are held to assist cooperating teachers in working with interns. In those settings, the teachers in the school have made a commitment to welcome you to the building.

There are many varieties of professional development schools, including the immersion program concept, shown in the bottom part of Figure 6.3. In an immersion setting, a cohort of certification candidates work in a school building for an entire year. They teach, advise, tutor, and participate in many different aspects of the school. Like the clinical site and PDS, the immersion concept is new, but it seems to be an improvement on the older, more traditional apprenticeship model with a single exemplary cooperating teacher. One key benefit may be that the school system which has invested so much in your preparation will feel that you would be the best candidate for any openings that might develop (although that may also happen at a individual placement site). If you have a chance to enter a program that uses a clinical site, PDS, or immersion model, do so. We think they are usually advantageous to the student teacher.

Getting Started and Being Successful

Student teachers often enter student teaching with a mix of apprehensions and excitements. We recently asked a group of mathematics, English, science, and social studies certification candidates for their major concerns about starting to teach. Their statements reveal many of the common anxieties faced by new teachers:

Will I Be Able To . . . ?

Reach the kids

Individualize lessons to fit the students

Answer their questions

Avoid lesson plans that bomb

Speak clearly

Use discipline and patience

Understand the rules of the school

Be an effective role model

Get around paperwork and school policies that block learning

Work in someone else's classroom

Respond to students who do not understand what I am telling them

Not resort to traditional practices

Prepare clear lesson plans

Keep discipline problems from disrupting learning

Connect to the students

Be an agent of change

Work with other teachers and get along with my cooperating teacher

Absorb all that is needed to be a good teacher (in a short time)

It is reasonable to feel apprehensive about succeeding in a situation in which you have had little prior experience. Most new teachers need time to figure out for themselves the best ways to handle the myriad demands they face in the role of classroom instructor. It is true that some student teachers just seem to have a natural way of running a classroom and working with kids. This leads to the popular notion that teaching is an art. In this view, some can do it and some cannot. While the idea of a "natural" who simply walks into the classroom and succeeds masterfully represents an attractive image, it is far from the reality of schools.

A different, more empirical, explanation for those who easily do well as teachers is that they have spent a lot of time playing and working with kids as they have grown up. They may come from a larger family and have experience negotiating interactions with that kind of competitive group. They may have worked in summer camp, day school, as baby sitters, or in church and community programs. One way or another they have had practice defining themselves in relation to kids. They have figured out what they hope to gain from teaching-like situations, and they have a sense of the boundaries with youngsters. If there is one thing we would urge those of you thinking of becoming teachers to do, it is to gain as much experience as possible interacting with kids before you apply to or begin a teacher education program.

The most common initial pressure you will face as you begin to teach is trying to be friends with your students. It is difficult, but important, to separate "being a friend" from "being friendly." Novices often deeply want to be liked by their students; some are trying hard to be different from unfriendly or uncaring teachers they remember having in school. College-age student teachers in particular tend to be ambivalent about their own authority in the classroom. Some of them have only recently been students and they find the transition to assuming the authority and concomitant power of the teacher a difficult one.

The power between teacher and student is highly unequal, and it stands in sharp contrast to the dynamics of a friendship where two individuals are relatively equal in their relationship. In wanting to be friends, student teachers tend to get confused about the boundaries that they must maintain between themselves and their students. From the complicated boundary of, for example, when it is appropriate or not appropriate to touch students, to the even more complicated connections of being a teacher, counselor, and confidant, the student teacher has to learn for her or himself all the subtleties of maintaining appropriate separations between themselves and their students while still connecting to them.

The Dialectic of Student Teaching

There is a dialectic that occurs almost predictably in student teaching. The student teacher assumes the role with idealism, energy, and relative inexperience. The students, after some brief hours of a willing suspension of disbelief, start responding to their new teacher. They may challenge, they may resist, they may complain, they may wonder aloud when their real teacher is going to teach them again. Whatever the form it takes, some students usually provide an antithesis to the student teacher's initial actions.

An experienced cooperating teacher will recognize that the "student teacher/students-in-the-class dialectic" is part of the developmental process of becoming a teacher and will not get in its way. When you become a student teacher, he or she will guide and navigate the situation but will allow you, as much as possible, to work out your own resolutions to classroom dynamics. This means staying close enough to be a resource but not taking over your role in the classroom.

Student teachers, however, must recognize that cooperating teachers have a primary allegiance to their own students and a secondary allegiance to their student teacher. When teachers feel that their students are being mistreated or are being deprived of adequate lessons, they are prompted to intervene. Cooperating teachers most often step in, and sometimes attempt to take back a class, when they feel a student teacher is not taking his or her work seriously. If your cooperating teacher senses you are not prepared, or are coming to class and "winging it," she or he will quickly lose patience. If this happens, it is very hard for you to regain your teacher's confidence or the respect of the students.

At different points as a student teacher, you will need to dig in and, in the words of one of our students, develop "emotional stamina." This means continuing to work hard, preparing for class even more thoroughly, and dealing honestly and straightforwardly with those students who are "in your face" or who reveal their resistance by turning away from learning. To earn the respect of students and maintain one's confidence as a teacher, it is necessary to critically analyze what you are getting back from your students. Often this means searching for new ways to approach learning, creating different ways of organizing classes, and relating to kids in ways that are true to yourself and to the kind of teacher you want to become.

Teaching Kids

Throughout the practicum, a student teacher faces constant tensions around how to motivate and inspire students. As clear as that goal may seem, the reality of education is that kids come to schools with immensely complicated stories that directly affect the way they respond in class. For some students, school is the safest and most secure place in their day. For others, school is a game they must play until they get to a point that they can be independent. For still others, school is a place to meet friends, play sports, grow up, and develop their identities. You will confront all these complexities and more in the classroom, and you may struggle at times to find a path through all the elements of students' experiences to a place where your teaching is relevant to their lives.

It is no wonder that many student teachers feel the issues of boundaries between themselves and their students difficult to negotiate. Student teachers will learn the stories of their students, but they must be aware that they cannot take responsibility for many of the elements of those stories. It is important to listen and hear, but student teachers must realize that sometimes that is all they can, and should, do. At other times, they must recognize when what a student presents as an issue or conflict is beyond their capability and responsibility to handle. They need to become familiar with school support systems and resources so they can appropriately refer individuals in need of specialized health and psychological services.

Building positive, respectful relationships in classrooms begins with how you conduct yourself in the student teacher role. Adolescents test student teachers about how serious they are, what they are doing, and how much they respect and care about them. Some youngsters are, at least on the outside, trying to prove they are tougher than any adult. They may be willing to push the limits of the student-teacher boundaries by being openly defiant or inappropriately disrespectful. For example, one of our more youthful-looking student teachers had a young man in her class behave in a blatantly disrespectful manner in front of the other students. She sensed the other students watching, some with quiet glee and others with discomfort, to see how she would handle the situation.

She chose to respond to the public insult right there, in the moment, explaining to the students what she expected in terms of respectful behavior in the classroom. Her message was heard by the students, and a better classroom atmosphere was the result. It took considerable intellectual, psychological, and emotional resolve to abandon the lesson and deal with the inappropriateness of the situation. She proved that it is not necessarily age or appearance that determines how students relate to their teachers, but rather an adult's personal sense of presence and ability to take oneself seriously enough to command the respect of students.

The key for student teachers is to earn the respect of students, which is not an easy feat. As one student put it, "in a class full of individuals, it is hard to get things right for everyone." Here are a few steps you can take to establish a good rapport with, and a productive environment for, your students:

Decide what name you prefer in class and after school, and make it clear to your students. Some student teachers are comfortable with Ms. or Mr. Others prefer to be known by their first names, but many schools insist that students not refer to teachers on a first-name basis. Often, students will avoid the situation altogether and just say "Miss" or "Teacher." Discuss the name issue directly, first with your cooperating teacher, and then with your students so it is clear at the outset.

Include your students as much as possible in making decisions about the issues in your class that affect their lives—from classroom rules to curriculum content. Adolescents are searching for personal space and personal voice, and this means they need opportunities to express their ideas. As you teach kids, work with them to create the ground rules for group projects, build homework assignments and grading criteria collectively, and conduct discussions about how discipline or curriculum decisions get made. This does not mean agreeing with students all of the time or allowing them to control everything that happens in the room. Rather, it means giving them respect by including them in classroom decision making.

Get ready for questions about your views. In many cases, kids will ask you your views about politics, drugs and alcohol, religion, sex, abortion, divorce, gay and lesbian families, or other school or community issues. Bear in mind that they may be asking about your life in order to tell you about their lives. Adolescents are continually trying to make sense of their experiences, and they need genuine responses from the adults who are their teachers.

Try to be a resource to kids. You may be able to refer students to community services that can help them deal with personal issues. As you seek to answer their inquiries, you must recognize the balance between being forthright with students and maintaining the boundaries of your own private and public lives. You always have the option of not disclosing personal or political preferences when it may be unsafe for you personally or professionally to have your views known. If you decide not to discuss an issue, tell students clearly that this is a topic you do not discuss with people at school. Sometimes, the length of student teaching may make the decision about what to say for you. Your time in the school may be too short for you to be a real resource for the students, so deciding not to speak about particular issues may be the right choice.

Gendered Interactions

One of the things that is seldom talked about in teacher education programs is how much sexual energy there is in middle and high school classrooms. When a teacher takes the time to learn the stories of students, that teacher often becomes one of the few individuals in an adolescent's life to listen to him or her seriously. Attraction can arise from this interest and respect. To deny the attraction that students often have for their student teachers, or the attraction a student teacher may have for some of his or her students, is to deny reality.

Given that personal feelings usually exist on both the part of students and student teachers, the real challenge is how to manage the behavior appropriately. Occasionally we read in the paper about a teacher who has had an affair with a student and the exploitation of power and situation that such relationships usually involve. As a student teacher, you must clearly understand that your role does not extend beyond that of teacher, mentor, and caring adult.

There is another seldom discussed gender dynamic present in student teaching. We have had female student teachers tell us of the harassment they receive from their male students—everything from being asked out on dates to threatening sexual innuendos. One student teacher had one of her students approach her during cafeteria duty. In a loud voice, so that his friends sitting nearby could hear, he asked her to the senior prom. The story spread throughout the school. A sad part of the situation was that the principal was almost prepared to remove the student teacher. He assumed she must have encouraged the male students to treat her in this way.

Judith Harmon Miller has written thoughtfully about the special complexities female student teachers may face in their student teaching, and her article would be an important one for both male and female student teachers to read.[17] Her findings document the sexually charged language used against some women in the classroom, the sense women feel of not being taken seriously as teachers, and the insensitivity of male administrators and many colleagues to the issues facing females in schools. Miller urges women teachers to support each other and to work with supportive male educators, to change unsafe hallways into corridors of respect and collaboration.

Staying out of the Coffee Room

Reflecting on his student teaching a few years ago, one of our certification graduates concluded, "I love teaching, but I hate schools." The kids were great and "I felt really successful as a teacher," our student continued. "It was the other adults in the building who were the problem." The challenges posed by other adults during student teaching surface again and again as an important theme when our student teachers recall their experiences in the role. "I felt burned out by the teachers who were burned out," a social studies candidate observed last year. "The attitude of teachers in the lunchroom was appallingly negative," recalled a prospective English teacher.

Every new educator must wrestle with the dilemmas of how to deal with other adults in the school with whom they may not agree. Common sources of tension and disagreement include colleagues who are tired, cynical, and constantly complaining about today's students; adults who talk and gossip about specific kids; teachers who openly dismiss ideas for change; or groups of staff who are in constant opposition to school administrators.

A familiar platform for teacher discontent is the coffee room. Every school has such a place where the teachers gather to talk about their daily experiences. Many times these conversations become gripe sessions, loaded with negativism and hopelessness. New teachers, largely unaware of the politics of the building, find it hard to avoid getting drawn into these discussions. It is not easy to disagree with veteran educators in their own space, and many times the interaction pattern demands an "us versus them" stance. To avoid the cynicism that seems to pervade many informal gatherings in schools, and to maintain your own sense of who you are in the school, take the advice to stay out of the coffee room.

If succeeding in student teaching means avoiding negative people, it also means finding positive allies. In every school, there are like-minded, forward-looking teachers who can be sources of inspiration and support. Seek out these individuals and cultivate relationships with them. They, too, may be feeling isolated within the faculty culture, and they may welcome your fresh energy and ideas. Of course, this may also mean going beyond the minimum by co-teaching an extra class, working on an extracurricular activity, or serving on a school-wide planning committee. Your extra investment of time and energy will be worth it. A faculty ally is the kind of person who could become your mentor during student teaching, and a long-term resource and friend during the rest of your professional career.

A Transformative Experience

We have discussed some of the complexities, tensions, and difficulties of student teaching, but there is no doubt the practicum is a compelling and rewarding process. Semester after semester, we have the privilege of watching our students enter the student teaching role feeling a little tentative, apprehensive, and unsure of themselves. At the end of the experience we often have those student teachers speak to other students in the program who have yet to do their practicums. Whether the student teacher is a traditional undergraduate, an older graduate student, or a non-traditional adult who has been out of college for a number of years, the experience of student teaching almost always seems to be transformative.

Newly certified teachers who have completed student teaching have tested and been tested. They have reached deeply into themselves to face the hard times of student teaching. They have stayed up late into the night studying their subject matter and preparing their lessons, and many know the material better than they ever did before they taught it. Their talents and intelligence have been fully challenged. They have felt the fun of working with students whose sense of potential seems unavoidable, and they have felt the sadness of working with students whose development seems thwarted and diverted. They have learned first hand about the complexities of schooling. Now, after successfully negotiating the passage of student teaching, they are ready for their first job as a teacher.

NOTES

1. Sonia Nieto, *Affirming Diversity: The Sociopolitical Context of Multicultural Education* (New York: Longman, 1992).

2. Portia Elliott, personal correspondence with the author, June 1998.

3. David Labaree, "The Trouble with Ed Schools," *Educational Foundations* 10, no. 3 (Summer 1996), 27–45.

4. R. S. Peters, ed., *The Philosophy of Education* (London: Oxford University Press, 1973).

5. Fenstermacher, "Controlling Quality and Creating Community."

6. Deborah P. Britzman, *Practice Makes Practice: A Critical Study of Learning to Teach* (Albany, NY: State University of New York Press, 1991).

7. Labaree, "The Trouble with Ed Schools."

8. Donald A. Schon, *The Reflective Practitioner: How Professionals Think in Action* (New York: BasicBooks, 1983).

9. Steven Zemelman, Harry Daniels, and Arthur Hyde, *Best Practice: New Standards for Teaching and Learning in America's Schools* (Portsmouth, NH: Heinemann, 1993), 4–5.

10. Rebecca Herman and Sam Stringfield, *Ten Promising Programs for Educating All Children: Evidence of Impact* (Arlington, VA: Educational Research Service, 1997), 116–123.

11. "Youth Services California Affiliates Briefing" (San Anselmo, CA: Youth Services California, May 1977).

12. Robert Coles, *The Call of Service: A Witness to Idealism* (Boston: Houghton Mifflin, 1993), xvi–xvii.

13. Ibid., xix.

14. Robert A. Rhoads, *Community Service and Higher Learning* (Albany: State University of New York Press, 1997).

15. Ibid., 219.

16. Ibid., 177.

17. Judith Harmon Miller, "Gender Issues Embedded in the Experience of Student Teaching: Being Treated Like a Sex Object," *Journal of Teacher Education* 48, no. 1 (January–February 1997), 19–28.

7

Finding Your First Job in Teaching

Where do you want to teach? In an urban, suburban, or rural community; North, South, East, or West; near the ocean, the mountains, or the desert; close to family and friends or far from home in a new situation? Along with the possibilities of place, consider what type of school interests you the most: large or small, traditional structure or alternative model, comprehensive curriculum or special academic theme, well-established school or newly opened building? Thinking carefully about where you want to teach is a great way to start a successful job search.

This chapter focuses on resources and strategies for finding your first job in teaching. Making the transition from professional preparation to professional employment requires clear plans of action and knowledge of the job search process. Matching your talents and interests with available jobs means knowing how to communicate effectively to schools hiring new teachers.

We concentrate on three essential dimensions of the job search process:

- Looking for positions and places by using newspapers, career centers, the Web, and your own personal network
- Letting schools know who you are by preparing a compelling résumé, assembling strong letters of reference, writing an effective cover letter, doing substitute teaching, and completing school system job applications
- Getting the job you want by developing a professional teaching portfolio, interviewing successfully, and understanding the rules for accepting a position and signing a contract

LOOKING FOR POSITIONS AND PLACES

When do schools advertise teaching positions? Surprisingly, all the time. Schools hire as need arises; many large school systems have openings throughout the year, especially in high shortage areas like mathematics or bilingual and special education. In general, however, the hiring pattern goes as follows:

- Jobs are listed early, even in January and February, for a school year that begins in August or September. Some of you may be student teaching and job searching simultaneously.

- The hiring season goes late, even into September and October. Do not stop if you do not have a job in the latter part of the summer. Some districts hire as the school year begins.

- Many jobs are listed as "anticipated," meaning school budgets are not yet set, or future plans of veteran teachers are not finalized. To prepare for possible vacancies, many schools start early, bringing people in for interviews, creating a ranking of the best candidates, and hiring when budgets are set (usually between March and May) or when staff leave their current positions. Other systems are known for hiring late, filling most of their openings in the summer.

You can begin your search for a teaching job in newspapers and college career centers. Both provide multiple listings of openings in school systems. Newspapers run advertisements for a limited time, so you need to keep going back to find the latest postings. A comprehensive college career center generally maintains an ongoing listing of positions for you to consult. Some career centers bring school system recruiters to campus to interview those who are completing their certification programs.

Consider subscribing to a newspaper that lists jobs in the locale where you want to teach. For each state there is a newspaper of record in which school systems advertise. In many cases, it is a large metropolitan newspaper such as *The New York Times, Miami Herald, Boston Globe, Rocky Mountain News, Los Angeles Times*, and *Seattle Times and Post Intelligencer*. Look in the largest city newspaper near where you want to teach between January and September, and you will find ads for teaching positions.

A map and the Web help to geographically locate communities with openings. Send résumés and cover letters to the principals and schools you are interested in as soon as you can. Getting a school system job application at this point is also a great advantage. You will have more time to prepare thoughtful responses to questions before submitting your credentials.

Cybersearching

As you probably know, an essential part of a new teacher's job search strategy includes looking online. Over 94 percent of college students have access to the Web, and more than half have used it to seek a job.[1] Given the time involved in poring over employment listings and newspaper ads, cybersearching makes great sense.

Link to the department of education Web page for each state on your job-possibilities list (see Part II for the Web addresses of teacher licensing agencies by state). The Web provides information about schools in the state, student enrollments, standardized test scores, certification rules, education reform initiatives, finance statistics, legislative developments, curriculum materials, museum and library resources, and much more.

School systems and individual schools, both domestic and international, are also creating their own home pages. Check out *Web 66*, an Internet site maintained by Hillside Elementary School in Cottage Grove, Minnesota, for hundreds of listings (http://web66.coled.umn.edu/schools.html). School Web pages vary, but most have information about students, curriculum, facilities, and community. Some include entries about the teaching faculty, so you can get a glimpse of future colleagues. Others list teacher openings, and some have a job application for you to download. Spend time with School Web pages. You will appear well-organized in an interview if you demonstrate that you have looked at the online materials and internalized the information.

Listed below are several good Web sites for job searching:

- http://www.gsn.org/hotlist/index.html—Information about school districts, demographics, weather and climate, and other topics in fifty states
- http://www.wm.edu/csrv/career/stualum/edempl.html—Public and private schools, schools abroad, and teacher placement agencies
- http://www.isiminc.com.mm.html#Positions—Job openings for independent schools across the country
- http://www.edutech-1.com—Jobs in California by region and subject field
- http://www.petersons.com/—Peterson's On-Line Guide to education careers
- http://www.ajb.dni.us/cgi-bin/websrch.cgi—America's Job Bank; openings by field and region

You can also look for positions by using one of the major Internet search engines. Type in a key word descriptor such as "public school teaching jobs" and you will be led to many potential employment opportunities.

Look at the Internet sites of the major newspapers, radio and television stations, large companies, human service and government agencies, historical associations, and museums/cultural organizations in communities where you may want to teach. Check out local chambers of commerce plus the state's department of travel and tourism. Just about any organization who might connect with your professional and personal life as a teacher has electronic information available for your review.

Probe for the meanings beneath the statistics and information you gather. For example, per-pupil expenditures invite comparisons between what different communities are spending on education and what resources may be available to support your teaching. Enrollment data, combined with numbers of schools and teachers, tell how crowded a given system is at this point in time. (See Part II for state-by-state data.) Tax information, recent election results, and economic reports may reveal the political climate and the amount of support education has in particular places.

Unfortunately, public education is not as advanced as corporations and universities in using new technologies for recruiting employees. In the high tech field, two of every three new jobs are filled using the Internet. In education, not all jobs are posted electronically; only some schools have Web pages, and only some administrators or personnel directors search for applicant résumés online. You might consider moving ahead of the curve by creating your own home page and posting your materials for schools to review.

Building a Network

Broadly defined, a network is a "web" of interrelated people through which new teachers build connections with other educators in the field. Networking is effective in job searching. It combines "who you know" with thoughtful attention to the substance of what different school systems are looking for in new teachers.

Many new teachers find jobs as a result of a "someone who knows someone who knows someone" set of linkages. In many ways, working through acquaintances and contacts is easier than applying blindly to job ads in newspapers or career service listings. The idea of an "it's who you know" network has negative connotations for many people because it suggests an "old boys'" club that has long denied women and people of color access to professional, managerial, and technical positions. Or, it implies that certain jobs are "wired" in advance for well-placed applicants with only minimal consideration given to qualifications or skills. Such practices are indefensible in education or any field.

Our vision of networking for jobs is quite different. You build a network of people with whom you are in regular (or semi-regular) contact. Once started, a network can grow and expand, encompassing your changing needs and interests. It may provide ideas about finding a job, developing exciting curriculum, expanding professional knowledge, launching innovative projects, entering graduate degree programs, making conference presentations, engaging in overseas study, and so on. The reality is this: Without a network, you deal with many unknown people and situations; with a network, you can search out good employment situations with more support and less uncertainty.

Here are some ideas for starting and sustaining a network:

Build your network now. Many undergraduates tell us that since they know few people in education, they have no basis for a network. Begin your network with people who know you: college professors, former public school teachers, employers, family members, friends, and co-workers. Tell them about your plans and goals for your academic and post-academic life. As one of our students told us, instead of people back home saying, "Jane is away at school majoring in something or other," she wanted them to know that "Jane is at college preparing to become a teacher."

Use your time in schools to meet teachers and administrators. Most teacher education programs ask you to spend many hours in schools even before your student teaching semester. Use that time to learn about other teachers' interests and to get involved with their projects. A teacher coordinating the school science fair, directing a musical production, or running an after-school computer club may welcome your help, particularly if you have knowledge and skills to bring to the effort. Your interest in their work will interest them in yours.

One graduate of our program starting coaching the girls' junior varsity basketball team at a local high school while she was still an undergraduate at the university. She made a point of talking with coaches, athletic directors, teachers, and principals from the schools her team played each season. When she began looking for a job, she knew school people throughout the region. Her network worked well; some of her references knew each other and she had up-to-date information about the schools to which she was applying. Today she is a highly respected young teacher in our area.

Stay in contact with your teachers. Your former public school teachers can be wonderful personal and professional resources. People in schools know other educators, and they may be able to connect you to job openings around a region. The most direct link, a job at your former school recommended by a former teacher, does not happen very often. Administrators often want to hire a former student, but there may not be an opening in your field when you are ready to enter the job market.

A more likely scenario is a former teacher telling you about a colleague in another school system doing interesting things in your field. You may hear about a science educator who is teaching environmental topics using satellite data from the Internet, or a math teacher who is doing problem-solving activities using census figures. Visit these teachers at their schools and observe instructional and curricular approaches that make sense to you. Your efforts may lead to contacts with other educators who are pursuing similar interests. Keep enlarging your network by staying in touch with interesting and innovative people. As you gain new ideas and build new relationships, job prospects may follow.

LETTING SCHOOL SYSTEMS KNOW WHO YOU ARE

Once you identify job openings in your field, you must convince school personnel that you are the best teacher for the job. A résumé, letters of recommendation, a cover letter, and your responses to school system job applications are essential tools. Personnel directors and search committees rely heavily on such materials to evaluate which of many applicants to interview. Your goal is to show you have the knowledge, experiences, and credentials to do outstanding teaching. Organize your professional materials the way you would organize a class or curriculum unit. You are teaching readers about yourself. The overall message needs to be: "I know my subject; I understand and respect kids; I am ready to teach."

A Compelling Résumé

The term *résumé* means to summarize or reiterate; to provide a short account of one's career and qualifications for a position. How important is your résumé to an effective job search? Opinions differ widely. Some regard a résumé as "first among equals" in your job materials, so you must make the résumé the lead document in your application. Otherwise, a thoughtful statement of educational philosophy or a comprehensive professional portfolio may never be read fully. Others struggle with the résumé. They may be uncomfortable with presenting themselves on paper, inferring that exaggeration is part of job-seeking.

The fact is, you need a compelling résumé. Every school district wants an easy-to-read, informative, factually accurate, and philosophically consistent summary of each teaching candidate. Your résumé must look professional, otherwise personnel directors and superintendents may quickly dismiss the application assuming that it was quickly or shoddily put together. The résumé should be a formal document, word-processed and laser printed on résumé stationery with matching paper for your cover letters and envelopes. The color of the paper and style of the presentation is your choice; many students prefer off-white or light gray paper.

Résumés are individual creations. There is no ideal formula for condensing your experiences onto paper that will guarantee you a job. In business, the conventional advice is to prepare a one-page résumé, so career counselors often communicate this idea to people in all fields. While four or five pages is excessive, people in schools want enough detail to show who you are and what you have done. If you have the experiences to warrant a two- or even three-page résumé, then that is the right length for you.

To paraphrase a statement often made about the process of authoring a book, you do not write a résumé, you rewrite it over and over again until it works for you and your readers. It will probably take several drafts to compose effective summaries of your experiences and what you have learned from them. Here are basic points to follow when writing your résumé:

Begin with your name, address, telephone, and e-mail, followed by your educational experiences. The first and most important thing a reader should see at the top of the page is your name and how to contact you in bold letters. Next, as shown in Figure 7.1, list the schools you attended, the degrees you hold, and when you graduated. This is the place for information about subject area major, academic minors and specializations, grade point average, honors, international experiences, and educational certifications. Include the certification numbers for all the states where you are licensed.

Clearly state your educational and employment record. After listing your educational background, present the job experiences most closely related to public school teaching, including student teaching, tutoring, camp counseling, or activities in which you worked with a diverse range of children and youth. Then include non-education-related work, arranged chronologically from most to least current. It is important to give the job title, place of work, and address as well as the dates of employment.

Provide short, descriptive summaries of the work you did in each position. Readers want to know what you did as a tutor, counselor, lab technician, project assistant, sales manager, community volunteer, or student leader. If you have been in the Peace Corps, Americorps, or military service, include these with summaries. List your presentations, publications, and performances, giving each its own section if you have more than one. If you developed curriculum units, did substitute teach-

Figure 7.1
Sample Educational Experiences Section of a Résumé

Education

May 1998   **Master of Education**
                University of Massachusetts–Amherst
                Amherst, Massachusetts
                Concentration: English Education

April 1997   **Massachusetts Teacher Certification**
                English, Grades 9–12 (Certificate No.: 000000)

May 1996   **Bachelor of Fine Arts**
                Emerson College
                Boston, Massachusetts
                Concentration: Writing, Literature, Publishing

Fall 1991   **Emerson College Semester Abroad**
                European Institute for International Communication
                Maastricht, the Netherlands
                Concentration: Literature, Creative Writing, Dutch Culture, and
                International Relations

ing, or taught in private or non-traditional settings, document these experiences clearly.

Ideally, the dates on your résumé follow one another in a chronological manner, from most recent to the beginning of college study or initial jobs. A reader will then easily follow your timeline in college, summer and part-time employment, your first job in your field, and so on. Admittedly, not everyone's career follows this neat pattern. If you left school before graduating, or took time away from your career to raise a family, say so. Your non-teaching experiences are relevant to your overall professional profile. The key is not to leave gaps or confusions in your history. At best, having time unaccounted for looks careless and inefficient; at worst, it may appear as though you have something to hide.

Be relentlessly concrete. Strive for concreteness in descriptions of your work. It is easy to be too general, too short, or too long. Generalities leave readers with little substantive information; too many words make it difficult to scan. Compare the following summaries of her student teaching by a new social studies teacher.

First Draft

Developed and taught multiperspective lessons for World History class.

Revised Statement

Developed and taught daily 9th grade World History course for 16 weeks on block schedule.

The first draft lacks key specifics found in the revised statement. The second entry lets readers know how long she taught, that a block schedule was in use, and that she designed many of her own units and taught them. On a longer document she might add more about her courses, which included units on women in medieval Europe; indigenous cultures in Asia, Africa, and Latin America; and peasant perspectives during the French Revolution.

Give yourself appropriate credit for what you have done. First-time résumé writers tend to err by understating or overinflating what they have done personally and professionally. Try to create a balance that accurately portrays your experiences and accomplishments. It is easy to be too modest, especially when the work was outside of education. "I was only a waitress," one student told us about her job at a local restaurant failing to give herself credit for the management experiences and job promotions she had earned. Perhaps many of you have had interesting experiences and impressive accomplishments: unusual summer work; overseas travel; athletic performances; musical, dance, or artistic expressions; internships; independent studies; or volunteer activities. Do not hesitate to include these events on your résumé, too.

At the same time, do not make the job of a summer temp or work/study student employee into a position of higher importance. Many times the vagueness of such roles lets you use impressive language, but alert readers will see through the words. It is not necessary to "pump up" a résumé, even if you have little experience outside of going to college, doing well in your subject field, and successfully completing your education courses and student teaching.

Include relevant skills and interests. When we asked students in our classes to list their special skills and talents for the personal interest section of their résumés, many had difficulty. Initially, it was hard to talk about themselves in terms of uniqueness. Some felt they did not measure up to others they knew in terms of abilities or accomplishments. "If I had more time, I could dance and play music," one student told us. "I used to be more interesting," another said, "Now I just study and write papers." Some questioned the value of a skills and interests category because it seemed excessive to cite reading, quilting, or hiking as personally meaningful activities.

Despite initial hesitation, our students eventually listed numerous items for the skills section, including speaking languages other than English; computer proficiencies with word-processing, spreadsheets, and databases as well as familiarity with Macintosh and/or IBM platforms; desktop publishing; Internet skills; research activities; publishing stories, poetry, or magazine articles; photography; and work in radio, television or other entertainment fields. Interests included personal fitness and training; being on a college athletic team; amateur performances of music, dance, art, theater; and lifeguarding with a knowledge of CPR.

The reason for including skills and interests on your résumé is to convey your well-roundedness and ongoing personal accomplishment. You want to describe yourself fully in a competitive situation. A school that recently came online will be interested in your knowledge of computers. Your outside-of-school interest in quilting or dance may also translate into interesting approaches to teaching history. Your daily jogging routine may open up the opportunity to help coach the track team.

Add your references. At the end of the résumé, it is customary to list references. You have three choices of how to do so. First, you could provide the names, addresses and phone numbers of the individuals who have agreed to give you a recommendation for a teaching job. Second, you could give the name of the college career center or placement service where your references are on file. Third, if you are still developing your list of recommendations, say "References available upon request."

Letters of Recommendation

Personnel directors, school principals, and hiring committees use letters of recommendation to form impressions about the kind of person you are and the kind of teacher you will be in their schools. Admittedly, such letters are a subjective way of assessing candidates for a teaching position. Your goal is to use these materials to help put your academic expertise, teaching abilities, and professional experience front and center for everyone to see.

Most schools ask for the names of at least three individuals who can discuss your readiness to teach in their system. Some districts ask for three letters plus the names of additional people whom they can contact. People providing references may be asked to write a general letter, respond to a school district form, or talk about an applicant in a telephone interview. Many of your former teachers and college professors will be happy to be references. They view writing recommendations as part of the job of an educator.

Try to get letters from individuals who can provide schools with one or more of the following types of references:

Academic references. As a subject matter specialist, you will benefit from letters from arts and sciences college professors who taught one or more of the classes in your field of study or who served as your academic advisor. School systems want assurance that you know your subject field well, and academic references will expand upon your grade point average and other accomplishments.

Professional references. As a teacher, you must have a letter or two that speaks to your ability to motivate students to learn while managing classrooms effectively. In a best-case scenario, your cooperating teacher writes one of these letters. This is the person who has seen you work directly with kids for an extended period of time during your student teaching. School people value the opinions of other teachers. In the case where you may not have had a great relationship with your cooperating teacher, or that person might not have seen many of your lessons first-hand, your college supervisor or an education professor can write a professional reference. Ideally, your cooperating teacher, college supervisor, and your education professor each affirm your success as a new teacher.

Personal references. You also want a letter in your file that describes your ability to be a mature, responsible employee who meets work demands easily and pleasantly. Former educational or non-educational employers are good sources of such personal references. Such letters show that you know how to work in a people-intensive job—everything from arriving on time to balancing the demands of personal and professional life. They may also convey a sense of you as a person of integrity and responsibility.

Confidential versus non-confidential letters. Many new teachers ask about requesting confidential or non-confidential letters. You can use a college placement service and include only confidential letters in your file. At a district's request, the service sends the letters. Or, you can send letters that you have seen with your other application materials. This can work well when you are applying to many schools and want to reduce the expense involved in using a service. A third option is to use some confidential and some non-confidential letters.

Ask about each district's policy concerning confidential letters. Some will review non-confidential letters because they can talk with references by telephone later; others insist on confidential letters only. It is entirely possible that not every letter will be the glowingly positive description that you yourself might write. Obviously, letters with uninspiring or negative comments are not going to help you get a job, so try to use only those references who you trust will write positive recommendations.

Transcripts

At some point, along with your letters of recommendation, you will be asked to send copies of your college transcripts. This can be expensive since many schools charge for official transcripts, and some students have attended more than one school. When sending multiple applications at the early stage of the job search, unofficial transcripts are generally acceptable to school systems. These materials are much less costly to reproduce while still providing an overview of your academic background.

Be sure to include copies of transcripts from all the schools you attended, even if your grades in some cases were not the best. Add a statement about the transcripts if you have issues to clarify such as incomplete courses or low grades. You can use this statement to explain how successful work performance contrasts with a less-than-distinguished undergraduate record. When you are offered a position, you will need to provide official transcripts.

The Cover Letter

The cover letter is an invitation to readers to learn more about you as an educator and a person. Without it, your application materials run the risk of being misplaced or misunderstood. With it, you are directing your correspondence to the right people for the right reasons at the right time—all of which are clearly stated in your letter.

A cover letter is generally the first item people see when they open your file. Those involved in the hiring process use it to start forming an impression of you as a potential teacher in their schools. Be sure to word-process or type the letter. Make it neat and free from factual or spelling errors. Address it to the appropriate person at the correct place, and make sure it is dated and signed. Include your return address, telephone, and e-mail address so that people can reach you quickly and easily.

As you prepare your cover letter, keep in mind the following ideas.

Convey enthusiasm. Begin by letting people know you are happy to be applying for this particular position: "It is with great interest that I apply for the position of . . ." You might include how you found out about the opening: "I spoke with . . ." or, "The placement office informed me of an opening at . . ." You want to create a sense of positive energy about your application right from the start.

Showcase your strengths. Briefly state your professional background. This can be a difficult task for a new teacher who may not have a lot of on-the-job experience. Begin with your teaching experiences; for example, "I completed my student teaching in an urban school where I worked with a range of ninth and tenth graders." Stay with the facts and do not embellish your record by trying to appear more qualified than you are. Refer to your academic coursework and major. Reviewers want to see your qualifications in your subject field. If you are already certified, say so. If you have tutoring experience or other work with youth, refer to these activities specifically. Perhaps you have recently received a special recognition or award, or have recently returned from an exciting personal endeavor. Tell readers about these activities. Bland letters are not necessarily better!

Preview your abilities as an educator. To convey the kind of teacher you intend to be, briefly share your ideas about instructional methods, classroom management, tests and assessments, the teacher's role in the school, or other parts of the job. You might mention a high point from your student teaching or previous work with students to illustrate your points. Let readers know that the practical realities of the job are not new to you. Say what you think, be tactful, but do not worry about saying the wrong thing to a potential employer. If you and a school system are not compatible philosophically, it is better to know this sooner than to wait until you have signed a contract and then realize that that system is not the place for you.

Follow the procedures. Inform the personnel director or hiring committee that you have followed their directions for the job application. If a district asks for an application, a résumé, and the names of three references, state in your cover letter that this is what you have provided. Inquire if they want or need additional information. In the last paragraph, let the contract person know that you will be following up to make sure everything is in place.

School System Job Applications

In addition to your other materials, many school districts will require you to complete a formal "application for professional employment." At first, a district's job application may appear redundant, asking for much of the same data that is already in your résumé or cover letter. The application, however, is a school system's way of collecting information it finds important. Just as you get to design your résumé and arrange your materials to create the best possible impression, school hiring committees use applications to assess how prospective teachers measure up to local priorities and concerns.

Despite our computerized society, many school system applications are still designed with typewriters or even handwriters in mind. They generally consist of four to six pages of questions and checklists. Lines are narrow, and the space provided is often not adequate for answering the questions. Copies of the application are generally not available on disk, and few districts are equipped to handle electronic submissions.

School system job applications are very important; many districts pay more attention to their materials than to yours. Type or neatly print responses, or ask if the district accepts answers that you word-process on separate sheets of paper. If so, include attachments for answers to questions over two to three lines.

Applications often include questions about your educational and career goals. They may ask you for examples of your educational philosophy in action: how you plan to prepare students for a multicultural society, how you will approach classroom management, or how you will include students with special needs in your classes. Consider writing draft statements about your professional interests, personal background, teaching philosophies, and classroom practices, saving them on your computer, and then customizing your responses for each application.

Substitute Teaching

Substitute teaching is another way of letting school systems know who you are, and it can enhance your application when you do apply for a full-time position. Schools everywhere desperately need substitutes, and there are nowhere near enough to go around. The average teacher misses nine days a year due to illness, professional development, or personal reasons. Multiply that figure times the number of teachers in a school system, and you see the high demand for substitute teachers. In Massachusetts, it is estimated that there are five thousand substitutes working in classrooms across the state on any given school day.

On the one hand, being a substitute in schools is not easy. The pay, around $50–$80 a day, is low, although some schools are now offering more money and choice of school placement to attract people to the job. With no permanent home base, you constantly move from school to school, books and calculators in hand. Stepping into an unfamiliar classroom is another complexity of the role. You do not know the kids, and they do not know you. Sometimes the lesson plans left by the regular teacher are unclear, or do not represent your way of teaching the material. You may be asked to work well outside your discipline; for example, a history major taking over a Spanish class.

On the other hand, substituting is one of the best ways to get known in a school system. It affords you the chance to meet just about everyone involved in the hiring process for new teachers, from principals to parents, and it allows you to preview the school system, the curriculum, and the students. You are able to field test some of your own teaching ideas and bring the results to a job interview. In effect, substitute teaching may be viewed as an educational apprenticeship, and proving yourself in the role may show school personnel that you are a good candidate to take over a classroom on your own.

Individuals moving to a new community or state, or finishing their student teaching in December, may find substitute teaching is one of the best ways to build connections in schools. One of our graduates, who moved to Denver, Colorado, after the school year had already begun, opted to substitute teach. She made up a business card identifying herself as a certified teacher and announcing her availability to substitute in all grades, all subjects. She sent her card and a letter of introduction to schools throughout the area. She soon had steady work and developed a great network to use in the following year's successful job search.

GETTING THE JOB YOU WANT

Once your application materials have been sent, you must wait to see if you "make the cut" and move from "applicant" to "candidate" in the next phase of the job-search process. A candidate is someone who, in the eyes of a school district, stands out enough to be strongly considered for a teaching position. If you are applying in high-shortage areas like mathematics or physics, you may be a candidate in many different places. It will be more difficult to find employment in subject fields with fewer shortages. In these cases, you may get more rejections than invitations, depending on how admissions people view your materials.

Schools will evaluate you as a potential employee. Likewise, you get to assess them as a future employer. They have collected data about you from transcripts, letters of recommendation, and your application materials. Now, you can gather information about them by finding out graduation rates, teacher salaries, cost of living, academic focus, and the like. If they call you in for an interview, be ready to ask them thoughtful, well-researched questions about how education happens in the schools.

What information do schools review in making hiring decisions? According to one study of teacher recruitment practices, large urban schools look at the following.

- Student teaching assessment—100 percent (for new teachers)
- Recommendations of previous employers—100 percent (for experienced teachers)
- Informal interviews assessing aptitude/characteristics—87.1 percent
- Assessment of classroom performance—69 percent
- Overall college GPA—56 percent
- Grades in specific education methods courses—56 percent
- Grades in specific academic discipline courses—around 50 percent
- Test scores—41 percent (25 percent said teacher test scores were not useful)
- Parent recommendations—23 percent (33 percent said these were not useful)

- Video-taped sample lesson—15 percent (43 percent said these were not useful)[2]

Many items on the above list—grades, references, and test scores—are communicated in the form of objective data. But as the application process moves along, the person replaces the paper and you become the center of attention. A strong professional teaching portfolio and a successful presentation of yourself in an interview are now keys to getting offered the job you want.

A Professional Teaching Portfolio

A professional teaching portfolio is an alternative way of presenting what you have accomplished academically and professionally. It is a compilation of the work you have done that you feel best shows your capabilities and talents as a teacher. According to many education reformers, portfolios offer a more authentic way to assess a person's work. Unlike short-answer or fill-in-the-blank exams, evaluators get to see what someone can do in terms of actual performance. Given the popularity of portfolios, many school systems are using them to evaluate prospective teachers.

Portfolios have long been a feature of the way individuals in other fields present themselves professionally. Architects, interior and fashion designers, painters, photographers, glassblowers, musicians, writers, poets, and house builders all collect samples of their work to show to prospective employers or customers. Similarly, teachers can gather samples of their work to complement their résumé and other application materials. The portfolio provides hiring committees with a more "up close and personal" look at an applicant.

Here are some suggestions for organizing your professional teaching portfolio.

Collection folders and display folders. Even as you start your teacher education program, it is useful to create a collection folder and a display folder. A collection folder is the running record of your work as a new teacher. It is a place for all the "artifacts" or products associated with your teaching: résumé, transcripts, lesson plans, curriculum units, class handouts, student writing and tests, in-class and homework assignments, evaluations from supervisors, comments from students or parents, letters of recommendation, newspaper articles about your projects, professional conferences and presentations, personal writing and publications, and photographs, videotapes, or audiotapes.

A display folder is a carefully chosen subset of the collection folder for use in the job search (see Figure 7.2). This becomes the professional teaching portfolio you share with other educators. Choose from among

Figure 7.2
Contents of a New Teacher's Display Portfolio

Résumé

Copy of teaching license

Letters of recommendation

Lesson plans featuring multiple teaching methods

Approaches to assessment

Approaches to classroom management

Samples of student work

Related professional activities and accomplishments

the pages and pages of raw materials in your collection folders those items that create the view of yourself you want others to see. Your display invites principals, personnel directors, teachers, and students to assess your potential as a teacher in their schools based on what you have done and how you have done it. Front and center in your portfolio is the "best of your best" for their review.

Create an organized, attractive presentation of materials. Use a three-ring binder or an expandable legal file as your portfolio container. Many students place materials inside plastic sleeves within their binder to keep the material from getting wrinkled or damaged and to make turning from section to section easy. Put your name and address on the outside so it is easily identifiable as your portfolio.

Include a Reader's Guide to your portfolio. Even the most interesting materials by themselves will not achieve the goal of clearly presenting yourself to others. To facilitate the viewer's understanding of your portfolio, consider creating a "Reader's Guide." The reality of the hiring process is that personnel directors and search committees are generally pressed for time and have multiple candidates to assess. They tend to scan through application materials, stopping at different places that interest them rather than reading each page completely. Given the time demands faced by interviewers, you will need to decide how lengthy and inclusive to make your portfolio. Your "Reader's Guide" should be composed of guideposts for readers in the form of tabs on the outside of pages to mark off sections, or include a concise, easy-to-follow table of contents.

Include content and process. Candidates for middle and high school positions must demonstrate their abilities to teach academic content and use multiple teaching methods. Include lesson plans and class activities that showcase both content and process in your portfolio. You cannot include everything, so make thoughtful choices. One mathematics teacher chose lessons on probability and statistics, fractions, problem solving, word problems, and measurement that also showed how he incorporated discussions, role playing, and student writing in his classes. A history teacher included a cooperative learning activity from a unit on social activism in the 1960s. It enabled her to demonstrate knowledge of academic content (contemporary U.S. history) and use of innovative teaching methods (groupwork and primary sources).

Many successful portfolios also include personal reflections and commentaries on the items included in the file. For example, if you feel a certain lesson or unit shows your best work, tell readers, "I am really proud of this work because . . ." If you genuinely value the comments of students, the feedback of supervisors, or correspondence from parents, then explain why this is the case. Use the introductions to different sections, or annotations on individual pages, to convey personal messages of importance.

The Job Interview

Rarely will anyone get a job in education without at least one interview with a prospective employer. Interview formats vary widely. Some are one-on-one or small-group meetings with the superintendent of schools or the building principal and department chairperson. In other places, teachers, parents, community members, and students are invited to ask you questions. Often you will be expected to teach a demonstration lesson in your field to a class of students while members of the interview team watch your performance.

Depending on the district, you may also be asked to write an essay during the interview (often on how you would use a particular educational methodology like active learning or cooperative groups); answer content questions from the state or district's Advanced Placement Exam; or respond to questions about teaching process and pedagogy (for instance, explain how you accommodate students with special needs). In many cases, you will go through an interview process that involves more than one step. You might meet with a committee and then complete a writing sample. Some districts call finalists back for a second set of interviews after the first round are completed.

Is interviewing the best way to assess a candidate for a teaching position? Most educators will probably say no, preferring instead to see a person actually teach for an extended period of time. Since repeatedly observing a prospective teacher is not possible outside of a professional development school context or in cases where a candidate is a long-term substitute in the district, interviews take on great importance in the hiring process. Employers see the individual-in-action during the interview, and they form immediate, sometimes lasting, impressions. It is your job to make those impressions positive ones.

In an interview, you have the opportunity to show what you know while at the same time learning more about a potential school in which to teach. You may be able to minimize feelings of tentativeness and uncertainty by setting up a mock interview with a friend who will ask you questions. Before the actual interview, outline some of your answers in advance so you are not trying to invent everything on the spot. Relax, and treat the meeting as a time to discuss learning and teaching with other educators. You will learn from them, they will learn from you, and if the fit is good, you may get a job offer to consider.

The most essential ingredient in every interview is your "personal vision" of yourself as a teacher. As you present yourself to superintendents, principals, teachers, parents, students, and others in the hiring process, show them you have a "positive, forward-looking, make-good-things-happen-for-kids attitude." No other factor is more important than how the hiring committee perceives this aspect of your approach to the work of a teacher.

In addition to the potential to make a difference in the lives of kids, here are four other essential qualities one outstanding principal told us he looks for when hiring new teachers:[3]

- An ability to work in highly interactive and cooperative ways
- A readiness to participate in networks of learning
- A commitment to ongoing inquiry into learning and teaching
- A high personal capacity for change

Interviewing Basics

Personal vision, collegiality, participation in networks of learning, commitment to ongoing inquiry, and capacity for change are made concrete by how you conduct yourself in the interview itself. Your answers to questions, the questions you ask, even your body language and appearance and the materials you bring with you for the interviewers to review communicate your sense of who you are and who you will be as a teacher. To create a positive presentation of yourself as an educator, use the following basic strategies for interviewing.

Strategy 1: Project Confidence. It seems to go without saying, but you must dress and conduct yourself in a professional manner. Use a firm handshake and find out the names and positions of the persons with whom you are talking. Establish eye contact with each person in the room; do not address your answers only to the person who is asking the questions. Make sure you answer the question that was asked, and if you do not know the answer, say so. Ask for clarification if you do not understand a question or if you think your answer to a question was not understood.

Strategy 2: Research the School. It is important to find out information about the school and community to which you have applied before coming to the interview. You want to show your interest by doing some basic research about the academic programs and the students who attend the school. In this way, you avoid asking questions that display a lack of knowledge about the school system. Use the Web or call the school and ask for copies of the student handbook, teacher policies and procedures, and any materials that are sent home to parents. Some possible topics to research include the percentage of students going on to post secondary education; students' performance on state-wide or district-wide graduation exams; academic, athletic or other co-curricular accomplishments; enrollment trends; class, race, gender, and language statistics; leading industries and health of the local economy; and recent political and economic developments in the area.

Strategy 3: Bring a Résumé and Portfolio. Even if you have sent this material previously, bring your résumé and a portfolio of your best work as a teacher. If appropriate, find a time in the interview to share at least one interesting and significant example of your teaching from your portfolio. Less is more in this context; explaining one teaching idea well is better than a hurried discussion of many different topics. You can also use the portfolio to showcase different instructional approaches. Many schools want to see if you can contribute to their vision of school-wide change by doing more than just lecturing in the classroom.

Strategy 4: Showcase Your Problem-Solving Skills. You may be asked to discuss a lesson or teaching plan that did not go as planned and how you responded. How you problem solve tells interviewers a lot about you as a new teacher. One of our English teachers described how after a particularly bad start to a class, he decided to simply sit quietly at his desk till the group behaved more appropriately. The students were quite taken back by his action; soon they were pleading for him to return to the front of the room and teach. Since the class was studying persuasive writing, he asked them to complete an essay convincing him to return to teaching. The students took up the challenge and responded with some of the best writing of the term. In turning the situation around, this teacher demonstrated the ability to adjust, adapt, and acclimate when plans for the day change quickly.

Strategy 5: Outline Answers to Questions in Advance. In the pressure of the interview, it is not easy to remember everything you want to say. Write down the key points you want to make in your opening statement and in your answers to questions from the committee. Although interviews vary greatly, you can expect some of the following questions:

What would you like to tell us about yourself?

Why do you want to teach?

What are your special talents (artist, coach, writer, dancer, researcher)?

What are your academic content knowledge specialties?

What are you going to do above and beyond the ordinary as a teacher?

What are you going to be doing in five years?

What are three words that best describe you as a teacher?

How are you going to integrate technology into your teaching?

What are your approaches to classroom management?

When have you had a problem with a student, and how did you solve it?

What are your best teaching methods (critical thinking, multiple intelligences, performance-based learning) and how do you plan to use them?

How do you plan to teach important ideas in your subject to a diverse group of students?

Strategy 6: Prepare an Effective Demonstration Lesson. As a part of the interview process, some districts ask finalists to come to the school to teach a demonstration lesson. They will ask you to teach a class similar to the ones you would be expected to teach if you were hired. You will most likely be observed by the students' regular teacher, the department chairperson, and perhaps the principal. How do you prepare for such a pressure-laden situation?

Design a self-contained lesson that can be accomplished from beginning to end in the time period that you have. Do not plan something too complex or too lengthy for the fifty minutes of the class. Focus on a significant idea in the curriculum area that you have been assigned, one that you find compelling and which you think you can make engaging for the students. Do not lecture during the entire period. Do your best to make the class interactive and fun, but don't overreach. The students will know why you are there. They will most likely be willing to cooperate; but if you ask them to do something that is too uncomfortable, they may resist.

Think back to your student teaching and reconstruct some of your best lessons. Did you establish a problem for students to solve? Did you simulate a situation and then have the students reflect on it? Did you take something that seems obvious, for example, the idea of the + sign in mathematics, and explore its history, what it means, and how it functions? Did you teach a basic idea such as the concept of property and examine it from more than one point of view? The notion is to develop a lesson that allows you to demonstrate you at your best: engaging, imaginative, and able to command the attention of the students.

Your students will respond to you better if you know their names. Ask the teacher whose class you will be teaching to send you a class list and if possible a seating chart ahead of time. Study the list and the chart and memorize the names and their seating locations if possible. Or, when you enter the class, ask your students to write their names in big bold lettering on a piece of paper and place it on the top or edge of their desks so that you can see it.

Follow common courtesy. Introduce yourself and tell your students a little about yourself: where you grew up, where you went to high school, college, and what you are doing there. Make that brief and consider asking the students to go around the room and briefly introduce themselves by giving their name and perhaps one of their interests.

Admittedly this process of introduction may take ten minutes from your lesson plan, but it will show the students and those observing that you are interested in them. In addition, as the lesson progresses, you may be able to tie the discussion to something one of your students mentioned about him- or herself at the beginning of the class. The genuine respect you show to the students, along with a vital, interactive, and intellectually interesting lesson, will serve your candidacy well.

Negotiating a Contract and Accepting an Offer

If you are offered a teaching position, you want to confirm some basic information before you accept it. Find out how many classes, what class levels, what tracking level, if any, and how many different preparations will you have? A course load of four or five classes in a non-block-schedule school is fairly standard; on a block schedule, three classes is common.

In addition to knowing how many classes you will have, it is important to know how many different classes you will have to prepare for each night. You need to know if the school groups its students heterogeneously or uses tracking and groups them homogeneously. Some schools have very intricate systems of classifying students and classes. In tenth grade, they may have four levels of classes, sometimes called basic, standard, college preparatory, and advanced placement.

If your assignment is to teach five tenth grade classes, and all are at the standard level, you may have only one preparation a night. If you have two tenth grade classes, one at the standard level and one at the advanced level, and you have two eleventh grade classes, one at the standard level and one at the basic level, then you would have four different preparations a night. A reasonable number of different preparations for a beginning teacher is two or three. Both you and the school hiring you should want to set the teaching load so that you can succeed.

In addition to knowing what your class assignment will be, you will want to know what other non-instructional assignments you will have.

Will you have time during the school day to prepare, plan, or grade papers? Or will you have your non-teaching periods assigned to cafeteria, study, or hall duty? Will you have the opportunity to supervise extracurricular activities or will you be required to do so? Will there be the opportunity to earn extra money, if you choose, through teaching in the summer, participating in curriculum development programs, or through coaching?

Other questions to ask include: Does the school offer any support if you decide to go to graduate school for further professional development? Does the school have a sabbatical or leave policy in place for its teachers? Will you have your own classroom, or will you be expected to move from classroom to classroom? Is there office space for teachers? These are all conditions of work that will affect your experience teaching in any school. It is perfectly reasonable for you to clarify each one of these issues before you accept your position.

Of course, salary is a major consideration. Ask to see your prospective school district's salary schedule. Compare it to the salary schedule of neighboring districts. A school system will have a beginning salary and a schedule of increments for each year of experience. In addition, the school will have a different beginning salary for teachers depending on whether they hold a bachelor's or master's degree or have graduate credit beyond the master's.

Principals and superintendents may not have a great deal of flexibility as to where they place you on the salary schedule. On a technical level, they have to follow contractual guidelines. On a functional level, they have to make sure that the salaries they offer new teachers are equitable in relation to those of the experienced faculty. But they do have some flexibility to assess your experience level before they automatically place you on step one of the salary schedule. If you have worked in other areas relevant to teaching, you may be given credit for that experience on the salary schedule and start your teaching at a slightly higher step on the salary schedule.

CONCLUSION

The end of a successful job search is the beginning of a career that matters. Despite all the contradictions that are embedded in the work of teachers, teaching is a meaningful, fulfilling occupation. If you are committed to your subject, love learning, and respect the potential in each and every one of your students, you will have the foundation for what it takes to become an outstanding teacher. Despite the anti-intellectualism that characterizes much of the discourse in our country, you will have the pleasure of doing intellectual work and continuing to learn during your entire worklife. Despite the boundaries you must keep between you and your students, you will have the opportunity to touch their lives through your teaching. We wish you well.

NOTES

1. N'Gai Croal, "Want a Job? Get Online," *Newsweek*, 9 June 1997, 81–82.

2. Segun C. Eubanks, *The Urban Teacher Challenge: A Report on Teacher Recruitment and Demand in Selected Great City Schools* (Belmont, MA: Recruiting New Teachers, 1996), 11, 23.

3. Mario Cirillo, personal communication with the author, April 1998.

PART II

PROFILES AND RESOURCES

8

State-by-State Profiles for New Teachers

The following state-by-state profiles offer key educational facts and essential certification information for prospective middle and high school teachers. They include the addresses of state licensing agencies; teacher salaries, student enrollments, per pupil spending, and number of teachers in states across the country; the type of teacher test required for certification by state; the names of institutions of higher education preparing secondary level teachers in each state; the colleges and universities that are accredited by the National Council for Accreditation of Teacher Education (NCATE); and the schools that were included in the 1999 *U.S. News & World Report* Top 50 rankings. We know of no other source where this material is listed in one place for easy and convenient reference. The data is up-to-date and accurate as of 1999.

Even though some of the facts will change, the categories themselves will remain important to new teachers. The names and numbers cited here serve as a way for you to orient yourself to the field of education, and to make more informed choices about your plans for teacher education.

TEACHER LICENSING AGENCIES

We include the name, mailing address, and web address of each state's department of education or state teacher licensing agency. Interacting with these organizations is essential for new teachers since they administer the certification regulations and policies in their state, including requests to obtain and maintain the license to teach.

TEACHER SALARIES

We list beginning and average teacher salaries as a way to look at issues of pay in the profession, and to allow future teachers to make comparisons between states. Data comes from the National Center for Education Statistics, *Digest of Education Statistics 1997* (Washington, D.C.: U.S. Department of Education, 1997) pages 86, 85. The Digest is updated every year and is available in libraries or on-line from the Department of Education.

STUDENT ENROLLMENTS, PER PUPIL EXPENDITURES, NUMBER OF TEACHERS

Figures related to student population, per pupil expenditure, and number of teachers offer evidence of the condition of education in each state. For example, the comparative ratio of the number of students to the number of teachers can be used to assess the demand for educators in a state or region. Similarly, the level of spending per pupil suggests the level of resources that are available to support schools. Data comes from the *Digest of Education Statistics 1997*, pages 53, 170, 76.

TEACHER TESTS

The move to widespread teacher exams makes testing an important, but rapidly changing, category. We list the teacher testing requirements for earning a license in each of the states that require a test. In some states, and in some colleges and universities within states, new teacher candidates must also pass a test before entering a certification program. Information on teacher tests comes from the Educational Placement Consortium, *Teacher Testing Requirements 1998* (Madison, WI: University of Wisconsin-Madison, 1998); Theodore E. Andrews, ed., *The NASDTEC Manual on the Preparation and Certification of Educational Personnel 1998–1999*) (Dubuque, IA: Kendall/Hunt Publishing Company, 1998), G-2–G4; and Web pages of the Educational Testing Service and various state education agencies. Consult these sources as well as individual states and institutions of higher education for the most recent developments.

COLLEGES AND UNIVERSITIES PREPARING SECONDARY TEACHERS

We include the institutions of higher education who are approved by the states to prepare secondary teachers. It is intended as a guide to use in thinking about what college or university teacher education program to attend. It is important to note that not every school offers a certification program in every teaching area, and some smaller schools specialize in just a few teaching fields. Our information comes from the *NASDTEC Manual 1998–1999*, section I-1–I-58.

NCATE ACCREDITATION

We identify institutions of higher education accredited by the National Council for Accreditation of Teacher Education (NCATE) by state as a way for prospective teachers to make more informed decisions about what college or university to attend. Every year there are a small number of changes to the list as schools gain or lose NCATE status. It is a good idea to ask the schools you are interested in about their relationship, if any, with NCATE. Data comes from an NCATE publication entitled *A List of Professionally Accredited Schools, Colleges, and Departments of Education* (Washington, D.C.: National Council for Accreditation of Teacher Education, 1999), and from the organization's website.

1999 *U.S. NEWS & WORLD REPORT*'S TOP FIFTY RANKINGS

The top 50 rankings from *U.S. News & World Report* are provided as another way for new teachers to think about potential schools. The list changes yearly, and is printed in a special career issue of the magazine.

ALABAMA

Alabama Department of Education
Teacher Education & Certification Office
PO Box 302101, Montgomery, AL 36130–2101
334–242–9977
http://www.alsde.edu

Beginning Salary
$24,824

Average Salary
$32,206

Enrollment
741,933

Per Pupil Spending
$4,405

Number of Teachers
44,056

Teacher Test
Alabama Basic Skills Test (for admission to undergraduate certification programs)

State Approved Secondary Teacher Education Institutions (*NCATE Accreditation)

Alabama A & M University, Normal, 35762*
Alabama State University, Montgomery, 36101–0271*
Athens State University, Athens, 35611*
Auburn University, Auburn, 36849–3501, and Montgomery, 36124–4023*
Birmingham–Southern College, Birmingham, 35254*
Faulkner University, Montgomery, 36109–3398
Huntingdon College, Montgomery, 36106–2148
Jacksonville State University, Jacksonville, 36265*
Judson College, Marion, 36756
Miles College, Birmingham, 35208
Oakwood College, Huntsville, 35896*
Samford University, Birmingham, 35229*
Spring Hill College, Mobile, 36608
Stillman College, Tuscaloosa, 35403–9990
Troy State University, Troy, 36082–0001, and Dothan, 36304*
Tuskegee University, Tuskegee, 36088*
University of Alabama, Tuscaloosa, 35487–0231*
University of Alabama, Birmingham, 35294*
University of Alabama, Huntsville, 35899
University of Mobile, Mobile, 36663–0220
University of Montevallo, Montevallo, 35115–6030*
University of North Alabama, Florence, 35632–0001*
University of South Alabama, Mobile, 36688*
University of West Alabama, Livingston, 35470*

1999 *U.S. News & World Report*'s **Top Fifty**: None

ALASKA

Alaska Department of Education
Teacher Education and Certification
801 W. 10th Street, Suite 200
Juneau, AK 99801–1894
907–465–2831
http://www.educ.state.ak.us

Beginning Salary
$34,800

Average Salary
$51,036

Enrollment
126,015

Per Pupil Spending
$8,963

Number of Teachers

7,379

Teacher Test

Praxis I PPST *or* CBT: Reading, Writing, Math

State Approved Teacher Education Institutions

University of Alaska, Anchorage, 99508
University of Alaska, Fairbanks, 99775–7480
University of Alaska Southeast, Juneau, 99801
Sheldon Jackson College, Sitka, 99835

1999 *U.S. News & World Report*'s Top Fifty: None

ARIZONA

Arizona Department of Education
Certification Unit
1535 West Jefferson Street, PO Box 6490
Phoenix, AZ 85007–6490
602–542–4367
http://www.ade.state.az.us

Beginning Salary	**Average Salary**
$24,042	$33,411
Enrollment	**Per Pupil Spending**
749,759	$4,778

Numbers of Teachers

38,017

Teacher Test

Arizona Teacher Proficiency Assessment: Professional Knowledge and content area test; a college course or appropriate examination on the Arizona and U.S. Constitutions

State Approved Secondary Teacher Education Institutions

Arizona State University, Tempe, 85287–0112
Grand Canyon University, Phoenix, 85061–1097
Northern Arizona University, Flagstaff, 86001
Prescott College, Prescott, 86301
Southwestern College, Phoenix, 85032–7042
University of Arizona, Tucson, 85721
University of Phoenix, Phoenix, 85040

1999 *U.S. News & World Report*'s **Top Fifty:**

24. Arizona State University, Tempe
40. University of Arizona, Tucson

ARKANSAS

Arkansas Department of Education
Teacher Education & Licensure
4 State Capitol Mall, Room 106B
Little Rock, AR 72201–1071
501–682–4342
http://arkedu.state.ar.us

Beginning Salary   **Average Salary**
$21,189 $30,159

Enrollment   **Per Pupil Spending**
457,076 $4,459

Number of Teachers

26,449

Teacher Test

Praxis II Core Battery: Professional Knowledge and Praxis II Specialty
Area Tests

**State Approved Secondary Teacher Education Institutions
(*NCATE Accreditation)**

Arkansas State University, Jonesboro, 72467*
Arkansas Technical University, Russellville, 72801–2222*
Harding University, Searcy, 72149–0001*
Henderson State University, Arkadelphia, 71999–0001*
Hendrix College, Conway, 72032*
John Brown University, Siloam Springs, 72761*
Lyon College, Batesville, 72503–2317*
Ouachita Baptist University, Arkadelphia, 71923*
Philander Smith College, Little Rock, 72202*
Southern Arkansas University, Magnolia, 71753*
University of Arkansas, Fayetteville, 72701*
University of Arkansas, Little Rock, 72204–1099*
University of Arkansas, Monticello, 71656–3478*
University of Arkansas, Pine Bluff, 71601–2799*
University of Central Arkansas, Conway, 72035–0001*
University of the Ozarks, Clarksville, 72830*
Williams Baptist College, Walnut Ridge, 72476

1999 *U.S. News & World Report*'s Top Fifty: None

CALIFORNIA

Commission of Teacher Credentialing
1900 Capitol Avenue
Sacramento, CA 95814–4213
916–445–7254
http://www.ctc.ca.gov

Beginning Salary $25,762	**Average Salary** $43,465
Enrollment 5,535,312	**Per Pupil Spending** $4,992

Number of Teachers

230,849

Teacher Test

California Basic Educational Skills Test (CBEST); Praxis II Specialty Area Tests; *or* Multiple Subjects Assessment for Teachers (MSAT)

State Approved Secondary Teacher Education Institutions (*NCATE Accreditation)

California Polytechnical State University, San Luis Obispo, 93407
California State University, Bakersfield, 93311–1099*
California State University, Chico, 95929
California State University–Dominguez Hills, Carson, 94747–9960*
California State University, Fresno, 93740–0057*
California State University, Fullerton, 92634*
California State University, Hayward, 94542–3000*
California State University, Long Beach, 90840–0106
California State University, Los Angeles, 90032*
California State University, Northridge, 91328*
California State Polytechnic University, Pomona, 91768–4019
California State University, Sacramento, 95819–6048
California State University, San Bernardino, 92407–2397
California State University–Stanislaus, Turlock, 95382*
San Diego State University, San Diego, 92182–0136,* and Imperial Valley, 92251
San Francisco State University, San Francisco, 94132*
San Jose State University, San Jose, 95192*
Sonoma State University, Rohnert Park, 94928
University of California, Berkeley, 94720–5800

University of California, Davis, 95616–8507
University of California, Irvine, 92717
University of California, Los Angeles, 90095
University of California, Riverside, 92521–0139
University of California–San Diego, La Jolla, 92093
University of California, San Francisco, 94143
University of California, Santa Barbara, 93106
University of Santa Cruz, Santa Cruz, 95064
Azusa Pacifica College, Azusa, 91702–7000
Bethany College, Scotts Valley, 95066–2898
Biola College, La Mirada, 90639–0001
California Baptist College, Riverside, 92504
California Lutheran College, Thousand Oaks, 91360
Chapman University, Orange, 92866
Christian Heritage College, El Cajon, 92019
Claremont Graduate School, Claremont, 91711
College of Notre Dame, Belmont, 94002
Concordia University, Irvine, 92612
Dominican College, San Rafael, 94901–2298
Fresno Pacific College, Fresno, 93702
Holy Names College, Oakland, 94619
Humboldt State University, Arcata, 95521–8299
John F. Kennedy University, Orinda, 94563
La Sierra University, Riverside, 92515–8247
Loyola Marymount University, Los Angeles, 90045*
Master's College, Newhall, 91321
Mills College, Oakland, 94613
Mount St. Mary's College, Los Angeles, 90049
National University, San Diego, 92037
Occidental College, Los Angeles, 90041
Pacific Union College, Angwin, 94508
Pepperdine University–Los Angeles, 90230
Pepperdine University–Malibu, 90263–4392
Point Loma Nazarene College, San Diego, 92106–2899
Saint Mary's College of California, Moraga, 94575–4800
Santa Clara University, Santa Clara, 95053
Simpson College, Redding, 96003
Southern California College, Costa Mesa, 92626
Stanford University, Palo Alto, 94305
United States International University, San Diego, 92131–1799
University of La Verne, La Verne, 91750–4443
University of the Pacific, Stockton, 95211–0197*
University of Redlands, Redlands, 92373–0999
University of San Diego, San Diego, 92110

University of San Francisco, San Francisco, 94117–1080
University of Southern California, Los Angeles, 90089–0031
Westmont College, Santa Barbara, 93108
Whittier College, Whittier, 90608

1999 *U.S. News & World Report*'s Top Fifty:

 3. Stanford University
 4. University of California–Los Angeles
 5. University of California–Berkeley
31. University of Southern California
40. University of California–Santa Barbara

COLORADO

Colorado Department of Education, Educator Licensing
State Office Building, 201 E. Colfax Avenue, Room 105
Denver, CO 80203–1704
303–866–6628
http://www.cde.state.co.us

Beginning Salary
$21,472

Average Salary
$36,373

Enrollment
673,438

Per Pupil Spending
$5,443

Number of Teachers

35,388

Teacher Test

Program for Licensing Assessments for Colorado Educators (PLACE)

**State Approved Secondary Teacher Education Institutions
(*NCATE Accreditation)**

Adams State College, Alamosa, 81102*
Colorado Christian University, Lakewood, 80226–7499
Colorado College, Colorado Springs, 80903
Colorado State University, Fort Collins, 80523–0015*
Fort Lewis College, Durango, 81301
Mesa College, Grand Junction, 81502–2647
Metropolitan State College of Denver, Denver, 80217–3362*
Regis College, Denver, 80221–1099
University of Colorado, Boulder, 80309–0030*

University of Colorado, Colorado Springs, 80933–7150*
University of Colorado, Denver, 80217–3364*
University of Denver, Denver, 80208
University of Northern Colorado, Greeley, 80639*
University of Southern Colorado, Pueblo, 81001–4901
Western State College, Gunnison, 81231

1999 *U.S. News & World Report*'s Top Fifty:

29. University of Colorado–Boulder

CONNECTICUT

Connecticut State Department of Education
Bureau of Teacher Certification & Professional Development
165 Capitol Avenue, Box 2219, Room 243
Hartford, CT 06145–2219
860–566–4561
http://www.state.ct.us/sde

Beginning Salary	**Average Salary**
$28,840	$51,688
Enrollment	**Per Pupil Spending**
523,054	$8,817

Number of Teachers

36,070

Teacher Test

Praxis I PPST *or* CBT: Reading, Writing, Math and Praxis II Specialty Area Tests

State Approved Secondary Teacher Education Institutions (*NCATE Accreditation)

Central Connecticut State University, New Britain, 06050*
Connecticut College, New London, 06320–4195
Eastern Connecticut State University, Willimantic, 06226
Fairfield University, Fairfield, 06430–5195
Quinnipiac College, Hamden, 06518
Sacred Heart University, Fairfield, 06432–1000
St. Joseph College, West Hartford, 06117
Southern Connecticut State University, New Haven, 06515
University of Bridgeport, Bridgeport, 06602
University of Connecticut–Storrs, 06269*

University of Hartford, West Hartford, 06117*
University of New Haven, New Haven, 06516
Wesleyan University, Middletown, 06457
Western Connecticut State University, Danbury, 06810–9972
Yale University, New Haven, 06520–8234

1999 *U.S. News & World Report***'s Top Fifty:**

46. University of Connecticut–Storrs

DELAWARE

Delaware Department of Education
Office of Certification
PO Box 1402, The Townsend Building
Dover, DE 19903
302–739–4686
http://www.doestate.de.us/

Beginning Salary	**Average Salary**
$24,300	$41,689
Enrollment	**Per Pupil Spending**
110,549	$7,030

Number of Teachers

6,463

Teacher Test

Praxis I PPST: Reading, Writing, Math; *or* Praxis I CBT: Reading, Writing, Math; *or* exemptions based on other standardized tests

State Approved Secondary Teacher Education Institutions (*NCATE Accreditation)

Delaware State University, Dover, 19901–2277*
University of Delaware, Newark, 19716
Wesley College, Dover, 19901–3875

1999 *U.S. News & World Report***'s Top Fifty**: None

DISTRICT OF COLUMBIA

Teacher Education & Licensure Branch
215 G Street NE, Room 101A
Washington, DC 20002
202–724–4250
http://www.k12.dc.us

Beginning Salary
$25,937

Average Salary
$44,947

Enrollment
79,159

Per Pupil Spending
$9,335

Number of Teachers

5,305

Teacher Test

Praxis I PPST *or* CBT: Reading, Writing and Math; Praxis II Specialty Area Tests

State Approved Secondary Teacher Education Institutions (*NCATE Accreditation)

American University, Washington, 20016–8001
Catholic University of America, Washington, 20064*
Gallaudet, Washington, 20002–3695*
George Washington University, Washington, 20052*
Howard University, Washington, 20059*
Trinity College, Washington, 20017
University of the District of Columbia, Washington, 20008

1999 *U.S. News & World Report*'s Top Fifty:

34. George Washington University

FLORIDA

Florida Department of Education
Bureau of Teacher Certification
325 West Gaines Street
Room 201, Turlington Building
Tallahassee, FL 32399–0400
850–488–2317
http://www.firn.edu/doe

Beginning Salary
$23,508

Average Salary
$34,281

Enrollment
2,240,283

Per Pupil Spending
$5,718

Number of Teachers

114,938

Teacher Test

Praxis I PPST *or* CBT: Reading, Writing, Math; Florida Professional Education Test; College Level Academic Skills Test (CLAST); Praxis II Specialty Area Tests

State Approved Secondary Teacher Education Institutions (*NCATE Accreditation)

Barry University, Miami, 33161
Bethune–Cookman College, Daytona Beach, 32114–3099*
Eckerd College, St. Petersburg, 33711
Flagler College, St. Augustine, 32085–1027
Florida A&M University, Tallahassee, 32307–3200*
Florida Atlantic University, Boca Raton, 33431–0991*
Florida Institute of Technology, Melbourne, 32901–6975
Florida International University, Miami, 33199*
Florida Memorial College, Miami, 33054
Florida Southern College, Lakeland, 33801–5698
Florida State University, Tallahassee, 32306–2400*
Jacksonville University, Jacksonville, 32211
Palm Beach Atlantic, West Palm Beach, 33416–4708
Rollins College, Winter Park, 32789
St. Leo College, St. Leo, 33574–6665
Southeastern College of the Assemblies of God, Lakeland, 33801
Stetson University, DeLand, 32720*
St. Thomas University, Miami, 33054
University of Central Florida, Orlando, 32816–0111*
University of Florida, Gainsville, 32611*
University of Miami–Coral Gables, Miami, 33124*
University of North Florida, Jacksonville, 32224*
University of South Florida, Tampa, 33620*
University of Tampa, Tampa, 33606–1490
University of West Florida, Pensacola, 32514*
Warner Southern College, Lake Wales, 33858

1999 *U.S. News & World Report*'s Top Fifty:

36. University of Florida
40. Florida State University

GEORGIA

Georgia Professional Standards Commission
205 Butler Street, Twin Towers East
Atlanta, GA 30334

404–657–9000
http://www.doe.kl2.ga.us

Beginning Salary
$24,693

Average Salary
$34,972

Enrollment
1,321,239

Per Pupil Spending
$5,193

Number of Teachers
79,480

Teacher Test

Praxis I PPST *or* CBT: Reading, Writing, Math; Praxis II Specialty Area Tests

State Approved Secondary Teacher Education Institutions (*NCATE Accreditation)

Agnes Scott College, Atlanta, 30030
Albany State College, Albany, 31705–2796*
Armstrong Atlantic State University, Savannah, 31419–1997*
Augusta State University, Augusta, 30904–2200*
Berry College, Mt. Berry, 30149–0159*
Brewton–Parker College, Mt. Vernon, 30445–0197
Clark Atlanta University, Atlanta, 30314*
Clayton College and State University, Morrow, 30260*
Columbus State College, Columbus, 31907–5645*
Covenant College, Lookout Mountain, 37350
Emory University, Atlanta, 30322
Fort Valley State University, Fort Valley, 31030–3298*
Georgia College and State University, Milledgeville, 31061*
Georgia Southern University, Statesboro, 30460*
Georgia Southwestern State University, Americus, 31709*
Georgia State University, Atlanta, 30303–3083*
Kennesaw State University, Marieta, 30144–5591*
LaGrange College, LaGrange, 30240
Mercer University, Macon, 31207–0001
North Georgia College & State University, Dahlonega, 30597*
Oglethorpe University, Atlanta, 30319–2797
Paine College, Augusta, 30901–3182
Piedmont College, Demorest, 30535
Shorter College, Rome, 30165–4298
Spelman College, Atlanta, 30314*
State University of West Georgia, Carrollton, 30118*
Toccoa Falls College, Toccoa Falls, 30598
University of Georgia, Athens, 30602*

Valdosta State University, Valdosta, 31698*
Wesleyan College, Macon, 31210

1999 *U.S. News & World Report*'s Top Fifty:

18. University of Georgia

HAWAII

State of Hawaii, Department of Education
Office of Personnel Services—Teacher Recruitment
PO Box 2360
Honolulu, HI 96804
808–586–3420
http://www.kl2.hi.us

Beginning Salary	**Average Salary**
$25,436	$36,829
Enrollment	**Per Pupil Spending**
188,485	$6,078

Number of Teachers

10,500

Teacher Test

Praxis I PPST *or* CBT: Reading, Writing, Math; *or* CBT Praxis II Specialty Area Tests; Principles of Learning and Teaching (PLT)

State Approved Secondary Teacher Education Institutions

Brigham Young University–Hawaii, Laie, Oahu, 96762
Chaminade University of Honolulu, Honolulu, 96816
University of Hawaii, Hilo, 96720–4091
University of Hawaii–Manoa, Honolulu, 96822
University of Phoenix–Hawaii, Honolulu, 96813

1999 *U.S. News & World Report*'s Top Fifty: None

IDAHO

Idaho State Department of Education, Teacher Certification
PO Box 83720
Boise, ID 83720–0027
208–332–6880
http://www.sde.state.id.us/dept/

Beginning Salary $19,667	**Average Salary** $31,772
Enrollment 245,252	**Per Pupil Spending** $4,210

Number of Teachers

12,784

Teacher Test

No Test

State Approved Secondary Teacher Education Institutions (*NCATE Accreditation)

Boise State University, Boise, 83725*
College of Idaho, Caldwell, 83605
Idaho State University, Pocatello, 83209–2698*
Lewis-Clark State College, Lewiston, 83501–2698*
Northwest Nazarene, Nampa, 83686*
University of Idaho, Moscow, 83844–4253*

1999 *U.S. News & World Report*'s Top Fifty: None

ILLINOIS

Illinois State Department of Education
Division of Professional Preparation, Certification & Placement
100 N. First Street
Springfield, IL 62777
217–782–2805
http://www.state.il.us/educate/

Beginning Salary $26,753	**Average Salary** $42,086
Enrollment 1,961,299	**Per Pupil Spending** $6,136

Number of Teachers

113,538

Teacher Test

Illinois Certification Testing System (ICTS) Basic Skills Test & subject-matter test

State Approved Secondary Teacher Education Institutions (*NCATE Accreditation)

Augustana College, Rock Island, 61201–2296*
Aurora College, Aurora, 60506–4892
Barat College, Lake Forest, 60045
Benedictine University, Lisle, 60532–0900
Blackburn College, Carlinville, 62626
Bradley University, Peoria, 61625*
Chicago State University, Chicago, 60628*
College of St. Francis, Joliet, 60435–6188
Columbia College, Chicago, 60605
Concordia University, River Forest, 60305*
DePaul University, Chicago, 60604*
Dominican University, River Forest, 60305–1099
Eastern Illinois University, Charleston, 61920–3099*
Elmhurst College, Elmhurst, 60126–3296*
Eureka College, Eureka, 61530
Governors State University, University Park, 60466
Greenville College, Greenville, 62246–0159
Illinois College, Jacksonville, 62650–2299
Illinois State University, Normal, 61761*
Illinois Wesleyan University, Bloomington, 61702–2900
Judson College, Elgin, 60123–1498
Knox College, Galesburg, 61401
Lake Forest College, Lake Forest, 60045–2239
Lewis University, Romeoville, 60446
Loyola University, Chicago, 60611
MacMurray College, Jacksonville, 62650
McKendree College, Lebanon, 62254
Millikin University, Decatur, 62522
Monmouth College, Monmouth, 61462
National-Louis University, Evanston, 60201
North Central College, Naperville, 60566
Northeastern Illinois University, Chicago, 60525
Northern Illinois University, Dekalb, 60115*
North Park University, Chicago, 60625–4987
Northwestern University, Evanston, 60208
Olivet Nazarene University, Kankakee, 60901–0592
Principia College, Elsah, 62028
Quincy College, Quincy, 62301–2699
Rockford College, Rockford, 61108
Roosevelt University, Chicago, 60605*
St. Xavier College, Chicago, 60655

Southern Illinois University, Carbondale, 62901*
Southern Illinois University, Edwardsville, 62026–1045*
Trinity Christian College, Palos Heights, 60463
Trinity International University, Deerfield, 60015
University of Chicago, Chicago, 60637
University of Illinois, Chicago, 60680
University of Illinois, Springfield, 62794
University of Illinois–Urbana-Champaign, Urbana, 61801
Western Illinois University, Macomb, 61455–1390*
Wheaton College, Wheaton, 60187–5593*

1999 *U.S. News & World Report*'s Top Fifty:

11. University of Illinois–Urbana-Champaign
18. Northwestern University

INDIANA

Indiana Professional Standards Board
251 E. Ohio, Suite 201
Indianapolis, IN 46204
317–232–9010
http://www.doe.state.in.us

Beginning Salary
$24,216

Average Salary
$38,750

Enrollment
984,610

Per Pupil Spending
$5,826

Number of Teachers

55,821

Teacher Test

Praxis II Core Battery: General Knowledge, Communication Skills, Professional Knowledge; Praxis II Specialty Area Tests

State Approved Secondary Teacher Certification Institutions (*NCATE Accreditation)

Anderson University, Anderson, 46012*
Ball State University, Muncie, 47306*
Bethel College, Mishawaka, 46545*
Butler University, Indianapolis, 46208*
Calumet College of St. Joseph, Whiting, 46394
DePauw University, Greencastle, 46135*
Franklin College, Franklin, 46131*

Goshen College, Goshen, 46526*
Grace College, Winona Lake, 46590
Hanover College, Hanover, 47243*
Huntington College, Huntington, 46750*
Indiana State University, Terre Haute, 47809*
Indiana University–Bloomington, Bloomington, 47405*
Indiana University East, Richmond, 47374–1289*
Indiana University–Kokomo, Kokomo, 46904–9003*
Indiana University Northwest, Gary, 46408*
Indiana University–Purdue University, Ft. Wayne, 46805–1499*
Indiana University–Purdue University, Indianapolis, 46202–5143
Indiana University–South Bend, South Bend, 46634*
Indiana University-Southeast, New Albany, 47150–6405*
Indiana Wesleyan University, Marion, 46953–9980*
Manchester College, North Manchester, 46962–0365*
Marian College, Indianapolis, 46222*
Oakland City University, Oakland City, 47660*
Purdue University, West Lafayette, 47907*
Purdue University–Calumet, Hammond, 46323*
St. Francis College, Fort Wayne, 46808*
St. Joseph's College, Rensselaer, 47978*
St. Mary's College, Notre Dame, 46556*
St. Mary-of-the-Woods College, St. Mary of the Woods, 47876*
Taylor University, Upland, 46989–1001*
Tri-State University, Angola, 46703
University of Evansville, Evansville, 47722–0329*
University of Indianapolis, Indianapolis, 46227–3697*
University of Southern Indiana, Evansville, 47712*
Valparaiso University, Valparaiso, 46383*
Wabash College, Crawfordsville, 47933–0352

1999 *U.S. News & World Report*'s Top Fifty:

13. Indiana University–Bloomington

IOWA

Board of Educational Examiners
Licensing Bureau
Grimes Office Building
East 14th and Grand Street
Des Moines, IA 50319–0146
515–281–3245
http://www.state.ia.us/educate/depteduc

Beginning Salary	**Average Salary**
$21,338	$33,296

Beginning Salary
$21,338

Average Salary
$33,296

Enrollment
504,511

Per Pupil Spending
$5,483

Number of Teachers

32,318

Teacher Test

No Test

State Approved Secondary Teacher Education Institutions (*NCATE Accreditation)

Briar Cliff College, Sioux City, 51104–0100
Buena Vista College, Storm Lake, 50588
Central College, Pella, 50219
Clarke College, Dubuque, 52001
Coe College, Cedar Rapids, 52402
Cornell College, Mt. Vernon, 52314–1098
Dordt College, Sioux Center, 51250
Drake University, Des Moines, 50311
Graceland College, Lamoni, 50140*
Grand View College, Des Moines, 50316–1599
Grinnell College, Grinnell, 50112
Iowa State University, Ames, 50011–2010
Iowa Wesleyan College, Mt. Pleasant, 52641
Loras College, Dubuque, 52004–0178
Luther College, Decorah, 52101*
Maharishi International University, Fairfield, 52557
Marycrest International University, Davenport, 52804
Morningside College, Sioux City, 51106*
Mt. Mercy College, Cedar Rapids, 52402
Mt. St. Clare College, Clinton, 52732–2967
Northwestern College, Orange City, 51041*
St. Ambrose College, Davenport, 52803
Simpson College, Indianola, 50125
University of Dubuque, Dubuque, 52001
University of Iowa, Iowa City, 52242–1396
University of Northern Iowa, Cedar Falls, 50614–0018
Upper Iowa University, Fayette, 52142
Wartburg College, Waverly, 50677–0903*

Westmar College, LeMars, 51031–2697
William Penn College, Oskaloosa, 52577

1999 *U.S. News & World Report*'s Top Fifty:

27. University of Iowa

KANSAS

Kansas State Board of Education, Certification Section
120 SE 10th Avenue
Topeka, KS 66612–1182
913–296–2288
http://www.ksbe.state.ks.us

Beginning Salary	**Average Salary**
$21,607	$36,136
Enrollment	**Per Pupil Spending**
465,140	$5,817

Number of Teachers

30,729

Teacher Test

Praxis I PPST: Reading, Writing, Math; Praxis II Core Battery: Professional Knowledge

State Approved Secondary Teacher Education Institutions (*NCATE Accreditation)

Baker University, Baldwin City, 66006*
Benedictine College, Atchison, 66002*
Bethany College, Lindsborg, 67456*
Bethel College, North Newton, 67117
Emporia State University, Emporia, 6680–5087*
Fort Hays State University, Hays, 67601–4099*
Friends University, Wichita, 67213*
Kansas Newman College, Wichita, 67213
Kansas State University, Manhattan, 66506*
Kansas Wesleyan, Salina, 67401–6196
McPherson College, McPherson, 67460
Mid-America Nazarene College, Olathe, 66062–1899
Ottawa University, Ottawa, 66067–3399
Pittsburg State University, Pittsburg, 66762*
St. Mary College, Leavenworth, 66048*
Southwestern College, Winfield, 67156–2499

Sterling College, Sterling, 67579
Tabor College, Hillsboro, 67063
University of Kansas, Lawrence, 66045*
Washburn University, Topeka, 66621*
Wichita State University, Wichita, 67260*

1999 *U.S. News & World Report*'s Top Fifty:

24. University of Kansas

KENTUCKY

Kentucky Department of Education
Office of Teacher Education & Certification, Div. of Certification
1024 Capitol Center Drive, Capitol Plaza Tower
Frankfort, KY 40601
502–573–4606
http://www.kde.state.ky.us

Beginning Salary	**Average Salary**
$22,457	$34,024
Enrollment	**Per Pupil Spending**
663,071	$5,217

Number of Teachers

39,120

Teacher Test

Praxis II Core Battery: Communication Skills, General Knowledge, Professional Knowledge; Praxis II Specialty Area Tests

State Approved Secondary Teacher Education Institutions (*NCATE Accreditation)

Alice Lloyd College, Pippa Passes, 41844
Ashbury College, Wilmore, 40390–1198
Bellarmine College, Louisville, 40205*
Berea College, Berea, 40404*
Brescia College, Owensboro, 42301
Campbellsville College, Campbellsville, 42718–2799
Centre College, Danville, 40422
Cumberland College, Williamsburg, 40769
Eastern Kentucky University, Richmond, 40475*
Georgetown College, Georgetown, 40324–1696
Kentucky Christian College, Grayson, 41143
Kentucky State University, Frankfort, 40601*

Kentucky Wesleyan College, Owensboro, 42302–1039
Morehead State University, Morehead, 40351*
Murray State University, Murray, 42071*
Northern Kentucky University, Highland Heights, 41099*
Pikeville College, Pikeville, 41501
Spalding University, Louisville, 40203*
Thomas More College, Crestview Hills, 41017–3248
Transylvania University, Lexington, 40508–1797
Union College, Barbourville, 40906–9989
University of Kentucky, Lexington, 40506–0032*
University of Louisville, Louisville, 40292*
Western Kentucky University, Bowling Green, 42101–3576*

1999 *U.S. News & World Report's* **Top Fifty**: None

LOUISIANA

Louisiana Department of Education
Bureau of Education, Teacher Certification, and Continuing Education
PO Box 94064
Baton Rouge, LA 70804–9064
504–342–3490
http://www.doe.state.la.us

Beginning Salary
$19,406

Average Salary
$27,565

Enrollment
777,570

Per Pupil Spending
$4,761

Number of Teachers
46,980

Teacher Test

Praxis II Core Battery: General Knowledge, Communication Skills, Professional Knowledge; Praxis II Specialty Area Tests

State Approved Secondary Teacher Education Institutions (*NCATE Accreditation)

Centenary College, Shreveport, 71104
Dillard University, New Orleans, 70122–3097
Grambling State University, Grambling, 71245*
Louisiana College, Pineville, 71359–6560
Louisiana State University and A&M College, Baton Rouge, 70803*
Louisiana State University, Shreveport, 71115*
Louisiana Technical University, Ruston, 71272*
Loyola University, New Orleans, 70118

McNeese State University, Lake Charles, 70609–2495*
Nicholls State University, Thibodaux, 70301*
Northeast Louisiana University, Monroe, 71209*
Northwestern State University, Natchitoches, 71497*
Our Lady of Holy Cross College, New Orleans, 70131–7399
Southeastern Louisiana University, Hammond, 70402*
Southern University and A&M College, Baton Rouge, 70813*
Southern University–New Orleans, New Orleans, 70126
University of New Orleans, New Orleans, 70148*
University of Southwestern Louisiana, Lafayette, 70503*
Xavier University of Louisiana, New Orleans, 70125*

1999 *U.S. News & World Report*'s Top Fifty: None

MAINE

Department of Education
Certification Office
23 State House Station
Augusta, ME 04333–0023
207–287–5944
http://www.state.me.us/education/

Beginning Salary
$20,725

Average Salary
$33,807

Enrollment
218,560

Per Pupil Spending
$6,428

Number of Teachers
15,392

Teacher Test

Praxis I PPST *or* CBT: Reading, Writing, Mathematics for vocational certificates only; Praxis II Core Battery: General Knowledge, Communication Skills, Professional Knowledge

State Approved Secondary Teacher Education Institutions (*NCATE Accreditation)

Colby College, Waterville, 04901
College of the Atlantic, Bar Harbor, 04609
University of New England, Biddeford, 04005
University of Maine, Farmington, 04938–1990*
University of Maine, Orono, 04469–5713*
University of Maine, Presque Isle, 04769
University of Southern Maine, Portland, 04104–9300*

1999 *U.S. News & World Report*'s **Top Fifty**: None

MARYLAND

State Department of Education
Division of Certification and Accreditation
200 West Baltimore Street
Baltimore, MD 21201
410–767–0412
http://www.msde.state.md.us/

Beginning Salary	**Average Salary**
$26,846	$42,334
Enrollment	**Per Pupil Spending**
818,947	$7,245

Number of Teachers
47,819

Teacher Test

Praxis I PPST *or* CBT: Reading, Writing, Math; Praxis II Core Battery: General Knowledge, Communication Skills, Professional Knowledge; Praxis II Specialty Area Tests

State Approved Secondary Teacher Education Institutions (*NCATE Accreditation)

Bowie State College, Bowie, 20715*
College of Notre Dame of Maryland, Baltimore, 21210
Columbia Union, Takoma Park, 20912
Coppin State College, Baltimore, 21216*
Frostsburg State College, Frostsburg, 21532
Goucher College, Baltimore, 21204
Hood College, Frederick, 21701–8575
Johns Hopkins University, Baltimore, 21218
Maryland Institute College of Art, Baltimore, 21217
Morgan State University, Baltimore, 21251*
Mount St. Mary's College, Emmitsburg, 21727
St. Mary's College of Maryland, St. Mary's City, 20686
Salisbury State College, Salisbury, 21801
Towson State College, Baltimore, 21252–0001
University of Maryland–Baltimore County, Baltimore, 21250
University of Maryland–College Park, College Park, 20742*
University of Maryland–Eastern Shore, Princess Anne, 21853
Washington College, Chestertown, 21620–1197
Western Maryland College, Westminister, 21157–4390

1999 *U.S. News & World Report*'s Top Fifty:

22. University of Maryland–College Park

MASSACHUSETTS

Massachusetts Department of Education, Office of Certification
350 Main Street, PO Box 9140
Malden, MA 02148–9140
617–388–3300
http://www.doe.mass.edu

Beginning Salary	**Average Salary**
$25,815	$43,479
Enrollment	**Per Pupil Spending**
936,794	$7,287

Number of Teachers

62,710

Teacher Test

Massachusetts Educator Certification Tests: Communication and Literacy Skills; Subject Matter Tests

State Approved Secondary Teacher Education Institutions (*NCATE Accreditation)

American International College, Springfield, 01109
Atlantic Union College, South Lancaster, 01561
Bay Path College, Longmeadow, 01106
Boston College, Chestnut Hill, 02167*
Boston University, Boston, 02215
Bradford College, Bradford, 01835
Brandeis University, Waltham, 02254–9110
Bridgewater State College, Bridgewater, 02325*
Clark University, Worcester, 01610–1477
College of the Holy Cross, Worcester, 01610
Eastern Nazarene, Quincy, 02170
Elms College, Chicopee, 01013
Emmanuel College, Boston, 02115
Fitchburg State College, Fitchburg, 01420–2697*
Framingham State College, Framingham, 01701–9101
Gordon College, Wenham, 01984
Harvard Divinity School, Cambridge, 02138
Harvard Graduate School, Cambridge, 02138
Lesley College, Cambridge, 02138–2790

Massachusetts College of Liberal Arts, North Adams, 01247–4100
Merrimack College, North Andover, 01845
Mt. Holyoke College, South Hadley, 01075
Northeastern University, Boston, 02115
Pine Manor College, Chestnut Hill, 02167
Regis College, Weston, 02193–1571
Salem State College, Salem, 01970*
Simmons College, Boston, 02115
Smith College, Northampton, 01063
Stonehill College, North Easton, 02357
Suffolk University, Boston, 02108–2770
Tufts University, Medford, 02115
University of Massachusetts–Amherst, Amherst, 01003*
University of Massachusetts–Boston, Boston, 02125–3393
University of Massachusetts–Dartmouth, Dartmouth, 02747–2300
University of Massachusetts–Lowell, Lowell, 01854*
Wellesley College, Wellesley, 02181
Westfield State College, Westfield, 01086
Western New England College, Springfield, 01119
Wheaton College, Norton, 02766
Worcester State College, Worcester, 01605

1999 *U.S. News & World Report*'s Top Fifty:

  1. Harvard University
31. Boston College

MICHIGAN

Michigan Department of Education
Office of Professional Preparation & Certification Services
PO Box 30008
Lansing, MI 48909
517–373–3310
http://www.mde.state.mi.us

Beginning Salary
$25,635

Enrollment
1,662,100

Number of Teachers
83,179

Average Salary
$46,074

Per Pupil Spending
$6,994

Teacher Test

Michigan Test for Teacher Certification (MTTC)

State Approved Secondary Teacher Education Institutions (*NCATE Accreditation)

Adrian College, Adrian, 49221–2575
Albion College, Albion, 49224
Alma College, Alma, 48801
Andrews University, Berrien Springs, 49104–0740*
Aquinas College, Grand Rapids, 49506–1799
Calvin College, Grand Rapids, 49546*
Central Michigan University, Mt. Pleasant, 48859*
Concordia College, Ann Arbor, 48105
Cornerstone College and Grand Rapids Baptist Seminary, Grand Rapids, 49505–5897
Eastern Michigan University, Ypsilanti, 48197*
Ferris State College, Big Rapids, 49307
Grand Valley State College, Allendale, 49401*
Hillsdale College, Hillsdale, 49242
Hope College, Holland, 49423*
Kalamazoo College, Kalamazoo, 49006–3295
Madonna University, Livonia, 48150–1173*
Marygrove College, Detroit, 48221–2599*
Michigan State University, East Lansing, 48824–1046
Michigan Tech, Houghton, 49931–1295
Northern Michigan University, Marquette, 49855*
Oakland University, Rochester, 48309–4401*
Olivet College, Olivet, 49076
Saginaw Valley College, University Center, 48710–0001*
Siena Heights College, Adrian, 49221
Spring Arbor College, Spring Arbor, 49283*
University of Detroit Mercy, Detroit, 48219–0900
University of Michigan, Ann Arbor, 48109
University of Michigan, Dearborn, 48128
University of Michigan, Flint, 45502
Wayne State University, Detroit, 48202*
Western Michigan University, Kalamazoo, 49008*

1999 *U.S. News & World Report*'s Top Fifty:

  8. University of Michigan–Ann Arbor
 13. Michigan State University

MINNESOTA

Minnesota Department of Children, Families, and Learning
Personnel Licensing Section
616 Capitol Square Building, 550 Cedar Street
St. Paul, MN 55101–2273
651–582–8691
http://www.educ.state.mn.us/

Beginning Salary
$23,998

Average Salary
$37,991

Enrollment
836,700

Per Pupil Spending
$6,000

Number of Teachers
46,971

Teacher Test

Praxis I PPST *or* CBT: Reading, Writing, Math

**State Approved Secondary Teacher Education Institutions
(*NCATE Accreditation)**

Augsburg College, Minneapolis, 55454*
Bernidji State University, Bernidji, 56601–2699*
Bethel College, St. Paul, 55112*
Carleton College, Northfield, 55057
College of St. Benedict, St. Joseph, 56374–2099*
College of St. Catharine, St. Paul, 55105*
College of St. Scholastica, Duluth, 55811
Concordia College, Moorhead, 56562*
Concordia University, St. Paul 55104–5494*
Gustavus Adolphus College, St. Peter, 56082–1498*
Hamline University, St. Paul, 55104–1284*
Macalester College, St. Paul, 55105
Mankato State University, Mankato, 56002–8400*
Moorhead State University, Moorhead, 56563*
St. Cloud State University, St. Cloud, 56301–4498*
St. Mary's University of Minnesota, Winona, 55987–1399
St. Olaf College, Northfield, 55057–1098*
Southwest State University, Marshall, 56258
University of Minnesota, Duluth, 55812–2496*
University of Minnesota–Twin Cities, Minneapolis, 55455*
University of Minnesota, Morris, 56267–2199*
University of St. Thomas, St. Paul, 55105*
Winona State University, Winona, 55987*

1999 *U.S. News & World Report's* **Top Fifty:**

10. University of Minnesota–Twin Cities

MISSISSIPPI

Mississippi Department of Education
Office of Educator Licensure
359 NW Street, PO Box 771
Jackson, MS 39205–0771
601–359–3483
http://mdek12.state.ms.us

Beginning Salary   **Average Salary**
$20,150 $28,482

Enrollment   **Per Pupil Spending**
504,168 $4,080

Number of Teachers

28,997

Teacher Test

Praxis I PPST *or* CBT: Reading, Writing, Math; Praxis II Principles of
Learning and Teaching; Praxis II Specialty Area Tests

**State Approved Secondary Teacher Education Institutions
(*NCATE Accreditation)**

Alcorn State University, Lorman, 39096*
Belhaven College, Jackson, 39202
Blue Mountain College, Blue Mountain, 38610
Delta State University, Cleveland, 38733*
Jackson State University, Jackson, 39217*
Millsaps College, Jackson, 39210*
Mississippi College, Clinton, 39058*
Mississippi State University, Mississippi State, 39762*
Mississippi University for Women, Columbus, 39701*
Mississippi Valley State University, Itta Bena, 38941–1400*
Rust College, Holly Springs, 38635
Tougaloo College, Tougaloo, 39174
University of Mississippi, University, 38677*
University of Southern Mississippi, Hattiesburg, 39406*
William Carey College, Hattiesburg, 39401–5499

1999 *U.S. News & World Report*'s Top Fifty: None

MISSOURI

Office of Teacher Certification
Department of Elementary & Secondary Education
PO Box 480
Jefferson City, MO 65102–0480
573–751–0051
http://www.dese.state.mo.us

Beginning Salary
$21,996

Average Salary
$34,292

Enrollment
883,327

Per Pupil Spending
$5,383

Number of Teachers
57,951

Teacher Test

Praxis II Specialty Area Tests

State Approved Secondary Teacher Education Institutions (*NCATE Accreditation)

Avila College, Kansas City, 64145
Central Methodist College, Fayette, 65248
Central Missouri State University, Warrensburg, 64093*
College of the Ozarks, Point Lookout, 65726
Columbia College, Columbia, 65216
Culver-Stockton College, Canton, 63435
Drury College, Springfield, 65802*
Evangel College, Springfield, 65802*
Fontbonne College, St. Louis, 63105
Hannibal La-Grange College, Hannibal, 63401
Harris-Stowe State College, St. Louis, 63103*
Lincoln University, Jefferson City, 65102–0029*
Lindenwood University, St. Charles, 63301
Maryville College, St. Louis, 63141–7299*
Missouri Baptist College, St. Louis, 63141–8698
Missouri Southern State College, Joplin, 64801*
Missouri Valley College, Marshall, 65340
Missouri Western State College, St. Joseph, 64507*
Northwest Missouri State University, Maryville, 64468*
Park College, Kansas City, 64152–9974

Rockhurst College, Kansas City, 64110–2561
St. Louis University, St. Louis, 63103–2097*
Southeast Missouri State University, Cape Girardeau, 63701*
Southwest Baptist University, Bolivar, 65613
Southwest Missouri State University, Springfield, 65804
Truman State University, Kirkville, 63501*
University of Missouri–Columbia, Columbia, 65211
University of Missouri–Kansas City, Kansas City, 64110*
University of Missouri–St. Louis, St. Louis, 63121*
Washington University, St. Louis, 63130–4899*
Webster University, St. Louis, 63119–3194
William Jewell College, Liberty, 64068
William Woods University, Fulton, 65251

1999 *U.S. News & World Report*'s Top Fifty:

34. University of Missouri–Columbia
39. Washington University, St. Louis

MONTANA

Office of Public Instruction, Certification Services
PO Box 202501
Helena, MT 59620–2501
406–444–3150
http://www.metnet.state.mt.gov

Beginning Salary
$19,992

Average Salary
$30,202

Enrollment
166,909

Per Pupil Spending
$5,692

Number of Teachers

10,076

Teacher Test

Praxis I PPST *or* CBT: Reading, Writing, Math; *or* any standard examination required for another state's certification

State Approved Secondary Teacher Education Institutions (*NCATE Accreditation)

Carroll College, Helena, 59625
Montana State University–Bozeman, Bozeman, 59717*
Montana State University–Billings, Billings, 59101–0298*

Northern Montana College, Havre, 59501
Rocky Mountain College, Billings, 59102
University of Great Falls, Great Falls, 59405
University of Montana, Missoula, 59802*
Western Montana College of the University of Montana, Dillon, 59725*

1999 *U.S. News & World Report*'s Top Fifty: None

NEBRASKA

Nebraska Department of Education
Teacher Certification Office
301 Centennial Mall S., Box 94987
Lincoln, NE 68509–4987
402–471–2496
http://nde4.nde.state.ne.us

Beginning Salary
$21,299

Average Salary
$32,395

Enrollment
292,121

Per Pupil Spending
$5,935

Number of Teachers

20,028

Teacher Test

Praxis I PPST *or* CBT: Reading, Writing, Math

**State Approved Secondary Teacher Education Institutions
(*NCATE Accreditation)**

Chadron State College, Chadron, 69337*
College of St. Mary, Omaha, 68124
Concordia College, Seward, 68434*
Creighton University, Omaha, 68178–0001*
Dana College, Blair, 68008–1099*
Doane College, Crete, 68333*
Hastings College, Hastings, 68901*
Midland Lutheran College, Fremont, 68025
Nebraska Wesleyan University, Lincoln, 68504*
Peru State College, Peru, 68421*
Union College, Lincoln, 68506*
University of Nebraska, Kearney, 68849*
University of Nebraska, Lincoln, 68588*
University of Nebraska, Omaha 68182*

Wayne State College, Wayne, 68787*
York College, York, 68467–2699

1999 *U.S. News & World Report*'s **Top Fifty**: None

NEVADA

Nevada Department of Education
1820 E. Sahara, Suite 205
Las Vegas, NV 89104
702–486–6455
http://www.nsn.k12.nv.us/nvdoe

Beginning Salary	**Average Salary**
$25,576	$37,199
Enrollment	**Per Pupil Spending**
282,131	$5,160

Number of Teachers

13,878

Teacher Test

Praxis I PPST or CBT: Reading, Writing, Math; Praxis II Core Battery: Professional Knowledge; Praxis II Specialty Area Tests

State Approved Secondary Teacher Education Institutions (*NCATE Accreditation)

University of Nevada–Las Vegas, Las Vegas, 89154*
University of Nevada–Reno, Reno, 89557*

1999 *U.S. News & World Report*'s **Top Fifty**: None

NEW HAMPSHIRE

New Hampshire Department of Education
Bureau of Credentialing
State Office Park South, 101 Pleasant Street
Concord, NH 03301–3860
603–271–2407
http://www.state.nh.us/doe/education.html

Beginning Salary	**Average Salary**
$23,510	$36,813
Enrollment	**Per Pupil Spending**
194,581	$5,859

Number of Teachers

12,346

Teacher Test

Praxis I PPST *or* CBT: Reading, Writing, Math

State Approved Secondary Teacher Education Institutions (*NCATE Accreditation)

Antioch New England Graduate School, Keene, 03431
Dartmouth College, Hanover, 03755
Franklin Pierce College, Rindge, 03461–0060
Keene State College, Keene, 03435*
New England College, Henniker, 03242
New Hampshire College, Manchester, 03106–1045
Notre Dame College, Manchester, 03104
Plymouth State College, Plymouth, 03264*
River College, Nashua, 03060–5086
St. Anselm College, Manchester, 03102
University of New Hampshire, Durham, 03824*
Upper Valley Teacher Training Program, Hanover, 03766

1999 *U.S. News & World Report*'s Top Fifty: None

NEW JERSEY

State of New Jersey, Department of Education
Office of Licensing and Credentials
100 Riverview Plaza, PO Box 500
Trenton, NJ 08625–0500
609–292–2070
http://www.state.nj.us/education

Beginning Salary
$31,435

Average Salary
$49,277

Enrollment
1,221,013

Per Pupil Spending
$9,774

Number of Teachers

86,706

Teacher Test

Praxis II Core Battery: General Knowledge for elementary teachers; Praxis II Specialty Area Tests for all others

State Approved Secondary Teacher Education Institutions (*NCATE Accreditation)

Caldwell College, Caldwell, 07006
The College of New Jersey, Ewing, 08628–0718*
College of St. Elizabeth, Morristown, 07960–6989
Fairleigh Dickinson University, Madison, 07940
Georgian Court College, Lakewood, 08701–2697
Kean University, Union, 07083–0411*
Monmouth University, West Long Branch, 07764–1898
Montclair State University, Upper Montclair, 07043*
New Jersey City University, Jersey City, 07305*
Princeton University, Princeton, 08544–0430
Ramapo College of New Jersey, Mahwah, 07430
Richard Stockton College of New Jersey, Pleasantville, 08240–9988
Rider University, Lawrenceville, 08648–3099*
Rowan University, Glassboro, 08028*
Rutgers State University of New Jersey, New Brunswick, 08903
St. Peter's College, Jersey City, 07306–5997
Seton Hall University, South Orange, 07079–2691
Westminster Choir College, Princeton, 08540
William Paterson University of New Jersey, Wayne, 07470*

1999 U.S. News & World Report's Top Fifty:

33. Rutgers State University, New Brunswick

NEW MEXICO

State of New Mexico Department of Education
300 Don Gaspar, Room 101
Santa Fe, NM 87501–2786
505–827–6587
http://sde.state.nm.us

Beginning Salary	**Average Salary**
$22,634	$29,904
Enrollment	**Per Pupil Spending**
330,522	$4,586

Number of Teachers

19,398

Teacher Test

New Mexico Teacher Assessments: Basic Skills, General Knowledge, Teacher Competencies

State Approved Secondary Teacher Education Institutions (*NCATE Accreditation)

College of the Southwest, Hobbs, 88240–9987
College of Santa Fe, Santa Fe, 87505–5634
Eastern New Mexico University, Portales, 88130*
New Mexico Highland University, Las Vegas, 87701
New Mexico Mining & Technical College, Socorro, 87801
New Mexico State University, Las Cruces, 88003–8001*
University of New Mexico, Albuquerque, 89131*
Western New Mexico University, Silver City, 88061

1999 *U.S. News & World Report*'s **Top Fifty**: None

NEW YORK

New York State Education Department
Office of Teaching, Cultural Education Center
Albany, NY 12234
518–474–3901
http://www.nysed.gov

Beginning Salary	**Average Salary**
$28,749	$49,488
Enrollment	**Per Pupil Spending**
2,825,000	$9,623

Number of Teachers

181,559

Teacher Test

New York State Teacher Certification Examinations (NYSTCE); *or* Praxis II Core Battery Tests (until 9/99)

State Approved Secondary Teacher Education Institutions (*NCATE Accreditation)

Adelphi University, Garden City, 11530
Alfred University, Alfred, 14802–1205
Barnard College, New York City, 10027–6598
Canisius College, Buffalo, 14208
City College, New York City, 10031
Colgate University, Hamilton, 13346
College of Mt. St. Vincent, Bronx, 10471
College of New Rochelle, New Rochelle, 10805–2339

College of Staten Island of the City University of New York, Staten Island, 10314–6600
College of St. Rose, Albany, 12203
Columbia University, Teachers College, New York City, 10027
Concordia College, Bronxville, 10708
Cornell University, Ithaca, 14850
Daemen College, Amherst, 14226–3592
Dominican College, Orangeburg, 10962
Dowling College, Oakdale, 11769–1999
D'Youville College, Buffalo, 14201
Elmira College, Elmira, 14901
Fordham University, Bronx, 10458*
Hartwick College, Oneonta, 13820–4620
Herbert H. Lehman College, Bronx, 10468
Hobart & William Smith Colleges, Geneva, 14456–3397
Hofstra University, Hempstead, 11549*
Houghton College, Houghton, 14744
Hunter College of the City University of New York, New York City, 10021–5085
Iona College, New Rochelle, 10801–1890
Ithaca College, Ithaca, 14850–7020
Keuka College, Keuka Park, 14478
LeMoyne College, Syracuse, 13214–1399
Long Island University, Brooklyn, 11201
Long Island University–C. W. Post College, Greenvale, 11548–1300
Long Island University–Southampton College, Southampton, 11968
Manhattan College, Riverdale, 10471
Manhattanville College, Purchase, 10577
Marist College, Poughkeepsie, 12601
Marymount College, Tarrytown, 10591
Marymount Manhattan College, New York City, 10021
Molloy College, Rockville Center, 11570
Mt. St. Mary College, Newburgh, 12550
Nazareth College of Rochester, Rochester, 14618–3790
New School for Social Research, New York City, 10011–8878
New York Institute of Technology, Old Westbury, 11568–8000
New York University, New York City, 10011
Niagara University, Niagara University, 14109*
Nyack College, Nyack, 10960
Pace University–White Plains, 10606
Pace University, New York City, 10038
Pace University, Pleasantville, 10570
Queens College of the City University of New York, Flushing, 11367–1597
Rensselaer Polytechnic Institute, Troy, 12180–3590

Roberts Wesleyan College, Rochester, 14624–1997
Rochester Institute of Technology, Rochester, 14623
Russell Sage College, Troy, 12180
St. Bonaventure University, St. Bonaventure, 14778–2284
St. Francis College, Brooklyn, 11201
St. John Fisher College, Rochester, 14618
St. John's University, Jamaica, 11439
St. John's University, Staten Island, 10301
St. Joseph's College, Brooklyn, 11205
St. Joseph's College–Suffolk, Patchogue, 11772–2603
St. Lawrence University, Canton, 13617
St. Thomas Aquinas College, Sparkhill, 10976
Siena College, Londonville, 12211–1462
State University of New York, Albany, 12222
State University of New York, Binghamton, 13902–6000
State University of New York, Buffalo, 14260
State University of New York, Stony Brook, 11794
State University of New York College at Buffalo, 14222*
State University of New York College at Cortland, 13045
State University of New York College at Fredonia, 14063
State University of New York College at Geneseo, 14454
State University of New York College at New Paltz, 12561–2443
State University of New York College at Old Westbury, 11568–0210
State University of New York College at Oneonta, 13820–4015
State University of New York College at Oswego, 13126
State University of New York College at Plattsburgh, 12901–2681
State University of New York College at Potsdam, 13676
State University of New York College at Purchase, 10577–1400
Syracuse University, Syracuse, 13244
Union College, Schenectady, 12308–2311
University of Rochester, Rochester, 14627–0251
Utica College of Syracuse University, Utica, 13502–4892
Vassar College, Poughkeepsie, 12604
Wagner College, Staten Island, 10301
Wells College, Aurora, 13026
Yeshiva University, New York City, 10033–3201
York College of the City University of New York, Jamaica, 11451–0001

1999 *U.S. News & World Report*'s Top Fifty:

 2. Columbia University, Teachers College
16. New York University
29. Cornell University
44. SUNY–Albany

46. Syracuse University
46. SUNY–Buffalo

NORTH CAROLINA

Department of Public Instruction, Licensure Section
301 North Wilmington Street, Education Building
Raleigh, NC 27601–2825
919–733–0377
http://www.dpi.state.nc.us

Beginning Salary
$20,620

Average Salary
$31,279

Enrollment
1,199,962

Per Pupil Spending
$5,077

Number of Teachers

73,201

Teacher Test

Praxis II Core Battery: Professional Knowledge; Praxis II Specialty Area Tests

State Approved Secondary Teacher Education Institutions (*NCATE Accreditation)

Appalachian State University, Boone, 28608*
Barton College, Wilson, 27893*
Belmont Abbey College, Belmont, 28012*
Bennett College, Greensboro, 27401–3239*
Campbell University, Bules Creek, 27506*
Catawba College, Salisbury, 28144*
Chowan College, Murfreesboro, 27855
Davidson College, Davidson, 28036*
Duke University, Durham, 27706*
East Carolina University, Greenville, 27858–4353*
Elizabeth City State University, Elizabeth City, 27909*
Elon College, Elon, 27244–2010*
Fayetteville State University, Fayetteville, 28301–4298*
Gardner–Webb University, Boiling Springs, 28017–9980*
Greensboro College, Greensboro, 27401–1875*
Guilford College, Greensboro, 27410*
High Point University, High Point, 27262–3598*
Johnson C. Smith University, Charlotte, 28216*

Lees–McRae University, Banner Elk, 28064*
Lenoir–Rhyne College, Hickory, 28603*
Livingstone College, Salisbury, 28144*
Mars Hill College, Mars Hill, 28754*
Meredith College, Raleigh, 27607–5298*
Methodist College, Fayetteville, 28311*
Montreat College, Montreat, 28757*
North Carolina A & T State University, Greensboro, 27411*
North Carolina Central University, Durham, 27707*
North Carolina State University, Raleigh, 27695*
North Carolina Wesleyan University, Rocky Mount, 27804*
Pfeiffer University, Misenheimer, 28109*
Queens College, Charlotte, 28274*
St. Augustine's College, Raleigh, 27610–2298*
Salem College, Winston-Salem, 27108*
Shaw University, Raleigh, 27601*
University of North Carolina, Asheville, 28804–3299*
University of North Carolina, Chapel Hill, 27599–2200*
University of North Carolina, Charlotte, 28223*
University of North Carolina, Greensboro, 27412*
University of North Carolina, Pembroke, 28372*
University of North Carolina, Wilmington, 28403*
Wake Forest University, Winston-Salem, 27109*
Warren Wilson College, Swannanoa, 28815*
Western Carolina University, Cullowhee, 28723*
Wingate University, Wingate, 28174*
Winston-Salem State University, Winston-Salem, 27110*

1999 *U.S. News & World Report*'s Top Fifty:

22. University of North Carolina–Chapel Hill
46. University of North Carolina–Greensboro

NORTH DAKOTA

Education Standards and Practices Board
Office of Certification
600 E. Boulevard Avenue
Bismarck, ND 58505–0540
701–328–2264
http://www.dpi.state.nd.us

Beginning Salary   **Average Salary**
$18,225 $27,738

Enrollment
118,427

Per Pupil Spending
$4,775

Number of Teachers
7,501

Teacher Test

No state-wide test required. Each accredited institution does exit testing of certification candidates; schools use a range of measures from tests to portfolios.

State Approved Secondary Teacher Education Institutions (*NCATE Accreditation)

Dickinson State College, Dickinson, 58601–4896*
Jamestown College, Jamestown, 58405
Mary College, Bismark, 58501
Mayville State University, Mayville, 58257–1299*
Minot State University, Minot, 58707*
North Dakota State University, Fargo, 58105*
University of North Dakota, Grand Forks, 58202*
Valley City State University, Valley City, 58072*

1999 U.S. News & World Report's Top Fifty: None

OHIO

State of Ohio Department of Education
Division of Professional Development & Licensure
65 South Front Street, Room 412
Columbus, OH 43215–4183
614–466–3593
http://www.ode.ohio.gov

Beginning Salary
$20,355

Average Salary
$38,914

Enrollment
1,841,095

Per Pupil Spending
$6,162

Number of Teachers
107,347

Teacher Test

Praxis II Core Battery: General and Professional Knowledge; Praxis II Specialty Area Tests

State Approved Secondary Teacher Education Institutions (*NCATE Accreditation)

Antioch College, Yellow Springs, 45387
Ashland College, Ashland, 44805*

Baldwin-Wallace College, Berea, 44017–2088*
Blufton College, Blufton, 45817
Bowling Green State University, Bowling Green, 43403*
Capital University, Columbus, 43209–2394*
Case Western Reserve University, Cleveland, 44106
Cedarville College, Cedarville, 45314–0601
Central State University, Wilberforce, 45384
Cleveland State University, Cleveland, 44115–2403*
College of Mt. St. Joseph, Cincinnati, 45233–1672
College of Wooster, Wooster, 44691
Defiance College, Defiance, 43512
Denison University, Granville, 43023
Franciscan University of Steubenville, Steubenville, 43952–6701
Heidelberg College, Tiffin, 44883–2434
Hiram College, Hiram, 44234
John Carroll University, University Heights, 44118*
Kent State University, Kent, 44242–0001*
Lake Erie College, Painesville, 44077
Malone College, Canton, 44709
Marietta College, Marietta, 45750–4005
Miami University, Oxford, 45056*
Mt. Union College, Alliance, 44601
Mt. Vernon Nazarene College, Mt. Vernon, 43050
Muskingum College, New Concord, 43762
Notre Dame College, Cleveland, 44121
Oberlin College, Oberlin, 44074
Ohio Dominican College, Columbus, 43219
Ohio Northern University, Ada, 45810*
Ohio State University, Columbus, 43210–1200*
Ohio University, Athens, 45701*
Ohio Wesleyan University, Delaware, 43015
Otterbein College, Westerville, 43081*
University of Akron, Akron, 44325*
University of Cincinnati, Cincinnati, 45221–0127*
University of Dayton, Dayton, 45469*
University of Findlay, Findlay, 45840*
University of the Rio Grande, Rio Grande, 45674
University of Toledo, Toledo, 43606–3398*
Urbana University, Urbana, 43078–2091
Walsh University, Canton, 44720–3396
Wilmington College, Wilmington, 45177
Wittenberg University, Springfield, 45501
Wright State University, Dayton, 45435*
Xavier University, Cincinnati, 45207
Youngstown State University, Youngstown, 44555–0001*

1999 *U.S. News & World Report'*s **Top Fifty:**

7. Ohio State University–Columbus

OKLAHOMA

Oklahoma Department of Education
Professional Standards Section
2500 N. Lincoln Blvd.
Oklahoma City, OK 73105–4599
405–521–3337
http://www.sde.state.ok.us

Beginning Salary	**Average Salary**
$24,187	$29,214
Enrollment	**Per Pupil Spending**
620,379	$4,845

Number of Teachers

39,364

Teacher Test

Oklahoma Teacher Certification Test

State Approved Secondary Teacher Education Institutions (*NCATE Accreditation)

Bartlesville Wesleyan, Bartlesville, 74006
Cameron University, Lawton, 73505*
East Central University, Ada, 74820*
Langston University, Langston, 73505*
Mid-America Bible College, Oklahoma City, 73170
Northeastern Oklahoma State University, Tahlequah, 74464*
Northwestern Oklahoma State University, Alva, 73714*
Oklahoma Baptist University, Shawnee, 74801*
Oklahoma Christian University of Science and Art, Oklahoma City, 73136–1100*
Oklahoma City University, Oklahoma City, 73106
Oklahoma Panhandle State University, Goodwell, 73939
Oklahoma State University, Stillwater, 74078
Oral Roberts University, Tulsa, 74171
Phillips University, Enid, 73701
Southeastern Oklahoma State, Durant, 74701*
Southern Nazarene University, Bethany, 73008*
Southwestern Oklahoma State, Weatherford, 73096*
University of Central Oklahoma, Edmond, 73734*

University of Oklahoma, Norman, 73019*
University of Science & Arts Oklahoma, Chickasha, 73018*
University of Tulsa, Tulsa, 74104*

1999 *U.S. News & World Report*'s Top Fifty:
46. University of Oklahoma

OREGON

Teacher Standards & Practices Commission
255 Capitol Street NE, Public Service Bldg., Suite 105
Salem, OR 97310
503–378–3586
http://www.ode.state.or.us

Beginning Salary   **Average Salary**
$24,592 $40,839

Enrollment   **Per Pupil Spending**
537,783 $6,436

Number of Teachers

26,680

Teacher Test

Praxis I PPST *or* CBT: Reading, Writing, Math; *or* California Basic Educational Skills Test (CBEST); Praxis II Core Battery: Professional Knowledge; Praxis II Specialty Area Tests

State Approved Secondary Teacher Education Institutions (*NCATE Accreditation)

Concordia University, Portland, 97221
Eastern Oregon University, LaGrande, 97850–2899
George Fox University, Newberg, 97132
Lewis & Clark College, Portland, 97219–7899
Linfield College, McMinnville, 97128
Oregon State University, Corvallis, 97331*
Pacific University, Forest Grove, 97116
Portland State University, Portland, 97207–0751*
Southern Oregon University, Ashland, 97520
University of Oregon, Eugene, 97401*
University of Portland, Portland, 97203
Warner Pacific College, Portland, 97215
Western Baptist College, Salem, 97301
Western Oregon University, Monmouth, 97361*
Willamette University, Salem, 97301

1999 *U.S. News & World Report*'s Top Fifty:

16. University of Oregon

PENNSYLVANIA

Pennsylvania Department of Education
Teacher Preparation & Certification
333 Market Street
Harrisburg, PA 17126–0333
717–787–2967
http://www.cas.psu.edu/pde.html

Beginning Salary	**Average Salary**
$29,514	$47,402
Enrollment	**Per Pupil Spending**
1,807,250	$7,109

Number of Teachers

104,921

Teacher Test

Praxis II Core Battery: General Knowledge, Communication Skills, Professional Knowledge; Praxis II Specialty Area Tests

**State Approved Secondary Teacher Education Institutions
(*NCATE Accreditation)**

Albright College, Reading, 19612–5234
Allegheny College, Meadville, 16335
Allentown College of St. Francis de Sales, 18034–9568
Alvernia College, Reading, 19607
Beaver College, Glenside, 19038
Bloomsburg University of Pennsylvania, Bloomsburg, 17815*
Bryn Mawr College, Bryn Mawr, 19010–2899
Bucknell University, Lewisburg, 17837
Cabrini College, Radnor, 19087–3698
California University of Pennsylvania, California, 15419–1394*
Carlow College, Pittsburgh, 15213
Cedar Crest College, Allentown, 18104–6196
Chatham College, Pittsburgh, 15232
Chestnut Hill College, Philadelphia, 19118–2693
Cheyney University of Pennsylvania, Cheyney, 19319
Clarion University of Pennsylvania, Clarion, 16214*
College Misericordia, Dallas, 18612
Delaware Valley College, Doylestown, 18901–2697

Dickinson College, Carlisle, 17013
Drexel University, Philadelphia, 19104
Duquesne University, Pittsburgh, 15282–0201
East Stroudsburg University of Pennsylvania, East Stroudsburg, 18301
Eastern College, Saint Davids, 19087–3696
Edinboro University of Pennsylvania, Edinboro, 16444
Elizabethtown College, Elizabethtown, 17022
Gannon University, Erie, 16541
Geneva College, Beaver Falls, 15010
Gettysburg College, Gettysburg, 17325–1484
Grove City College, Grove City, 16127–2104
Gwynedd-Mercy College, Gwynedd Valley, 19437
Holy Family College, Philadelphia, 19114
Immaculata College, Immaculata, 19345
Indiana University of Pennsylvania, Indiana, 15705*
Juniata College, Huntington, 16652
King's College, Wilkes-Barre, 18711
Kutztown State College, Kutztown, 19530*
LaRoche College, Pittsburgh, 15237
LaSalle University, Philadelphia, 19141–1199
Lebanon Valley College of Pennsylvania, Annville, 17003–0501
Lehigh University, Bethlehem, 18015
Lincoln University, Lincoln University, 15935
Lock Haven State College, Lock Haven, 17745*
Lycoming College, Williamsport, 17701–5192
Mansfield University of Pennsylvania, Mansfield, 16933*
Marywood University, Scranton, 18509*
Mercyhurst College, Erie, 16546
Messiah College, Grantham, 17027
Millersville University of Pennsylvania, Millersville, 17551*
Moravian College, Bethlehem, 18018
Muhlenberg College, Allentown, 18104
Neumann College, Aston, 19014–1298
Penn State University, University Park, 16802*
Penn State University Harrisburg Campus of the Capital College, Middletown, 17057–4898
Philadelphia College of Bible, Brookville, 19047–2990
Point Park College, Pittsburgh, 15222
Robert Morris College, Coraopolis, 15108–1189
Rosemont College, Rosemont, 19010–1699
Saint Francis College, Loretto, 15940
Saint Joseph's University, Philadelphia, 19131
Saint Vincent College, Latrobe, 15650
Seton Hill College, Greensburg, 15601–1599

Shippensburg University of Pennsylvania, Shippensburg, 17257*
Slippery Rock University, Slippery Rock, 16057*
Susquehanna University, Selinsgrove, 17870–1001
Swarthmore College, Swarthmore, 19081–1397
Temple University, Philadelphia, 19122–1803*
Theil College, Greenville, 16125
University of Pennsylvania, Philadelphia, 19104
University of Pittsburgh, Pittsburgh, 15260
University of Pittsburgh, Johnstown, 15904
University of Scranton, Scranton, 18510*
University of the Sciences in Philadelphia, Philadelphia, 19104–4495
Ursinus College, Collegeville, 19426
Villanova University, Villanova, 19085–1672
Washington & Jefferson College, Washington, 15301
Waynesburg College, Waynesburg, 15370–9930
West Chester University, West Chester, 19383*
Westminster College, New Wilmington, 16172
Widener University, Chester, 19013
Wilkes College, Wilkes-Barre, 18766
Wilson College, Chambersburg, 17201–1285
York College of Pennsylvania, York, 17405–7199

1999 *U.S. News & World Report*'s Top Fifty:

20. Temple University
20. University of Pennsylvania
27. Penn State University–Main Campus
37. University of Pittsburgh–Main Campus

RHODE ISLAND

Rhode Island Department of Education
Office of Teacher Education & Certification
255 Westminster Street, Shepard Building, 4th Floor
Providence, RI 02903
401–222–4600
http://instruct.ride.ri.net

Beginning Salary	**Average Salary**
$24,754	$43,363
Enrollment	**Per Pupil Spending**
51,181	$7,469

Number of Teachers
10,482

Teacher Test

Praxis II Core Battery: General Knowledge, Communication Skills, Professional Knowledge

State Approved Secondary Teacher Education Institutions (*NCATE Accreditation)

Brown University, Providence, 02912
Johnson & Wales University, Providence, 02903
Providence College, Providence, 02918
Rhode Island College, Providence, 02908*
Salve Regina College, Newport, 02840–4192
University of Rhode Island, Kingston, 02881*

1999 *U.S. News & World Report's* **Top Fifty**: None

SOUTH CAROLINA

South Carolina Department of Education
Teacher Certification Section
1600 Gervais Street, Suite C
Columbia, SC 29201
803–734–8466
http://www.state.sc.us/sde

Beginning Salary	**Average Salary**
$21,791	$32,524
Enrollment	**Per Pupil Spending**
648,980	$4,797

Number of Teachers

39,922

Teacher Test

Praxis II Principles of Teaching and Learning; Praxis II Specialty Area Tests

State Approved Secondary Teacher Education Institutions (*NCATE Accreditation)

Benedict College, Columbia, 29204
Bob Jones University, Greenville, 29614
Charleston Southern University, Charleston, 29423–8087
The Citadel–The Military College of South Carolina, Charleston, 29409*
Claflin College, Orangeburg, 29115
Clemson University, Clemson, 29634–5124*
Coastal Carolina University College, Conway, 29528

Coker University, Hartsville, 29550
College of Charleston, Charleston, 29424
Columbia College, Columbia, 29203
Converse College, Spartanburg, 29302
Erskine College, Due West, 29639
Francis Marion University, Florence, 29501–0547
Furman University, Greenville, 29613
Lander University, Greenwood, 29649
Limestone College, Gaffney, 29340
Morris College, Sumter, 29150–3599
Newberry College, Newberry, 29108*
Presbyterian College, Clinton, 29325
South Carolina State University, Orangeburg, 29117*
Southern Wesleyan University, Central, 29630
University of South Carolina, Columbia, 29208*
University of South Carolina, Aiken, 29801
University of South Carolina, Spartanburg, 29303*
Vorhees College, Denmark, 29042
Winthrop University, Rock Hill, 29733*
Wofford College, Spartanburg, 29303–3663

1999 *U.S. News & World Report*'s **Top Fifty**: None

SOUTH DAKOTA

South Dakota Department of Education & Cultural Affairs
The Office of Policy and Accountability
700 Governors Drive
Pierre, SD 57501–2291
605–773–3553
http://www.state.sd.us/state/executive/deca

Beginning Salary
$19,609

Average Salary
$27,098

Enrollment
142,910

Per Pupil Spending
$4,775

Number of Teachers
9,641

Teacher Test
No test

State Approved Secondary Teacher Education Institutions (*NCATE Accreditation)

Augustana College, Sioux Falls, 57197*
Black Hills State University, Spearfish, 57799–9502*
Dakota State University, Madison, 57042*
Dakota Wesleyan University, Mitchell, 57301
Huron University, Huron, 57350–2798
Mt. Marty College, Yankton, 57078–3724
Northern State University, Aberdeen, 57401*
Oglala College, Lakota Kyle, 57752
South Dakota State University, Brookings, 57007*
University of Sioux Falls, Sioux Falls, 57105*
University of South Dakota, Vermillion, 57069*

1999 *U.S. News & World Report*'s Top Fifty: None

TENNESSEE

Tennessee Department of Education
Office of Teacher Licensing & Career Ladder Certification
5th Floor, Andrew Johnson Tower, 710 James Robertson Pkwy.
Nashville, TN 37243–0377
615–532–4885
http://www.state.tn.us/education

Beginning Salary
$21,537

Average Salary
$34,071

Enrollment
891,101

Per Pupil Spending
$4,388

Number of Teachers
53,403

Teacher Test

Praxis II Principles of Teaching and Learning; Praxis II Specialty Area Tests

State Approved Secondary Teacher Education Institutions (*NCATE Accreditation)

Austin Peay State University, Clarksville, 37044*
Belmont University, Nashville, 37212–3757*
Bethel College, McKenzie, 38201
Bryan College, Dayton, 37321–7000
Carson-Newman College, Jefferson City, 37760*

Christian Brothers University, Memphis, 38104–5581
Crichton College, Memphis, 38115
Cumberland University, Lebanon, 37087
David Lipscomb University, Nashville, 37204–3951
East Tennessee State University, Johnson City, 37614*
Fisk University, Nashville, 37208–3051
Free Will Baptist Bible College, Nashville, 37205–0117
Freed–Hardeman University, Henderson, 38340*
George Peabody College of Vanderbilt University, Nashville, 37203*
King College, Bristol, 37620–2699
Lambuth University, Jackson, 38301
Lane College, Jackson, 38301
Lee University, Cleveland, 37311
LeMoyne–Owen College, Memphis, 38126
Lincoln Memorial University, Harrogate, 37752–0901
Maryville College, Maryville, 37804
Middle Tennessee State University, Murfreesboro, 37132*
Milligan College, Milligan, 37682*
Rhodes College, Memphis, 38112
Southern Adventist University, Collegedale, 37315*
Tennessee State University, Nashville, 37208*
Tennessee Technological University, Cookeville, 38505*
Tennessee Temple University, Chattenooga, 37404
Tennessee Wesleyan College, Athens, 37301–0040
Trevecca Nazarine University, Nashville, 37210–2877
Tusculum College, Greeneville, 37743
Union University, Jackson, 38305–3697
University of Memphis, Memphis, 38152*
University of Tennessee, Chattanooga, 37403*
University of Tennessee, Knoxville, 37996*
University of Tennessee, Martin, 38238*

1999 *U.S. News & World Report*'s Top Fifty:

  6. George Peabody College of Vanderbilt University
46. University of Tennessee–Knoxville

TEXAS

State Board for Educator Certification
1001 Trinity, Teacher Retirement System Building
Austin, TX 78701
512–469–3001
http://www.sbec.state.tx.us

Beginning Salary
$22,642

Average Salary
$32,913

Enrollment
3,809,186

Per Pupil Spending
$5,222

Number of Teachers
240,371

Teacher Test

Exam for Certification of Educators in Texas (ExCET); Alternate route requires Praxis I PPST *or* CBT: Reading, Writing, Math; Texas Academic Skills Program Test required for entrance to teacher preparation programs

State Approved Secondary Teacher Education Institutions (*NCATE Accreditation)

Abilene Christian University, Abilene, 79699-9000
Angelo State University, San Angelo, 76909
Austin College, Sherman, 75090–4440
Baylor University, Waco, 76798*
Concordia University, Austin, 78705–2799
Dallas Baptist University, Dallas, 75211–9800
East Texas Baptist University, Marshall, 75670–1498
Hardin-Simmons University, Abilene, 79698
Houston Baptist University, Houston, 77074–3298
Howard Payne University, Brownwood, 76801–2794
Huston-Tillotson College, Austin, 78702
Jarvis Christian College, Hawkins, 75765
Lamar University, Beaumont, 77710
Le Tourneau University, Longview, 75607
Lubbock Christian University, Lubbock, 79407
McMurry University, Abilene, 79697
Midwestern State University, Wichita Falls, 76308–2099
Our Lady of the Lake University, San Antonio, 78207–4689
Paul Quinn College, Dallas, 75241–4398
Prairie View A & M University, Prairie View, 77446*
Rice University, Houston, 77005
Schreiner College, Kerrville, 78028–5697
St. Edward's University, Austin, 78704
St. Mary's University, San Antonio, 78228–8503
Sam Houston State University, Huntsville, 77341*
Southern Methodist University, Dallas, 75275
Southwest Texas State University, San Marcos, 78666–4616
Southwestern Advent College, Keene, 76059
Southwestern University, Georgetown, 78626
Stephen F. Austin State University, Nacogdoches, 75962*

Sul Ross State University, Alpine, 79832
Sul Ross State University–Rio Grande College, Uvalde, 78801
Tarleton State University, Stephenville, 76402
Texas A & M International University, Laredo, 78041
Texas A & M University, College Station, 77843*
Texas A & M University, Commerce, 75429–3011
Texas A & M University, Corpus Christi, 78412
Texas A & M University, Kingsville, 78363
Texas A & M University, Texarkana, 75505–5518
Texas Christian University, Fort Worth, 76129
Texas College, Tyler, 75712–4500
Texas Lutheran University, Sequin, 78115
Texas Southern University, Houston, 77004
Texas Technical University, Lubbock, 79409–5005*
Texas Wesleyan University, Fort Worth, 76105–1536
Texas Woman's University, Denton, 76204–5765
Trinity University, San Antonio, 78212–4200
University of Dallas, Irving, 75062–4799*
University of Houston–University Park, Houston, 77204*
University of Houston, Clear Lake City, 77058–1080*
University of Houston, Houston, 77002
University of Houston, Victoria, 77901–4450
University of the Incarnate Word, San Antonio, 78209–6397
University of Mary Hardin Baylor, Belton, 76513
University of North Texas, Denton, 76203*
University of St. Thomas, Houston, 77006
University of Texas, Arlington, 76019
University of Texas, Austin, 78712
University of Texas, Brownsville, 78520
University of Texas, Dallas, 75083–0688
University of Texas, El Paso, 79968
University of Texas–PanAmerican, Edinburg, 78539–2999
University of Texas, San Antonio, 78249
University of Texas, Tyler, 75701–6699
Wayland Baptist University, Plainview, 79072
West Texas A & M University, Canyon, 79016
Wiley College, Marshall, 75670

1999 *U.S. News & World Report*'s Top Fifty:

11. University of Texas–Austin
45. Texas A & M University–College Station

UTAH

Utah State Office of Education
Certification & Personnel Department
250 East 500 South
Salt Lake City, UT 84111
801–538–7740
http://www.usoe.kl2.ut.us

Beginning Salary	**Average Salary**
$20,544	$31,461
Enrollment	**Per Pupil Spending**
478,085	$3,656

Number of Teachers

20,039

Teacher Test

No test

State Approved Secondary Teacher Education Institutions (*NCATE Accreditation)

Brigham Young University, Provo, 84602*
Southern Utah University, Cedar City, 84720
University of Utah, Salt Lake City, 84112
Utah State University, Logan, 84322*
Weber State University, Ogden, 84408–1015*
Westminster College of Salt Lake City, Salt Lake City, 84105

1999 *U.S. News & World Report*'s Top Fifty:
40. Utah State University

VERMONT

Vermont Department of Education
Licensing & Professional Standards Office
State Office Building, 120 State Street
Montpelier, VT 05620
802–828–2445
http://www.state.vt.us/educ

Beginning Salary	**Average Salary**
$24,445	$37,331

Enrollment   **Per Pupil Spending**
106,607 $6,750

Number of Teachers

7,676

Teacher Test

No test

**State Approved Secondary Teacher Education Institutions
(*NCATE Accreditation)**

Castleton State College, Castleton, 05735
College of St. Joseph, Rutland, 05701–3899
Goddard College, Plainfield, 05667*
Johnson State University, Johnson, 05656
Lyndon State College, Lyndonville, 05851
Middlebury College, Middlebury, 05753
Norwich University, Northfield, 05663
St. Michael's College, Winooski, 05439
School for International Training, Brattleboro, 05302–0676
Trinity College, Burlington, 05401
University of Vermont, Burlington, 05405*

1999 *U.S. News & World Report*'s Top Fifty: None

VIRGINIA

Department of Education, Office of Professional Licensure
Division for Compliance Coordination
PO Box 2120
Richmond, VA 23218–2120
804–225–2022
http://www.pen.k12.va.us

Beginning Salary   **Average Salary**
$25,500 $35,785
Enrollment   **Per Pupil Spending**
1,096,093 $5,327

Number of Teachers
74,731

Teacher Test

Praxis I PPST *or* CBT: Math, Reading, Writing; Praxis II Specialty Area
Tests

State Approved Secondary Teacher Education Institutions (*NCATE Accreditation)

Averett College, Danville, 24541
Bluefield College, Bluefield, 24605
Bridgewater College, Bridgewater, 22812–1599
Christopher Newport University, Newport News, 23606–2998
Clinch Valley College, Wise, 24293
College of William & Mary, Williamsburg, 23187–8795*
Eastern Mennonite University, Harrisonburg, 22802–2462*
Emory & Henry College, Emory, 24327–0947
Ferrum College, Ferrum, 24008
George Mason University, Fairfax, 22030–4444*
Hampton University, Hampton, 23668*
Hollins University, Hollins, 24020
James Madison University, Harrisonburg, 22807*
Liberty University, Lynchburg, 24502
Longwood College, Farmville, 23909*
Lynchburg College, Lynchburg, 24501
Mary Baldwin College, Staunton, 24401
Marymount University, Arlington, 22207–4299*
Mary Washington College, Fredericksburg, 24401–5358
Norfolk State University, Norfolk, 23504*
Old Dominion University, Norfolk, 23529–0050*
Radford University, Radford, 24142*
Randolph-Macon College, Ashland, 23005
Randolph-Macon Woman's College, Lynchburg, 24503
Regent University, Virginia Beach, 23464
Roanoke College, Salem, 24153
Saint Paul's College, Lawrenceville, 23805
Shenandoah University, Winchester, 22601
Sweet Briar College, Winchester, 24595
University of Richmond, Richmond, 23173
University of Virginia, Charlottesville, 22906*
Virginia Commonwealth University, Richmond, 23284*
Virginia Intermont College, Bristol, 24201–4298
Virginia Polytechnic Institute and State University, Blacksburg, 24061*
Virginia State University, Petersburg, 23806*

Virginia Union University, Richmond, 23220
Virginia Wesleyan College, Norfolk, 23502–5599

1999 *U.S. News & World Report*'s Top Fifty:

13. University of Virginia

WASHINGTON

Superintendent of Public Instruction
Professional Education and Certification Office
PO Box 47200
Olympia, WA 98504–7200
360–753–6773
http://www.k12.wa.us

Beginning Salary
$24,590

Average Salary
$38,933

Enrollment
971,903

Per Pupil Spending
$5,906

Number of Teachers

46,907

Teacher Test

ACT, SAT, *or* Washington Pre-College test (required for admission to teacher education programs)

State Approved Secondary Teacher Education Institutions (*NCATE Accreditation)

Central Washington University, Ellensburg, 98926*
Eastern Washington University, Cheney, 99004–2496*
Evergreen State College, Olympia, 98505
Gonzaga University, Spokane, 99258–0001*
Heritage College, Toppenish, 98948
Northwest College, Kirkland, 98083
Pacific Lutheran College, Tacoma, 98447*
Saint Martin's College, Lacey, 98503
Seattle Pacific University, Seattle, 98119*
Seattle University, Seattle, 98122*
University of Puget Sound, Tacoma, 98416*
University of Washington, Seattle, 98195
Walla Walla College, College Place, 99324–3000
Washington State University, Pullman, 99164–1046*
Western Washington University, Bellingham, 98225–5996*

Whitman College, Walla Walla, 99362
Whitworth College, Spokane, 99251*

1999 *U.S. News & World Report*'s Top Fifty:

24. University of Washington
37. Washington State University

WEST VIRGINIA

Department of Education
Office of Professional Preparation
1900 Kanawha Boulevard East
Building #6, Room 252
Charleston, WV 25305–0330
304–558–7010
http://wvde.state.wv.us

Beginning Salary
$22,011

Average Salary
$33,072

Enrollment
303,441

Per Pupil Spending
$6,107

Number of Teachers
21,073

Teacher Test

Praxis I PPST *or* CBT: Reading, Writing, Math *or* waiver based on ACT or SAT scores; Praxis II Specialty Area Tests; Praxis II Principles of Learning and Teaching

State Approved Secondary Teacher Education Institutions (*NCATE Accreditation)

Alderson-Broaddus, Philippi, 26416*
Bethany College, Bethany, 26032*
Bluefield State College, Bluefield, 24701*
Concord College, Athens, 24712*
Davis & Elkins College, Elkins, 26241
Fairmont State College, Fairmont, 26554*
Glenville State College, Glenville, 26351*
Marshall University, Huntington, 25755*
Salem Teikyo University, Salem, 26426
Shepherd College, Shepherdstown, 25443*
University of Charleston, Charleston, 25304*
West Liberty State College, West Liberty, 26074*
West Virginia State College, Institute, 25112–1000*
West Virginia University, Morgantown, 26506–6009*

West Virginia Wesleyan College, Buckhannon, 26201*
Wheeling Jesuit University, Wheeling, 26003

1999 *U.S. News & World Report*'s Top Fifty: None

WISCONSIN

Wisconsin Department of Public Instruction, Teacher Licensing
PO Box 7841
Madison, WI 53707–7841
800–441–4563 or 608–266–3390
http://www.dpi.state.wi.us

Beginning Salary	**Average Salary**
$24,560	$39,271
Enrollment	**Per Pupil Spending**
884,738	$6,930

Number of Teachers

55,033

Teacher Test

Praxis I PPST: Reading, Writing, Math; *or* any teacher examination that
includes reading, writing, and math skills required in other states

**State Approved Secondary Teacher Education Institutions
(*NCATE Accreditation)**

Alverno College, Milwaukee, 53234–3922*
Beloit College, Beloit, 53511
Cardinal Stritch College, Milwaukee, 53217–7516*
Carroll College, Waukeska, 53186
Carthage College, Kenosha, 53140
Concordia University, Mequon, 53097
Edgewood College, Madison, 53711*
Lakeland College, Sheboygan, 53802–0359
Lawrence University, Appleton, 54912
Marantha Baptist Bible College, Watertown, 53094
Marian College, Fond du Lac, 54935*
Marquette University, Milwaukee, 53201–1881*
Mount Mary College, Milwaukee, 53222
Mount Senario College, Ladysmith, 54848
Northland College, Ashland, 54806
Ripon College, Ripon, 54971
Saint Norbert College, De Pere, 54115
Silver Lake College, Manitowoc, 54220
University of Wisconsin, Eau Claire, 54701

University of Wisconsin, Green Bay, 54302
University of Wisconsin, La Crosse, 54601*
University of Wisconsin, Madison, 53706
University of Wisconsin, Milwaukee, 53201
University of Wisconsin, Oshkosh, 54901*
University of Wisconsin, Parkside, 53141–2000
University of Wisconsin, Platteville, 53818–3099*
University of Wisconsin, River Falls, 54022*
University of Wisconsin, Stevens Point, 54481–3897
University of Wisconsin, Stout, 54751
University of Wisconsin, Superior, 54880
University of Wisconsin, Whitewater, 53190*
Viterbo College, La Crosse, 54601*
Wisconsin Lutheran College, Milwaukee, 53226

1999 *U.S. News & World Report*'s Top Fifty:

9. University of Wisconsin–Madison

WYOMING

Professional Teaching Standards Board
Hathaway Building, 2nd Floor
2300 Capitol Avenue
Cheyenne, WY 82002–0050
307–777–7291
http://www.k12.wy.us

Beginning Salary	**Average Salary**
$21,900	$32,472
Enrollment	**Per Pupil Spending**
98,777	$6,160

Number of Teachers

6,734

Teacher Test

Coursework; *or* an appropriate examination on the Wyoming and U.S. Constitutions

State Approved Secondary Teacher Education Institution (*NCATE Accreditation)

University of Wyoming, Laramie, 82071*

1999 *U.S. News & World Report*'s **Top Fifty**: None

ADDITIONAL PROFILES

Guam Department of Education
PO Box DE
Agana, Guam 96932
617–475–0457
http://www.doe.edu.gu/

Puerto Rico Department of Education
PO Box 190759
San Juan, Puerto Rico 00919–0759
787–759–2000

University of Puerto Rico
San Juan, Puerto Rico 00936–4984

Virgin Islands: St. Croix
Government of the Virgin Islands of the United States
Department of Education
Sunny Isle Professional Building, Suite 1
Chritiansted, St. Croix, VI 00820
370–772–4144

Virgin Islands: St. Thomas and St. John
Department of Education
PO Box 11900
St. Thomas, VI 00801
340–774–4546

United States Department of Defense
Dependent Schools Certification Unit
4040 North Fairfax Drive
Arlington, VA 22203–1634
703–696–3081, ext. 133
http://www.educ.odedodea.edu

9

Directory of Resources

American Alliance for Health, Physical Education, Recreation, and Dance (AAHPERD)
1900 Association Drive
Reston, VA 20191–1599
(703) 476–3414 or (800) 321–0789

American Association for Employment in Education (AAEE)
820 Davis Street, Suite 222
Evanston, IL 60201–4445
(847) 864–1999
e-Mail: aaee@nwu.edu

American Council on Teaching of Foreign Languages (ACTFL)
6 Executive Plaza
Yonkers, NY 10701–6801
(914) 963–8830
e-Mail: actflhq@aol.com
http://www.actfl.org

Educational Placement Service
University of Wisconsin–Madison
1000 Bascom Mall
Box 29 Education Building
Madison, WI 53706–1398
(608) 262–1755

Educational Testing Service
Princeton, New Jersey 08541

(800) 772–9476
http://www.ets.org

Interstate New Assessment and Support Consortium (INTASC)
Council of Chief State School Officers
One Massachusetts Avenue NW Suite 700
Washington, D.C. 20001
(202) 408–5505
http://www.ccsso.org

International Society for Technology in Education (ISTE)
1787 Agate Street
Eugene, OR 97403–1923
(541) 346–4414
e-Mail: cust svc@ccmail.uoregon.edu
http://www.iste.org

National Association of State Directors of Teacher Education and Certification (NASDTEC)
3600 Whitman Avenue
N. Suite 105
Seattle, WA 98103
(206) 548–0116
http://www.nasdtec.org

National Board for Professional Teaching Standards
PO Box 839959
San Antonio, TX 78283–3959
(800) 532–1813
http://www.nbpts.org

National Center for Education Information
4401A Connecticut Avenue, NW Suite #12
Washington, D.C. 20008
(202) 362–3444

National Center for Education Statistics
Office of Educational Research and Improvement
U.S. Department of Education
555 New Jersey Avenue NW
Washington, D.C. 20208–5574
http://nces.ed.gov

National Center for Fair & Open Testing
342 Broadway
Cambridge, MA 02139

(617) 864–4810
http://www.fairtest.org

National Council of Accreditation for Teacher Education (NCATE)
2010 Massachusetts Avenue NW
Suite 500
Washington, D.C. 20036–1023
(202) 466–7496
http://www.ncate.org

National Council of Teachers of English (NCTE)
1111 Kenyon Road
Urbana, IL 61801
(800) 369–6283
http://www.ncte.org

National Council of Teachers of Mathematics (NCTM)
Department S
1906 Association Drive
Reston, VA 22091
http://www.nctm.org

National Council for the Social Studies (NCSS)
3501 Newark Street NW
Washington, D.C. 20016
(202) 966–7840
http://www.ncss.org

National Evaluation Systems (NES)
130 Gatehouse Road
PO Box 226
Amherst, MA 01004–0226
(413) 256–0444 ext. 899

NES California
PO Box 340813
Sacramento, CA 95834
(916) 928–0244

NES Texas
PO Box 140406
Austin, TX 78714
(512) 926–0469

National Middle School Association (NMSA)
2600 Corporate Exchange, Suite 370
Columbus, OH 43231

(614) 895–4730
http://www.nmsa.org

National Science Teachers Association (NSTA)
1840 Wilson Boulevard
Arlington, VA 22201–3000
(703) 243–7100
http://www.nsta.org

National Service-Learning Clearinghouse
University of Minnesota
1954 Buford Avenue, Room R460
St. Paul, MN 55108
(800) 808-SERV (7378)
http://www.nicsl.coled.umn.edu

Professional Development School Network
Massachusetts Field Center for Teaching and Learning
University of Massachusetts Boston
100 Morrissey Boulevard
Boston, MA 02125–3393
(617) 287–7660
http://omega.cc.umb.edu/~mafldctr/pds.htm

Teach for America
20 Exchange Place
New York, NY 10005
(212) 425–9039
(800) 832–1230
http://www.teachforamerica.org

Teacher Education Accreditation Council (TEAC)
One Dupont Circle, Suite 320
Washington, D.C. 20036–1110

United States Department of Education
600 Independence Avenue, SW
Washington, D.C. 20202–0498
(800) USA-LEARN
http://www.ed.gov

References

Adler, Mortimer J., ed. *The Paideia Program: An Educational Syllabus.* New York: Macmillan, 1984.

American Association for Employment in Education. *1998 Job Search Handbook for Educators.* Evanston, IL: American Association for Employment in Education, 1998.

American Association of Colleges for Teacher Education. *Teacher Education Policy in the States: A 50 State Survey of Legislative and Administrative Actions.* Washington, D.C.: American Association of Colleges for Teacher Education, 1995.

———. *Capturing the Vision: Reflection on NCATE's Redesign Five Years Later.* Washington, D.C.: American Association of Colleges for Teacher Education, February, 1993.

American Association of University Women. *Hostile Hallways: The AAUW Survey on Sexual Harassment in America's Schools.* Washington, D.C.: American Association of University Women, 1993.

———. *How Schools Shortchange Girls.* Washington, D.C.: American Association of University Women, 1992.

"America's Best Graduate Schools." *U.S. News & World Report,* 29 March 1999: 108–111.

Andrews, Theodore E., ed. *The NASDTEC Manual on the Preparation and Certification of Educational Personnel 1998–1999.* Dubuque, IA: Kendall/Hunt, 1998.

Ballou, Dale, and Stephanie Soler. *Addressing the Looming Teacher Crunch: The Issue Is Quality.* Washington, D.C.: Progressive Policy Institute, February, 1998.

Berliner, David, and Bruce J. Biddle. *The Manufactured Crisis: Myths, Fraud, and the Attack on America's Public Schools.* Reading, MA: Addison-Wesley, 1995.

Bowman, Mary Ann. "Metaphors We Teach By: Understanding Ourselves as Teachers and Learners." *Teaching Excellence* 8, no. 3 (1996–1997):1–2.

Britzman, Deborah P. *Practice Makes Practice: A Critical Study of Learning to Teach.* Albany, NY: State University of New York Press, 1991.

Bronfenbrenner, Urie. *The Ecology of Human Development: Experiments by Nature and Design.* Cambridge: Harvard University Press, 1979.

Brumberg, Joan Jacobs. *The Body Project: An Intimate History of American Girls.* New York: Random House, 1997.

Callahan, Raymond E. *Education and the Cult of Efficiency: A Study of the Social Forces That Have Shaped the Administration of the Public Schools.* Chicago: University of Chicago Press, 1962.

Cannella, G., and J. Reif. "Preparing Teachers for Cultural Diversity: Constructivist Orientations." *Action in Teacher Education* 26, no. 3 (1994):37–45.

Carnegie Council on Adolescent Development. *Turning Points: Preparing American Youth for the 21st Century—Abridged Version.* New York: Carnegie Council on Adolescent Development, 1990.

Chomsky, Noam. *Language and Mind.* New York: Harcourt Brace Jovanovich, 1972.

Choy, Susan P. *Teacher's Working Conditions: Findings from The Condition of Education, 1996,* no. 7. Washington, D.C.: U.S. Government Printing Office, 1996:5–7.

Clark, C. M., and P. L. Peterson. "Teachers' Thought Processes." In *Handbook of Research on Teaching,* 3rd ed., edited by M. C. Wittrock. New York: Macmillan, 1986:255–296.

Clarke, Susan R. *Taking Care: Women High School Teachers at Midlife and Midcareer.* Unpublished Ed.D. dissertation, University of Massachusetts–Amherst, 1998.

Cocke, Cornelia. *Cracking the Praxis II: NTE,* 2nd ed. New York: Random House, 1997.

Cohen, David K., Eleanor Farrar, and Arthur G. Powell. *The Shopping Mall High School: Winners and Losers in the Educational Marketplace.* Boston: Houghton Mifflin, 1985.

Coles, Robert. *The Call of Service: A Witness to Idealism.* Boston: Houghton Mifflin, 1993.

Cortes, Carlos. "Beyond Affirmative Action." *MLE Alumni Bulletin* 9 (June 1996): 1–5.

Croal, N'Gai. "Want a Job? Get Online." *Newsweek,* 9 June 1997:81–82.

Daley, Beth. "City Faces New Shortage of Teachers." *The Boston Globe,* 23 March 1998: A1, B10.

Darling-Hammond, Linda. *The Right to Learn: A Blueprint for Schools That Work.* San Francisco: Jossey Bass, 1997.

———. "The Current Status of Teaching and Teacher Development in the United States." *Educational Research Association Invitational Conference on Teacher Development,* May 6–8, 1996.

———. "Who Will Speak for the Children? How 'Teach For America' Hurts Urban Schools and Students." *Phi Delta Kappan* 76, no. 1 (1994):21–34.

———. "Teaching and Knowledge: Policy Issues Posed by Alternate Certification for Teachers." *Peabody Journal of Education* 67, no. 3 (Spring, 1990):123–154.

Darling-Hammond, Linda, Arthur E. Wise, and Stephen P. Klein. *A License to Teach.* Boulder, CO: Westview Press, 1995.

Education Week. "High Standards for All Children and Assessment Aligned with Those Standards." *Education Week*, 8 January 1998:80.

———. "Teachers Who Have the Knowledge and Skills to Teach to Higher Standards." *Education Week*, 8 January 1998:83.

Educational Placement Consortium. *Teacher Testing Requirements 1998*. Madison, WI: University of Wisconsin–Madison, 1998.

Eubanks, Segun C. *The Urban Teacher Challenge: A Report on Teacher Recruitment and Demand in Selected Great City Schools*. Belmont, MA: Recruiting New Teachers, 1996.

Feistritzer, Emily C. "The Truth Behind the 'Teacher Shortage.'" *The Wall Street Journal*, 28 January, 1998:A18.

Fenstermacher, Gary D. "Controlling Quality and Creating Community: Separate Purposes for Separate Organizations." *Journal of Teacher Education* 45, no. 5 (1994):329–336.

Frantz, Douglas, and Jon Nordheimer. "Giant of Exam Business Keep Quiet on Cheating." *New York Times* (Northeast edition), 28 September 1997:32.

Freire, Paulo. *Teachers as Cultural Workers: Letters to Those Who Dare Teach*. Translated by Donaldo Macedo, Dale Koike, and Alexandre Oliverira. Boulder, CO: Westview Press, 1998.

Gerald, Debra E., and William J. Hussar. *Projections of Education Statistics to 2005*. Washington, D.C.: U.S. Department of Education, 1995.

Goodlad, John I. *A Place Called School: Prospects for the Future*. New York: McGraw Hill, 1984.

Grossman, Pamela I. "Learning to Teach Without Teacher Education." *Teachers College Record* 91, no. 2 (Winter, 1989):191–208.

Guyton, Edith, and John D. McIntyre. "Student Teaching and School Experiences." In *Handbook of Research on Teacher Education*, edited by Robert W. Houston. New York: Macmillan, 1990.

Haberman, Martin. "Selecting and Preparing Culturally Competent Teachers for Urban Schools." In *Handbook of Research on Teacher Education*, 2d ed., edited by John Sikula, Thomas J. Buttery, and Edith Guyton. New York: Macmillan, 1996.

Hampel, Robert. *The Last Little Citadel: American High Schools Since 1940*. A Study of High Schools. Boston: Houghton Mifflin, 1986.

Haney, Walter, George Madaus, and Amelia Kreitzer. "Charms Talismanic: Testing Teachers for the Improvement of American Education." In *Review of Research in Education* 14, edited by Ernst Z. Rothkopf. Washington, D.C.: American Educational Research Association, 1987.

Hechinger, Fred. *Fateful Choices: Healthy Youth for the 21st Century*. New York: Hill & Wang, 1992.

Heck, Shirley F., and C. Ray Williams. *The Complex Roles of the Teacher*. New York: Teachers College Press, 1984.

Herman, Rebecca, and Sam Stringfield. *Ten Promising Programs for Educating All Children: Evidence of Impact*. Arlington, VA: Educational Research Service, 1997.

Hirsch, E. D., Jr. *Cultural Literacy: What Every American Needs to Know*. Boston: Houghton Mifflin, 1987.

Hofstadter, Richard. *Anti-intellectualism in American Life*. New York: Vintage Books, 1963.

Honan, William H. "The Ivory Tower Under Seige." *New York Times Education Life*, 4 January 1998:44.

Institute for Education in Transformation. *Voices from the Inside: A Report on Schooling from Inside the Classroom*. Claremont, CA: Institute for Education in Transformation, Claremont Graduate School, 1992.

Interstate New Teacher Assessment and Support Consortium. "Next Steps: Moving Toward Performance-Based Licensing in Teaching." Washington, D.C.: Council of Chief State School Officers, 1995.

Jackson, Philip W. *Life in Classrooms*. New York: Holt, Rinehart and Winston, 1968.

Jacobi Gray, Maryann, Sandra Geschwind, et al. *Evaluation of Learn and Serve America, Higher Education: First Year Report*, Vol. 1. Santa Monica: Rand, 1996.

Jones, Byrd L., and Robert W. Maloy. *Schools for an Information Age: Reconstructing Foundations for Learning and Teaching*. Westport, CT: Praeger, 1996.

Kozol, Jonathan. *Savage Inequalities: Children in America's Schools*. New York: HarperPerennial, 1991.

Labaree, David F. "The Trouble with Ed Schools." *Educational Foundations* 10, no. 3 (Summer 1996):27–45.

———. "Power, Knowledge, and the Rationalization of Teaching: A Genealogy of the Movement to Professionalize Teaching." *Harvard Educational Review* 62, no. 2 (1992):123–154.

LaFleur, Richard A. "Latina Resurgens: Classical Language Enrollments in American Schools and Colleges." *The Classical Outlook* (Summer 1997):125.

Lawall, Gilbert W. "Graduate Latin Teacher Preparation Programs." In *Latin for the 21st Century: From Concept to Classroom*, edited by Richard A. LaFleur. Menlo Park: Scott Foresman–Addison Wesley, 1997.

Lehr, Dick. "Classroom Buzz." *The Boston Globe*, 11 February 1997:E1, E6.

Levin, Tamar. "Where All Doors Are Open for Disabled Students." *New York Times*, 28 December 1997:1, 20.

Lieberman, Ann, and Lynne Miller. *Teachers, Their World, and Their Work: Implications for School Improvement*. Alexandria, VA: Association for Supervision and Curriculum Development, 1984.

Lucas, Christopher J. *Teacher Education in America: Reform Agendas for the Twenty-First Century*. New York: St. Martin's Press, 1997.

Maloof, David. "A Teacher's Repertoire of Roles." *Boston Globe*, 1 February 1998: C5–C7.

McCafferty, Dennis. "Master Your Computer—or Flunk." *USA Weekend*, 6–8 February 1998:28.

Mee, Cynthia S. *2,000 Voices: Young Adolescents' Perceptions & Curriculum Implications*. Columbus, OH: National Middle School Association, 1997.

Miller, Judith Harmon. "Gender Issues Embedded in the Experience of Student Teaching: Being Treated Like a Sex Object." *Journal of Teacher Education* 48, no. 1 (January–February 1997):19–28.

Murname, R. J., and Frank Levy. *Teaching the New Basic Skills: Principles for Ed-*

ucating Children to Thrive in a Changing Economy. New York: Free Press, 1996.

National Center for Education Statistics. *America's Teachers: Profile of a Profession, 1993–94*. Washington, D.C.: U.S. Department of Education, 1997.

National Commission on Teaching & America's Future. *What Matters Most: Teaching for America's Future*. Washington, D.C.: National Commission on Teaching & America's Future, 1996.

National Council for Accreditation of Teacher Education. *A List of Professionally Accredited Schools, Colleges, and Departments of Education*. Washington, D.C.: National Council for Accreditation of Teacher Education, November, 1997.

Nieto, Sonia. *Affirming Diversity: The Sociopolitical Context of Multicultural Education*. New York: Longman, 1992.

———. "We Speak in Many Tongues: Language Diversity and Multicultural Education." In *Multicultural Education for the 21st Century*, edited by C. Diaz. Washington D.C.: NEA Professional Library, 1992.

Orfield, G., with S. Schley, D. Glass, and S. Reardon. *The Growth of Segregation in American Schools: Changing Patterns of Separation and Poverty Since 1968*. Washington, D.C.: National School Boards Association, 1993.

Peters, R. S., ed. *The Philosophy of Education*. London: Oxford University Press, 1973.

Pugach, Marlene, and James D. Raths. "Testing Teachers: Analysis and Recommendations." *Journal of Teacher Education* 34, no. 1(January/February 1983):34–37.

Rhoads, Robert. *Community Service and Higher Learning*. Albany, NY: State University of New York Press, 1997.

Rigden, Diana Wyllie. "How Teachers Would Change Teacher Education." *Education Week on the Web*, 11 December 1996:1.

Roth, Robert A. "Standards for Certification, Licensure, and Accreditation." In *Handbook of Research on Teacher Education*, 2d ed., edited by John Sikula. New York: Macmillan, 1996.

———. "The University Can't Train Teachers? Transformation of a Profession." *Journal of Teacher Education* 45, no. 4 (September–October, 1994):261–268.

Sadkar, David, and Myra Sadkar. *Failing at Fairness: How America's Schools Cheat Girls*. New York: C. Scribner's Sons, 1994.

Schon, Donald A. *The Reflective Practitioner: How Professionals Think in Action*. New York: BasicBooks, 1983.

Sizer, Theodore R. *Horace's Compromise: The Dilemma of the American High School*. Boston: Houghton Mifflin, 1985.

Steinberg, Jacques. "Help Wanted in New York: 3,000 Teachers (Or Maybe 9,000)." *New York Times*, 10 August 1997:29–30.

"Survey Reveals Teaching Shortages in Many of Nation's Largest Cities." *The Recorder*, 22 May 1996:7

Tatum, Beverly Daniel. *"Why Are All the Black Kids Sitting Together in the Cafeteria?" and Other Conversations about Race*. New York: BasicBooks, 1997.

Tyack, David, and Larry Cuban. *Tinkering Toward Utopia: A Century of Public School Reform*. Cambridge, MA: Harvard University Press, 1995.

Tyack, David, and Elizabeth Hansot. *Learning Together: A History of Coeducation in American Public Schools*. New York: Russell Sage Foundation, 1992.

Tyack, David B. *The One Best System: A History of American Education.* Cambridge: Harvard University Press, 1974.

U.S. Department of Education. *Community Update,* no. 38. Washington, D.C.: U.S. Department of Education, August 1996.

U.S. Department of Education Initiative on Teaching. *Ensuring a Talented, Dedicated and Well-Prepared Teacher in Every Classroom.* Washington, D.C.: U.S. Department of Education, 1997.

"U.S. School Population Will Hit a Record." *USA Today,* 22 August 1997:3A.

Vygotsky, Lev. *Thought and Language,* translated by A. Kozulin. Cambridge, MA: MIT Press, 1987.

Walters, Laurel Shaper. "The Bilingual Education Debate." *The Harvard Education Letter* 14, no. 3 (May/June 1998):1–4.

Western Interstate Commission for Higher Education. *Knocking at the College Door: Projections of High School Graduates by Race/Ethnicity 1996–2012.* Boulder, CO: Western Interstate Commission for Higher Education, 1998.

Wise, Arthur, and Jane Leibbrand. "Accreditation and the Creation of a Profession of Teaching." *Phi Delta Kappan* 75, no. 2 (October 1993):133–157.

Young, Kenneth E., Charles M. Chambers, H. R. Kells, and associates with assistance from Ruth Cargo. *Understanding Accreditation: Contemporary Perspectives on Issues and Practices in Evaluation of Educational Quality.* San Francisco: Jossey-Bass, 1983.

"Youth Services California Affiliates Briefing." San Anselmo, CA: Youth Services California, May 1997.

Yugar, Yolanda. "The Positive Potential of Middle School Students." *National Dropout Prevention Newsletter* 10, no. 4 (Fall 1997):8.

Zemelman, Steven, Harry Daniels, and Arthur Hyde. *Best Practice: New Standards for Teaching and Learning in America's Schools.* Portsmouth, NH: Heinemann, 1993.

Index

About the Authors

ROBERT W. MALOY is a lecturer in the department of teacher education and curriculum studies in the School of Education of the University of Massachusetts–Amherst. He coordinates history and social studies teacher education in the Secondary Teacher Education Program, and co-directs "180 Days in Springfield," a professional development school partnership with the Springfield, Massachusetts, public schools. He also directs the TEAMS (Tutoring Enrichment Assistance Models for Schools) Project, a public service outreach tutoring project for culturally and linguistically diverse students in local public schools. He is the co-author of *Schools for an Information Age*, with Byrd L. Jones (Praeger, 1996); *Kids Have All the Write Stuff*, with Sharon A. Edwards (1992); and *Partnerships for Improving Schools*, with Byrd L. Jones (Greenwood Press, 1988).

IRVING SEIDMAN is a professor of education in the department of teacher education and curriculum studies in the School of Education of the University of Massachusetts–Amherst. He is director of teacher education for the Amherst campus, and he coordinates English teacher education in the School of Education's Secondary Teacher Education Program. A second edition of his *Interviewing as Qualitative Research* was published in 1998.